DESIGN
AND
TECHNOLOGY
IN
ARCHITECTURE
REVISED EDITION

DESIGN AND TECHNOLOGY IN ARCHITECTURE
REVISED EDITION

David Guise

Professor
City College of New York

VNR Van Nostrand Reinhold
New York

Case study drawings by Sandra K. Mintzes
Text design by Karin Gerdes Kincheloe

Copyright © 1991 by Van Nostrand Reinhold

Library of Congress Catalog Card Number 90-21156
ISBN 0–442–00618–7

Printed in the United States of America.

Van Nostrand Reinhold
115 Fifth Avenue
New York, New York 10003

Chapman and Hall
2–6 Boundary Row
London, SE1 8HN, England

Thomas Nelson Australia
102 Dodds Street
South Melbourne 3205
Victoria, Australia

Nelson Canada
1120 Birchmount Road
Scarborough, Ontario MIK 5G4, Canada

16 15 14 13 12 11 10 9 8 7 6 5 4 3 2 1

Library of Congress Cataloging-in-Publication Data
Guise, David
    Design and technology in architecture / David Guise. — rev. ed.
        p.   cm.
    Includes index.
    ISBN 0-442-00618-7
    1. Structural design. 2. Building. 2. Architecture. I. Title
TA658.G85   1991
624.1′7—dc20

                                        90-21156
                                        CIP

To my wife
Gretchen Grunenfelder Guise

Preface
to Revised Edition

I am pleased to have the opportunity to add additional case studies and to update building code and stress-value information in *Design and Technology in Architecture*. Ideally, I envision the case studies in a binder, permitting an ongoing insertion of significant buildings that would add to the data base averages, ultimately permitting an analysis of data by building type. This edition provides an opportunity to encourage others to add their own case studies to those contained herein. The greater the data base, the more accurate the rule-of-thumb design extrapolations they generate will become. The intention has always been for these case studies to serve as a format and starter model for others to add to and refine. My students have enjoyed investigating buildings of their own selection, discovering the relationship between a structure's ultimate form, texture, and technical systems.

ACKNOWLEDGMENTS

This text would not be a reality without the continued support of my original editor, Judith Joseph, now C.E.O. at Van Nostrand Reinhold, and her executive editor, Lilly Kaufman. It is with particular gratitude that I thank Wendy Lochner, the architectural editor who guided and nourished this effort, Liz Geller of Van Nostrand Reinhold, and David Banner and Herb Niemirow of Caliber/Phoenix Color Corp. who coordinated the work. Without the encouragement and support of Edward Allen, Forrest Wilson, Tom Peters, and Essy Baniassad, the effort might never have been undertaken.

David Guise

Preface
to First Edition

Design and Technology in Architecture provides an overview of the various physical forces that act on buildings and the framing systems that contain them. Through text and case studies of well-known examples of contemporary architecture, the reader can discover the hidden world of buildings: environmental comfort systems, and structural systems, which influence the outer appearance of any edifice. Lovers of architecture will understand and appreciate how the many systems that make up a building influence form, texture, and character.

This is primarily a book for architecture and design students, who will benefit from technical awareness in doing their own design work. It is also appropriate for a variety of readers, from the professional architect who is integrating form and function in each new design to the intelligent layperson and admirer of architecture. It should also serve the needs of the fine arts student who wishes to understand how the inner workings of a building affect its outer appearance.

The book is organized in two major sections. Part One is a brief introduction to the various technologies that influence design decisions: loads, framing and mechanical, people-moving and life-safety systems are surveyed. Part Two provides the student and practicing architecture with eighteen unique case studies of well-known contemporary buildings. Photographs, sections and plans reveal the inner and outer surfaces of such buildings as U.S. Steel, One Shell Plaza, and the Citicorp Building. The case studies include examples of both steel-framed and concrete-framed buildings. Included are more than 200 drawings and photographs, created specifically for this book.

It is hoped that readers will find in this book an exciting new dimension to the appreciation of architecture. Understanding technology can bring a new spirit to the work of the architectural designer.

Contents

Part One

FUNDAMENTALS

Milan Cathedral.

The Crypt de la Colonia Güell, built at the turn of the century with simple bricks and stone, used the inherent nature of its materials—capable only of resisting compression forces well—to produce a striking, almost supernatural, architectural mood. The major factor contributing to the unique quality of this space is the use of powerful tilting stone columns. The direction of the loads transmitted from the brick roof vaulting to the columns is slightly skewed from the vertical. The columns are precisely aligned to counteract these loads. By positioning his columns in this way the architect, Antonio Gaudi, minimized the need for them to resist bending and buckling tendencies, calling upon them to resist only compressive forces.

The surrealistic space that was created is the direct result of using a particular material, with a specific structural capacity, in a manner that exploits that capacity. Few architects have dared to tilt their columns; most choose to express them as verticals. The new arsenal of contemporary framing materials and sophisticated mechanical systems may also be utilized either to express an architectural concept or to help achieve a predetermined desired aesthetic effect.

❖

The earliest structures were small and built with easily obtainable materials. Basic shelters, simple and often elegant in shape and form, were created out of mud, straw, bricks, stones, and logs. These materials have continued to be used in construction throughout history. In the classical architecture of ancient Greece, formalized compositions of masonry walls and columns supported wood roofs. A thousand years later, solid, staid masonry walls supported wood roof trusses for most of Europe's major structures, including the basilican church, massive and a bit ponderous compared to the soaring delicacy of the Gothic cathedrals which slowly evolved from this simple form. The high Gothic style was the epitome of masonry architecture, with both form and structure true to its stone material. The horizontal thrusts of the high nave arches were conducted to the ground in a series of spectacular flying buttresses, often crowned with sculptured pinnacles.

The early uses of iron were confined to concealed connections and restraints. An example is the dome added to Florence Cathedral between 1420 and 1434 by the architect Brunelleschi. Iron-linked stone chains were used to contain the horizontal thrusts present at the base of the dome, eliminating the need for heavy masonry buttressing. Concealing the chains within the space between the inner and outer dome gave the building a visual lightness not otherwise possible with stone alone.

Crypt de la Colonia Güell, near Barcelona, Spain, built between 1898 and 1914.

Restored peasant house, Romania. Rubble stone walls, dirt floors, and a thatched roof.

Saint Appollinare in Classe, Ravenna, Italy, 534 A.D.

Notre Dame, Paris. 1163–1235

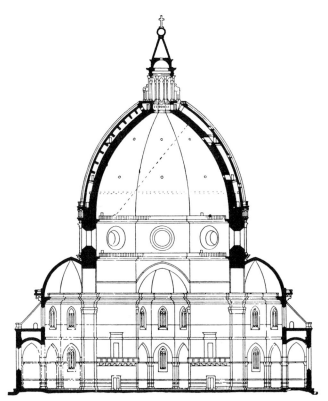

Section through the Florence Cathedral dome.

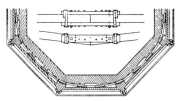

Half plan of the dome and detail showing the iron-linked stone chain.

Florence Cathedral. Between 1420 and 1434 the architect Brunelleschi added this dome to the original structure which was begun in 1298.

It was not until the early 1800s that iron framing systems came into use, followed by steel framing after the development of the Bessemer smelting process in 1855. Cast iron framing was the forerunner of today's steel. Iron, without the addition of carbon and other material, does not possess the strength of steel. An iron beam is therefore more brittle and far bulkier than a steel beam of comparable strength would be.

Since both materials lose their strength and become plastic when subjected to heat, iron and steel framing must be protected from exposure to fire. Only in large-span and/or low-rise structures such as exhibition halls and railroad train sheds is it safe to expose and express the actual shape of the framing. In such buildings the horizontal steel is high above the floor and safely remote from flames, and any occupants would be at or near ground level with easy access to safety in case of fire.

Wood beams and floors supported by load-bearing masonry walls have been in common use since the Middle Ages. Originally applied in the construction of guild halls, castles, and merchant palaces, this basic technique was used in building the early New England mills and factories. It is still a popular method for constructing town houses and small stores. The masonry walls, with their rich variety of textures, provide both vertical support and fire separation from adjacent buildings. This method of construction is so prevalent that most building codes refer to it as "ordinary construction."

The use of many small wooden members closely spaced for both vertical (studs) and horizontal (joists) support did not evolve until the advent of the machine-made nail in the 1830s. Nails made the joining process both quick and economically feasible, allowing the use of relatively light pieces of wood so that a small number of people could erect a house, church, or barn without rigging equipment. The vast majority of American homes built today are constructed with wood studs and joists.

With the demand for more working and living space came the development of the high-rise building. Masonry was not suitable for this type of building since the thickness required for masonry-bearing walls and columns would have severely limited the amount of usable occupant space. As cities entered the twentieth century, therefore, steel skeletons, protected against

A restored house in Mystic, Connecticut.

A traditional New England barn.

Plank and beam construction for a contemporary house in the woods.

A typical steel frame office building rises in Philadelphia, forming a backdrop for the brick face of traditional "ordinary construction."

High-rise reinforced concrete skeletons now compete with steel. Columns tend to be thicker and more closely spaced than in steel framing.

Concrete's plastic shapes as seen in Saarinen's TWA Terminal.

fire by a variety of insulating materials, became the dominant framing system for high-rise structures.

Early uses of concrete were monolithic and ponderous. The Romans used it as a liquid stone, often pouring it into masonry molds that also served as the final exposed finish. In modern times concrete reinforced with steel rods became a competitive framing choice for medium, and eventually high-rise, structures as technology devised ways to increase the spanning capacity of concrete beams and decrease the diameter of columns. The bulk of an individual concrete framing member will exceed that of a comparable steel member, resulting in a greater total building weight for a concrete framing system than for a similar steel system. Concrete's cost and ready availability, however, along with the advent of agile hoisting equipment, have made it competitive with steel framing for all but the very tallest structures or those requiring extremely long spans. The plastic shapes and forms that are obtainable, along with the rich variety of textures achievable only with concrete, are features of great appeal to architects.

Essentially we erect our buildings out of four basic materials: wood, masonry, steel, and reinforced concrete. Each has inherent characteristics, limits and capabilities, and architects subordinate, disguise or exploit these qualities for particular structural and aesthetic results.

Most buildings being built today are of a very modest size, and continue to utilize wood and masonry for their support systems. The principal innovations in private home and small building construction over the last hundred years have been in the available selection of finishing materials and heating, cooling and lighting methods. In contrast, our large commercial buildings, high-rise apartment structures, laboratories, and public edifices, with their requirements of greater height and larger span, have given rise to new structural framing methods along with new, sophisticated mechanical systems. It is with these large buildings that this book is mostly concerned.

Chapter 1

LOADS

Every structure, no matter how large or small, must support itself, plus all the other forces placed on it by nature and by the occupants of the building. Additional stresses can be induced by external forces such as wind, snow and ice, earthquakes and soil pressures.

LIVE AND DEAD LOADS

The weight of the structure itself and that of all its permanently attached components such as mechanical and building service equipment, fixed-in-place partitions and ceilings are called *dead loads*.

Superimposed loads produced by the nature of a building's use and occupancy are called *live loads*.

Live loads affect every floor in a building, and the amount of the load is based on the type of use the floor is subjected to. For example, a warehouse required to store paper goods might have to be designed to carry 300 to 400 pounds per square foot, while an apartment house would be required to support only the relatively light live loads of 40 pounds per square foot. Different parts of the same building could be used for different purposes and thus be required to support different loads.

Machinery can induce vibrations, and cars driven in a garage will generate horizontal forces that must be accounted for. Even the duration of a load can be a factor, especially if the framing material is wood, which can bounce back from a short-time-impact load such as a dropped object, but would take a permanent set under the long-term load induced by stored material.

WIND

Wind, which acts on the vertical surface of a building, is a more critical issue in a high-rise building than in low structures. It exerts a greater force particularly on the upper floors of high-rise buildings than on low-rise buildings, because wind speed increases with its height above the ground. Floor systems must be designed to transfer the wind loads from the exterior walls into the central core of a building, where the building's walls and/or columns will in turn transfer the wind forces down to the ground.

A building's outer wall or skin must be designed so that it will neither buckle from wind pressure nor

Crypt de la Colonia Güell, near Barcelona, Spain.

Pontiac Michigan's Silverdome Stadium

Plywood sheating on the exterior walls provided sufficient rigidity to keep this house intact during an earthquake in Alaska.

leak from wind-driven rain. One must realize that the nature of wind currents is such that they will cause negative pressures to build up on the leeward side of the building. These negative pressures often cause more damage than the positive pressure on the windward side. The architectural ramification of this phenomenon is the necessity of designing a curtain wall that will permit inside and outside pressures to equalize themselves. Glass failure during a wind storm is usually due to negative pressure: the glass is "sucked" from the building, falling into the street and posing a tremendous hazard.

The required resistive strength of glass is affected by its location. The higher one goes the greater the wind speed and pressure; if the glass panels are kept uniform in size, they will need to be increased in thickness as their height above the ground increases.

An additional common problem caused by wind is the uplift effect it can have on a roof, especially on gently curved roofs. The roof's reaction to wind is similar to that of an airplane wing. An area of negative air pressure is produced by the passing wind and this in turn will create a tendency for the roof to "fly," or, less dramatically, to lift slightly and then fall, ultimately causing cracks and leaks. If the roof is not made of sufficiently heavy material, such as a concrete slab, to balance the negative pressure then the architect might have to tie down the roof to prevent flutter. This is a serious issue with very light roof materials such as the fabrics and plastics used to cover air-supported tennis court roofs and even giant roofs such as those on the Minneapolis and Pontiac, Michigan stadiums.

EARTHQUAKE

Earthquakes are another of nature's forces which designers must take into consideration. It would be easy to say that one should not build where this danger exists, but a variety of social and economic pressures make it at least a viable choice to build in fairly high seismic zones and assume the added costs entailed. The issue here is how these forces affect buildings. If a building's parts are firmly interconnected, the building will act as a totality and be less susceptible to shaking apart. There are interesting photos of some residences in Alaska, taken after an earthquake. The houses were built with rigid plywood sheets, and even though they fell and settled unevenly, they remained intact and could therefore protect life and limb. If they had been built of many small pieces, they would have crumbled.

Both wind and earthquake forces induce lateral or horizontal stresses in a structure. Wind forces are proportional to the amount of exposed vertical surface a building has, while earthquake-induced loads are related to the total weight of the building.

TEMPERATURE

Building materials contract and expand with temperature changes. Changes in the horizontal elements of a building are accommodated by expansion joints that allow for some movement. Vertical expansion and contraction is not a problem if it is uniform throughout the building.

When an exterior column is exposed to freezing outdoor temperature and an interior column is maintained at the warm interior temperature of the building, a significant imbalance in the relative heights of the columns will result. The taller the building, the greater the potential for imbalance. In the winter, the columns on the outside will be shorter than those located in the warm interior; conversely, in the summer, if the building is air-conditioned, the interior columns will be shorter than the exterior ones. This difference in column length can result in cracks in the walls, stuck or broken doors and windows, and sloping floors, unless the arthitect makes some provisions to prevent these things from happening. This is usually accomplished by connecting the air space between the column and its cover with the controlled environment of the building's interior; and by insulating the exterior sides of the columns. The addition of insulation will increase the visual appearance of the protected columns. In most buildings, this whole issue is avoided by placing all of the columns completely indoors behind the protection of a curtain wall.

SNOW AND ICE

Snow and ice create loads on the roof of a building. If the building is located in an area of heavy winter precipitation, the load can be considerable. For example, as much as 90 pounds per square foot must be allowed for in some parts of New York State. An architect must respond to the elements with either a structure capable of supporting the weight of the snow and ice or a means of lessening its impact. A sloping roof that prevents the accumulation of snow is a familiar example of the latter.

SOIL

Soil types vary greatly, ranging from mud to sand to rock, and must be taken into account when planning a structure. The soil's weight-bearing capacity will determine the type of foundation system that will be required. In all cases, the building's total weight must be distributed over a large enough area to permit the soil under its columns and/or walls to support the structure and its loads.

In some cases where poor soil conditions exist, piles might be required to help take the loads down to a better bearing material. The soil ultimately must be capable of supporting the building and all the loads placed in and on it.

Soil contains moisture, and the foundation of even a small building must go deep enough so that it is below the freezing line of the moisture in the soil. Otherwise the freezing process will cause the building to heave. Soil also exerts horizontal pressures on the walls of basements and cellars. Sometimes, the soil quality can determine the material selection for the framing system. For example, a steel-frame skeleton weighs much less than a comparable reinforced concrete frame. A poor soil situation might dictate the use of a steel skeleton frame because a concrete frame would greatly increase the cost of the foundation work required to support it.

Chapter 2

FRAMING MATERIALS

The three most commonly used framing materials in current use are wood, steel, and reinforced concrete. Aluminum, plastic, and glass are used to form parts of a building's skin, but so far have not made any significant structural contributions. Steel and concrete are manufactured in a variety of different strengths, and the strength of lumber varies, depending on the type of tree it comes from and its overall quality.

To develop a sense of the relative capacities of these three framing materials, the accompanying chart shows the more commonly used values for the typical kinds of stresses that structural members must resist. The data in the chart are for the most frequently used quality or grade of a particular material, selected from the fairly extensive range that is available. Stresses are described in pounds per square inch (psi) and are the allowable stresses as opposed to the actual stresses that have been determined by laboratory testing. Allowable stresses are those that are considered acceptable—and safe—according to the building codes. The actual stress that a material can physically withstand is always higher than the allowable stress, because common sense and the building codes dictate that there must be a margin of safety. This factor of safety allows for possible flaws in the material and

COMMONLY USED STRESS VALUES

WOOD

Construction-Grade Douglas Fir-Larch

Average compressive strength	900–1250 psi
Average tensile strength	650–1000 psi
Average strength in bending	1200–1500 psi
Average strength in shear	85–95 psi
Average weight per cubic foot	30–35 lb
Depth to span ratio for a typical joist	1/18–1/20

Some grades of long-leaf yellow pine have values over 2400 psi for bending, and spruce has values under 600 psi.

STEEL

36,000 psi, nominal strength

Average compressive strength	20,000 psi
Average tensile strength	22,000 psi
Average strength in bending	24,000 psi
Average strength in shear	14,500 psi
Average weight per cubic foot	490 lb
Depth to span ratio for typical beam	1/20 to 1/24

The common stress range of steel today is from 24,000 psi (A–36) to over 100,000 psi for high-strength steels.

CBS Building, New York, New York.

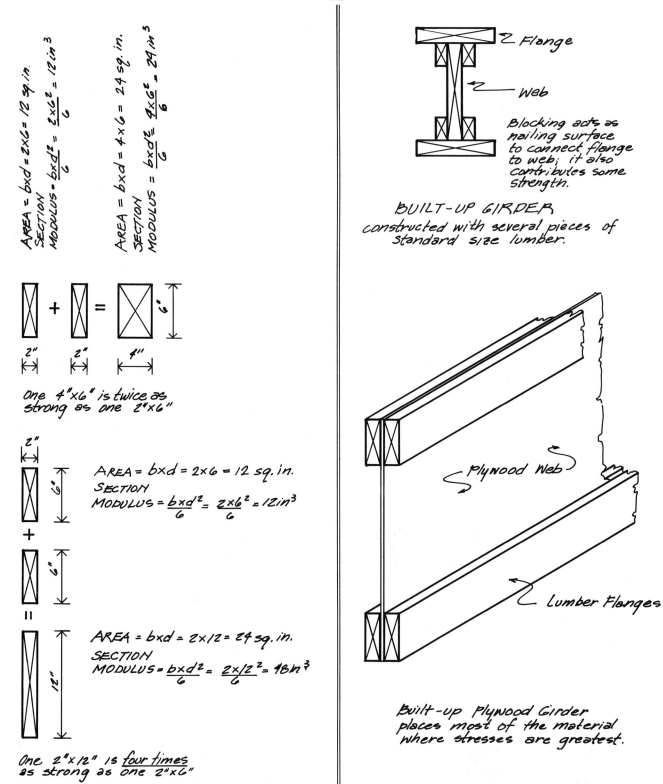

AREA = b×d = 2×6 = 12 sq.in.
SECTION
MODULUS = $\frac{b×d^2}{6}$ = $\frac{2×6^2}{6}$ = 12 in^3

AREA = b×d = 4×6 = 24 sq.in.
SECTION
MODULUS = $\frac{b×d^2}{6}$ = $\frac{4×6^2}{6}$ = 24 in^3

One 4"×6" is twice as strong as one 2"×6"

AREA = b×d = 2×6 = 12 sq.in.
SECTION
MODULUS = $\frac{b×d^2}{6}$ = $\frac{2×6^2}{6}$ = 12 in^3

AREA = b×d = 2×12 = 24 sq.in.
SECTION
MODULUS = $\frac{b×d^2}{6}$ = $\frac{2×12^2}{6}$ = 48 in^3

One 2"×12" is _four times_ as strong as one 2"×6"

Both the 4"×6" and the 2"×12" have the same area, but the 2"×12" is deeper and, therefore, stronger.

Flange

Web

Blocking acts as nailing surface to connect flange to web; it also contributes some strength.

BUILT-UP GIRDER
constructed with several pieces of standard size lumber.

Plywood Web

Lumber Flanges

Built-up Plywood Girder places most of the material where stresses are greatest.

REINFORCED CONCRETE

2500 to 5000 psi, nominal:

Average compressive strength	1125 to 2250 psi
Average tensile strength	Zero*
Average strength in bending compressive value as balanced by tensile value of steel reinforcement	Varies with the amount and type of reinforcing steel**
Average strength in shear	85 to 120 psi
Average weight per cubic foot	150 lb
Depth to span ratio for a typical beam	Between 1/16 to 1/18

The compressive strength of concrete ranges from 2,000 psi (used for mass footings) to 18,000 psi for special framing.

*The actual tensile capacity of concrete is about 10 percent of its compressive value.

**Area of steel varies from approximately 1–3% of beams; 2–8% of columns. Allowable stress range for the steel is between 20,000 to 32,000 psi.

workmanship, and provides a buffer between what a material can theoretically do and what an engineer or architect can prudently rely on it to do.

WOOD

Wood is a readily obtainable material in this country. It is easily joined together and is usually the most cost competitive framing material for small span structures such as private residences. Wood is unique among the materials used for framing members in that it is the only one that is grown. Aside from being cut to shape, it is used essentially as it is found in nature. Steel is an alloy of several metals, and concrete is a mixture of several substances. Wood, used in its natural state, can have a wide range of qualities, and thus a large variation in its ability to resist different kinds of stresses. The particular stress capacity and decay resistance of an individual piece of wood will vary, for example, according to the species of tree from which it is milled, the part of the log it comes from, the amount of moisture retained, and the quality of its grain.

Framing lumber can be obtained only by removing those parts of the log that are not needed. Structural lumber is rectangular, since cutting more complicated shapes is not practical. When engineering requires other shapes, and their cost can be justified, then built-up wood beams can be assembled by securing several pieces of lumber together.

Some defects, such as knotholes, can weaken the value of wood as a structural member. The amount of

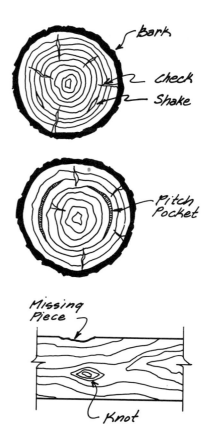

TYPICAL GRADE STAMP

a. Grading Organization's Name
b. Number of Mill
c. Grade of the wood
d. Species of the wood.
e. Moisture Content (s-dry = 19% or less)

Modern heavy timber construction enhances a shopping mall.

moisture content can affect the strength: a 1-percent change in moisture content will cause a 6-percent change in the crushing strength parallel to the grain of the lumber. Using green (unseasoned) lumber can cause the structure to warp, because it will eventually dry out and shrink. The direction of the grain is very important: the less parallel the grain is to the length of the beam, the weaker the beam will be.

Wood is also subject to several other defects as a structural member. These include wane, which consists of pieces of bark or missing wood along the edges; check, radial splits that occur during seasoning; shakes, a separation that occurs during growth (shakes can be between the growth rings or radial); and pitch pockets, openings between the growth rings that are filled with pitch.

All framing lumber that is required to have a dependable stress value is graded, either by inspection or by machine. Machine-graded wood is slightly more expensive and probably more accurately graded. Each individual piece of graded wood is stamped with a grade mark, which is the architect's assurance of the quality and strength specified.

Large wood timbers and laminated members consisting of layers of approximately 2-inch-thick lumber are available. Heavy timber construction is often seen in small commercial buildings, sports arenas, and as exposed frames in churches. The majority of construction lumber consists of relatively small pieces which permit easy handling and simple connections.

Wood joists are light, horizontal framing members 2 or 3 inches thick, usually 6 to 12 inches deep, and generally available in lengths up to 20 feet long. They are most often spaced 12 to 16 inches on center and are usually used to accommodate fairly light live loads (30 to 60 pounds per square foot). There are occasions when the architect is confronted with a situation where these size or span conditions are exceeded. For example, joists might be needed to span 24 feet and require 14-inch-deep lumber. The higher cost and difficulty of obtaining joists deeper than 12 inches or longer than 20 feet could affect the selection of wood as the framing material, or alter the framing system pattern by introducing the need for a girder to reduce the required length of the joists.

STEEL

Steel is a man-made material consisting of iron combined with carbon and small amounts of other alloys that are added to improve its strength and durability. It is readily available throughout the Western world,

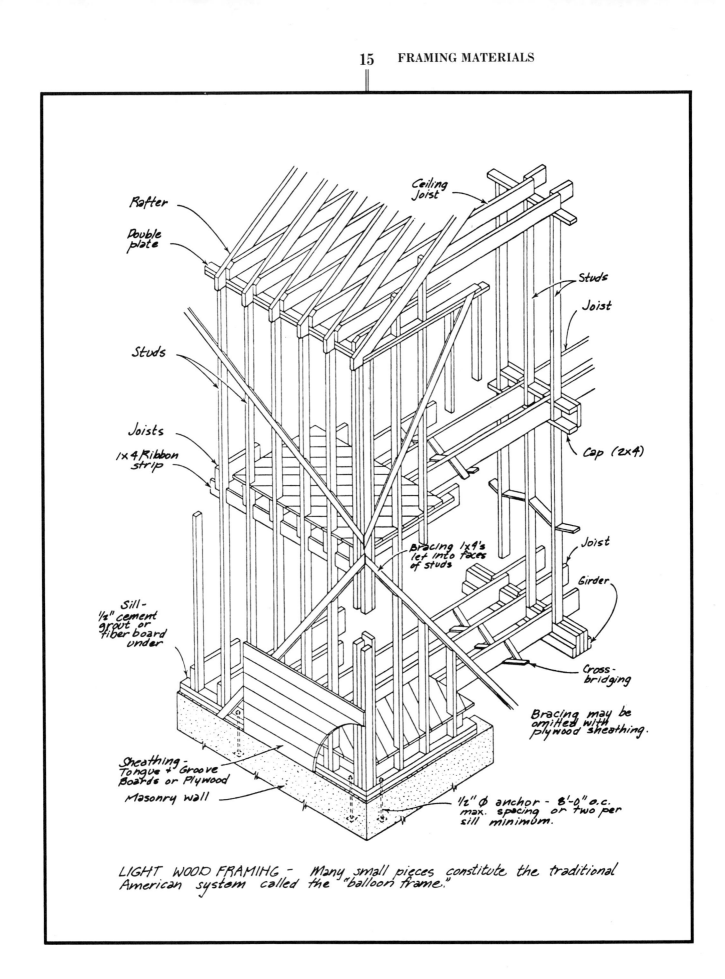

Rafter

Ceiling Joist

Double plate

Studs

Joist

Studs

Joists

1x4 Ribbon strip

Cap (2x4)

Bracing 1x4's let into faces of studs

Joist

Girder

Sill- ½" cement grout or fiber board under

Cross-bridging

Bracing may be omitted with plywood sheathing.

Sheathing- Tongue + Groove Boards or Plywood

Masonry wall

½" ⌀ anchor - 8'-0" o.c. max. spacing or two per sill minimum.

LIGHT WOOD FRAMING - Many small pieces constitute the traditional American system called the "balloon frame."

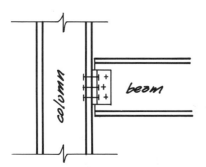

SIMPLE CONNECTION

transfers load only --
not bending stress.

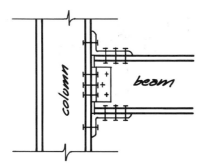

RIGID CONNECTION

transfers both load
and bending stress.

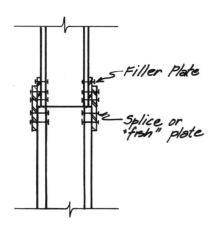

COLUMN SPLICE

- Filler Plate

- Splice or
"fish" plate

Angles, tees and plates are used
to connect one framing member
to another. The connections
are made either by bolting or
by welding.

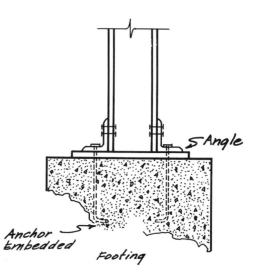

Angle

Anchor
Embedded

Footing

COLUMN BASE

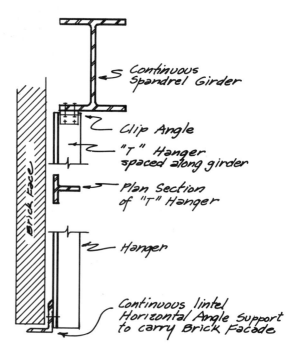

Continuous
Spandrel Girder

Clip Angle

"T" Hanger
spaced along girder

Plan Section
of "T" Hanger

Hanger

Continuous lintel
Horizontal Angle Support
to carry Brick Facade

TYPICAL SUPPORT FOR
OUTER FACE OF BUILDING

but is often scarce or totally unavailable in other parts of the world.

Steel has several major disadvantages. It is very heavy, weighing 490 pounds per cubic foot, and mechanical lifting equipment is required to hoist it into place. It must be protected against fire. It rusts if exposed to the elements, unless special high-cost alloys are added to prevent this. Finally, the methods used to connect framing members to each other require skilled labor and equipment, which adds to the construction expense.

Despite this, steel has important advantages. It can span larger distances than wood beams and is smaller than concrete beams carrying the same loads and spanning the same distances. Spans of 30 to 40 feet for steel are common, and spans up to 60 feet are not uncommon. The total framing weight of steel per square foot of floor area is less than that of reinforced concrete even though steel itself weighs much more per cubic foot (490 pounds for steel as opposed to 150 pounds for concrete). This is because the cross-sectional area of a steel-framing member is much smaller than that required for a concrete member spanning the same distance and carrying the same load. In addition, a concrete column will be much stouter than a steel one supporting the same load.

Structural steel became a glamour material at the turn of the century because it made possible tall, light buildings. The heavy masonry-bearing wall was replaced by a skeleton of steel beams, columns, and girders. Initially, the stress capacity of steel was low by today's standards. Joints were awkward and required innumerable rivets, but today, high-strength steel is fastened with bolts and/or is welded.

Steel framing members come in many shapes. The most commonly used beam looks like the letter H turned on its side and is called a *wide flange*. The largest wide flange beam available is 36 inches deep and weighs 360 pounds per linear foot, and the smallest is only 4 inches deep. This shape is used because it permits most of the material to be placed at the top and bottom of a beam, where the bending stress from its load is the greatest. The web in between acts to connect the two parts so that they can act together. The web also takes the load of the shear forces.

Other commonly available milled shapes of structural steel are angles, channels, and plates, all of which can be used individually or can be combined to make built-up members for special needs that cannot be met with the standard rolled shapes available from the mill.

Extra heavy wide flange shapes are used as columns. They are proportioned so that their flanges are approximately as wide as the depth of their web. The heaviest milled section weighs 730 pounds per foot, and has five inch thick flanges.

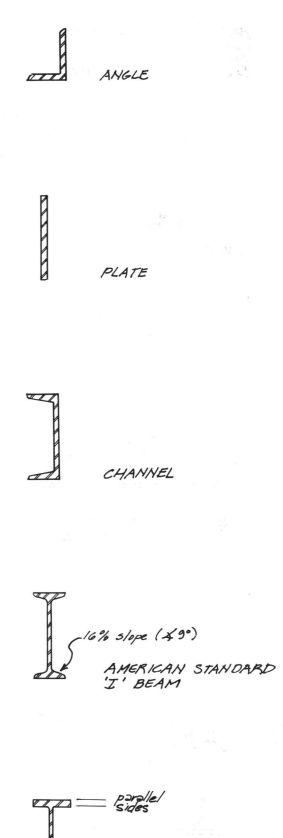

ANGLE

PLATE

CHANNEL

16% slope (≮9°)
AMERICAN STANDARD 'I' BEAM

parallel sides
WIDE FLANGE

Built-up girders and columns can be made from a combination of members to solve special situations.

BUILT-UP GIRDER

studs

COMPOSITE BEAM

Studs welded to top of beam to bond flange to concrete

Concrete Floor Slab

Extra plate added to bottom of beam in order to balance use of concrete at top

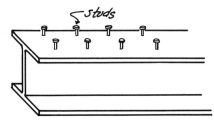

COMPOSITE BEAM

Composite construction is a way to make a steel beam more efficient by interconnecting its top flange with the concrete slab it supports. Anchoring the top flange into the concrete allows the beam and slab to act together to resist compression. A composite beam will be stiffer than a non-composite beam, permitting shallow members to be used.

Typical beams in high-rise buildings range in size from 1 to 2 feet in depth and weigh between 30 and 120 pounds per linear foot. When reading a framing plan (such as the ones in the case studies in Part Two), it is helpful to know the common symbols. W stands for wide flange, as in W21 × 82. The first number is the nominal depth; the second number is the weight per linear foot. For example, a plan would indicate a wide-flange beam 21 inches deep and weighing 82 pounds per foot as W21 × 82. American Standard beams bear the prefix S; C stands for channels; L, for angles; and other marks represent other special shapes.

Older drawings used the symbol W^F to designate wide-flange beams, and some architects and engineers continue to use this symbol out of habit. The current W21 × 82 designation was written as 21 W^F 82. Also, 12 I 24, formerly used to describe a 12-inch-deep American Standard I-beam weighing 24 pounds per linear foot, would now be written S12 × 24.

Since steel is a man-made material, there is every reason to believe that scientists can continue to improve its strength and perhaps its ability to withstand fire and resist oxidation.

CONCRETE

Basic concrete is a mixture of cement, water, sand, and gravel. The strength of this composition comes from the cement, which is essentially limestone and silica that has been ground and calcined. Cement and water are mixed to form a paste, to which an inexpensive filler or stretcher is added to make its bulk go further. This stretcher typically consists of a mixture of a fine material such as sand and a coarse material such as gravel. Fresh concrete is plastic, which means that it can take any reasonable shape when it is poured into a mold. This is one of its major advantages as a framing material.

Modern concrete often contains some chemical additives used to achieve some special property, such as a faster or slower curing time or a higher resistance on the part of cured concrete which is intended to be left exposed to the freeze-thaw cycle in areas where the winters are harsh.

The proportioning of concrete's ingredients is a complicated science and also a bit of an art. The final strength of concrete depends on the mixture proportions; generally, the greater the proportion of cement and the smaller the amount of water needed to make the mix plastic, the stronger the concrete will be. Unfortunately, cement is the most costly of the regular ingredients of concrete.

The size of the aggregate—which is usually gravel—depends on the use of the structure. For example, huge rocks would be included in a mix for construction of a dam, while 1 to 1½-inch-diameter gravel would generally be the maximum size aggregate used in a beam or a column. The type of material used to build the form-work that shapes the concrete also affects the surface, and therefore the appearance, of the cured concrete cast against it. Some architects have the wood form boards sandblasted, in order to leave a negative impression of wood grain on the finished concrete surface. Architects who do this believe that they are revealing the process. Others express horror over what they see as a dishonest gesture, that is, an attempt to make concrete look like wood.

The color of the cement, sand, and gravel can be selected to impart a particular color or texture to the finished concrete. A variety of textures can also be imparted to the concrete while it is in the early stages of curing and still plastic, and even the cured concrete can be etched or hammered to create a desired effect. The pattern of joints between successive pours and the rhythm of tie holes created by the form work can be used as an architectural expression, or carefully treated to leave no visible traces.

Roughly 28 days are required for concrete to obtain its full strength and load-carrying capacity. In theory, it never stops curing; but in 28 days, it is considered to have reached its final strength for engineering purposes. Normally concrete obtains sufficient strength within a week to support construction loads, thus permitting the forms to be removed and reused. This time factor is important to the builder, who needs to reuse the forms and be able to place loads (such as the next floor) on the concrete as soon as possible.

Nature sometimes causes problems. Concrete cannot cure properly if it becomes too hot or too cold during the process. A contractor must heat curing concrete in cold weather and keep it moist in hot weather. This added effort, especially the need to heat during the winter, obviously costs the builder money. Because of this, concrete is often ruled out as a framing material on construction projects scheduled for the winter months in areas that have cold winters. When a builder does need to pour concrete during freezing

Texture of wood boards and grain on the piers of Eero Saarinen's TWA Terminal.

Ridge texture cast into Paul Rudolph's Endo Laboratory Building.

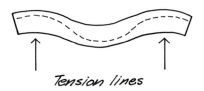

Tension lines

support

Location of steel bars in order to resist tensile stress

weather, it may be cost-effective to add chemicals that shorten the curing period and thus the heating time.

REINFORCED CONCRETE

Reinforced concrete is a combination of concrete and steel. Concrete, which can resist compressive forces but has very little ability to resist tensile stresses, pulls apart very easily—so easily that the building codes, which must be conservative, do not permit an architect to attribute any value to nonreinforced concrete's ability to withstand tension. Steel, by contrast, has excellent capacity to resist tension forces. The obvious solution, then, is to place steel along the lines of tensile stress in a concrete framing member. In actual practice, these stress patterns are stylized to permit easy fabrication, but in very special and difficult situations, the pattern of steel rods in concrete closely follows a pattern of engineering stress analysis. The high cost of the careful field work required to do this can be justified by the result.

Due to its strength, only relatively small amounts of steel are needed to reinforce concrete. Steel's ability to take tension is up to 10 times greater than concrete's ability to resist compression. Therefore, relatively little reinforcing steel is used in proportion to the amount of concrete used in a beam, and even less steel is needed in columns, which normally are subject to predominantly compressive stresses. The amount of steel generally ranges from 2 percent to 8 percent of the gross cross-sectional area of a column.

PRECAST CONCRETE

Many of the liabilities of poured concrete can be overcome when concrete framing members are precast in the factory. Construction-site time can be greatly reduced by using precast or factory-made concrete framing members, because they eliminate job-site waiting time required to cure poured concrete. The quality of workmanship and proper curing of the concrete members are much more easily controlled indoors. The in-the-field time and the cost of stripping off and rebuilding the forms is also avoided. Bad weather is never a factor when curing precast concrete in a factory. Openings for ductwork can be pre-engineered, and conduits for electric wiring can be embedded within the precast member. After being poured and cured, precast concrete members can be joined to each other in ways

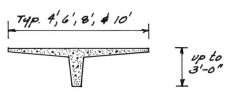

SINGLE TEE

Typ. 4', 6', 8', & 10'

up to
3'-0"

DOUBLE TEE

'I' GIRDER

beam and girder
size depends on
span and load.

BEAM WITH HAUNCH

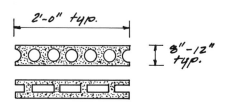

HOLLOW CORE SLABS

2'-0" typ.

8"-12"
typ.

Precast trusses span between poured-in-place columns.
BOSTON CITY HALL, KALLMANN, McKINNELL &
KNOWLES, Architects.

one precast framing member
can be joined to the next
by a variety of methods, each
one capable of many variations.

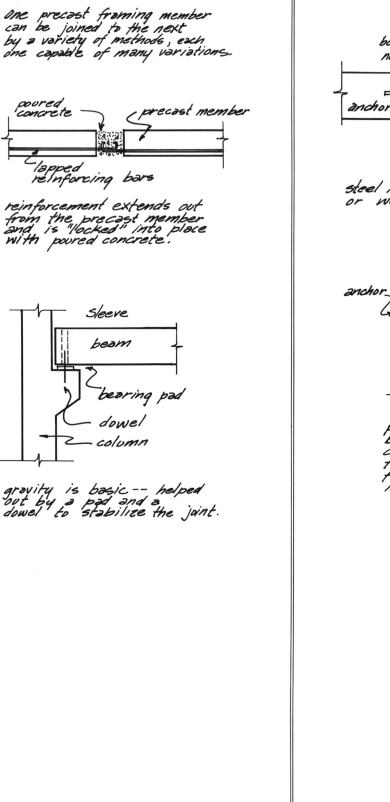

reinforcement extends out
from the precast member
and is "locked" into place
with poured concrete.

gravity is basic -- helped
out by a pad and a
dowel to stabilize the joint.

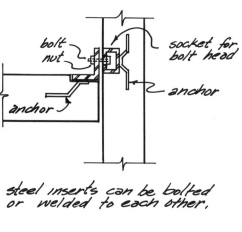

steel inserts can be bolted
or welded to each other.

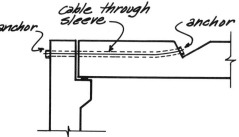

precast members can
be secured together by
cables or rods that are
then stretched (post-
tensioned) and locked
into place.

similar to those used for connecting steel or large timber members.

Precast concrete is not without its disadvantages. Precast members are often more difficult and costly to ship than the bulk cement and gravel ingredients used for mixing concrete on the job site. Giant cranes are needed to hoist these heavy hunks of concrete. Special care must be taken, during hoisting and placing, not to put stresses on them that are different from the ones they are designed to take in their final position in the structure. The steel reinforcement placed in precast concrete members is set in a specific pattern in order to resist a specific set of stresses. If a framing member or panel is subjected to a different kind of stress during the hoisting process, it may crack.

Perhaps the biggest general disadvantage of precast concrete framing systems is their basic lack of stability. A poured-in-place concrete building becomes one monolithic continuous whole. Individual precast members must be joined to each other, and this joint constitutes a weak point. Joining techniques are continually becoming more sophisticated, and new techniques are constantly being developed (and their costs reduced), but the solutions are not yet generally cost-effective when the stresses are high. Thus, this inherent instability of the framing joints tends to limit the use of precast concrete framing members to low- or medium-rise structures where stability is less critical.

PRE- AND POST-TENSIONED CONCRETE

There is another type of concrete construction in which steel wires or tendons are embedded within the concrete and subjected to a tensile stress imposed by jacks either before (pre-stressed) or after (post-stressed) the concrete is cured. The stress built into the beam by tensioning the steel in this way is essentially opposite and approximately equal to the stress that the live load of occupancy and use of the building will place on the beam.

An increase in efficiency over reinforced concrete is achieved by the tension put into the steel. The concrete in a stressed framing member is being squeezed by forces induced by the stressed wire. This means that all of the concrete is now working in compression. In a standard reinforced beam, only the top third or so of the concrete is put to work. The tension-stress capacity of the wire is so large (its average allowable working stress is 150,000 or more psi) that the total cross-sectional area of the stressing steel usually can

A twentieth century totem pole. Five story high precast concrete columns.

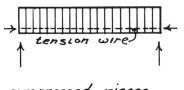

loose, uncompressed pieces will fall.

tension wire

compressed pieces stay together and, therefore, can act as a beam.

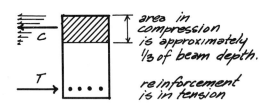

area in compression is approximately 1/3 of beam depth.

reinforcement is in tension

REINFORCED CONCRETE

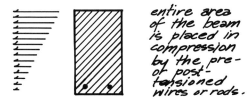

entire area of the beam is placed in compression by the pre- or post- tensioned wires or rods.

STRESSED CONCRETE

be less than one-half of 1 percent of the cross-sectional area of the beam.

Pre-stressing is used for precast concrete members. A wire or tendon is stretched over a frame; one end is anchored; and jacks are applied to the other end in order to pull the wire to its required degree of stress. Concrete is then poured into the beam form that parallels and encases the wire. The natural bonding coefficient between the steel and the concrete is fortunately so high that when the concrete has cured, the anchorage on the pre-stressed wire can be removed and the wire will not slip or pull away from the concrete surrounding it. The stress in the wire is transferred to the concrete by the bonding of the two materials.

Post-stressing is used in framing members that are poured in place at their final location. In the post-stressing process, a wire is placed within a flexible metal or plastic casing. (The casing is needed because stressing will take place after the concrete has been poured and cured.) The tubing is carefully placed within the empty formwork built for the framing member. One end of the wire is attached to an anchor that will be cast into the concrete when it is poured, and the other end is attached to a jacking collar that protrudes past the opposite end of the formwork. After the concrete has been poured and cured, the required amount of tensioning is applied to the collar by hydraulic or pneumatic jacks. The jacked end of the wire is then secured, and its stress is transferred to the beam, thus compressing it.

Post-tensioning is also used to join one piece of precast concrete to another, very much in the manner of stringing beads. When the tension force is applied after the pieces are strung together, they are locked in place by compression imparted from the stressing process and thus become secure and stable.

The increased efficiency of a beam that has been either pre- or post-tensioned permits it to have a shallower depth than a standard reinforced concrete member subject to the same span and load. A pre- or post-stressed member also has the capacity to span a greater distance than a standard reinforced concrete beam of the same size.

1. *This simple method of prestressing begins with screwing the pulling rod directly into the threaded center hole of the stressing ring.*

2. *The second step of the PI method is to slide the chair and ram into position on pulling rod and screw on the rear nut.*

3. *To obtain the proper tensioning force and elongation, operate the electrical pump.*

4. *Insert the holding shims between the stressing ring and the plate bearing on the concrete member.*

Tendon B has been tensioned and anchored. Note the use of increment shims to obtain proper tension. Also note identification mark visible for reference during tensioning.

Chapter 3

STRUCTURAL COMPONENTS

Beams, girders, and joists are the principal horizontal framing members utilized in most buildings, while columns and reinforced concrete bearing walls are the common vertical supports. Load-bearing masonry walls quickly become very thick on the lower floors of all but relatively low structures, severely limiting the amount of usable floor area. Trusses, along with rigid frames, concrete shells, space frames, and other exotic framing systems, are generally used in special situations. They are not part of the basic skeletal frame that is the subject of this discussion.

The ways that the horizontal and vertical framing members control and transmit the stresses to which they are subjected depends on the material that is used. The material also determines the size and proportions of the structural members.

FRAMING SYSTEMS

The framing system is the skeleton of a building. Like any skeleton, it supports the rest of the structure. The horizontal components of most framing systems fall into one of two basic categories: one-way and two-way. Multi-way systems exist, but they are less common than the other two systems. All horizontal framing systems distribute the loads and stresses that are placed on the building's floors until they can be picked up and transferred to the ground by vertical supports.

The vertical components of a framing system are not usually complicated with the necessity of dealing with ducts, lights, sprinkler piping, and other mechanical systems that must interface and/or cross with the joists, beams or girders of a floor system.

HORIZONTAL COMPONENTS

A beam is a horizontal framing member that receives part of a floor load and transmits it to a support that is usually located at each of its ends. The beam may be supported by a column, a wall, or another beam, usually placed at right angles to the first beam. A beam that receives the load of several other beams is called a *girder*. Smaller beams, which are used parallel to each other and are spaced fairly close together in relation to their span, are called *joists*. The hierarchy of girder-beam-joist depends not on the size of the individual units, but rather on their relative functions within the framing system.

Westcoast Transmission Co. Vancouver B.C.

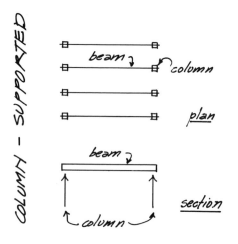

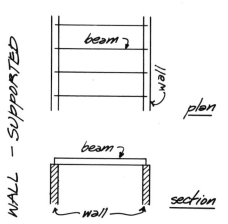

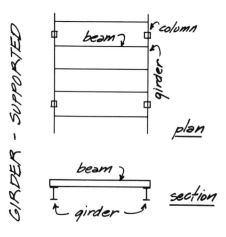

One-Way Systems

One-way framing systems are the most common. Most one-way systems consist of a sequential series of framing members that transfer their loads and stresses along a hierarchy of beams and girders. A one-way system can be identified by observing the stress path, which is always linear and goes in only one direction at a time. A load placed on a beam travels along its length to the points where the beam is supported. The load on each beam is apportioned to its support, which can be a column, a wall, or a girder. Joists spanning between two bearing walls is an example of the simplest type of one-way system.

Two-Way Systems

In a two-way system, the stresses imposed on the floor system are dispersed in two different directions at the same time, with each half running at right angles to the other. The major advantage of a two-way system is that each of the two framing members can be shallower than if they were carrying the entire load individually.

Many concrete buildings use a two-way rib system for their floor framing. Since all the ribs in both directions can be poured monolithically, the necessity of joining each segment of every rib to an adjacent rib is eliminated.

Two-way systems built of wood and steel are used for situations where the large number of joints needed can be justified by appearance and shallower structural depths.

Multiway Systems

A framing system that could distribute its loads in more than two directions would permit still shallower framing members provided the loads and spans remained constant. A framing system based on a triangular grid would be an example of a multi-way system.

Occasionally, the stress pattern induced in a monolithic floor system can be used to generate a beam or grid pattern. Stress-pattern grids such as those used by the Italian engineer-builder Nervi fall into a special category. They are much admired by architects and by the general public, since they are a true expression of the actual stresses. Unfortunately, their use is limited by the high cost of the special formwork shapes needed to build them.

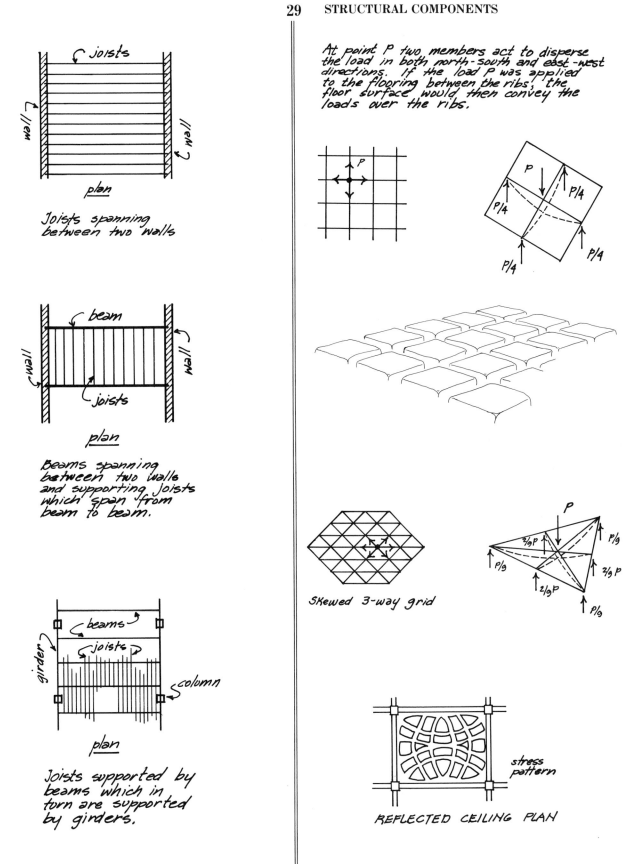

joists

wall   *wall*

plan

Joists spanning
between two walls

beam

wall   *wall*

joists

plan

Beams spanning
between two walls
and supporting joists
which span from
beam to beam.

beams

girder   *joists*

column

plan

Joists supported by
beams which in
turn are supported
by girders.

At point P two members act to disperse
the load in both north-south and east-west
directions. If the load P was applied
to the flooring between the ribs, the
floor surface would then convey the
loads over the ribs.

P

P/4   P   P/4

P/4   P/4

Skewed 3-way grid

P

²/₉P   P/₉

P/₉   ²/₉P

²/₉P   P/₉

*stress
pattern*

REFLECTED CEILING PLAN

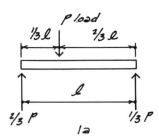

1a

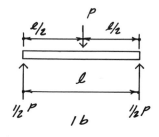

1b

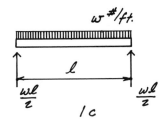

1c

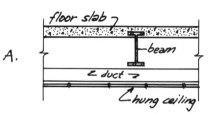

A.

Ducts can run under the deepest framing members and can be concealed from below by a hung ceiling.

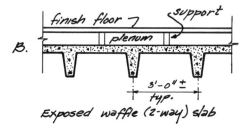

B.

Exposed waffle (2-way) slab

Ducts can run above the structural floor and a 'floating floor' walking surface can be placed above the ducts.

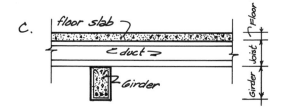

C.

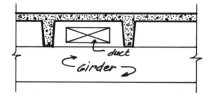

The ribs of a one-way system can be supported on the top of a girder. This method will permit the ducts to pass above the girder in the open spaces between the ribs.

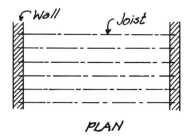

PLAN

2a

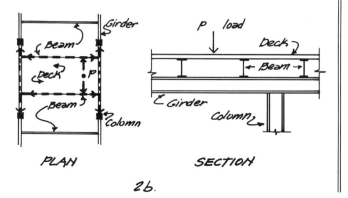

PLAN   SECTION

2b.

D.

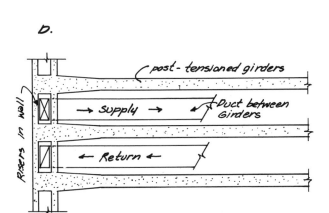

post-tensioned girders

→ Supply →

Duct between Girders

← Return ←

Risers in wall

(See PART II — American Life Case Study)

If a separate riser duct is provided for each horizontal duct, it will eliminate the need for any ducts to cross the direction of the framing members. A one-way framing system can be used to span the entire floor serviced by the duct.

E.

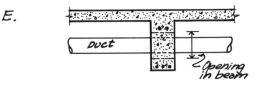

Duct

Opening in beam

This system is usually feasible only when the duct sizes are relatively small.

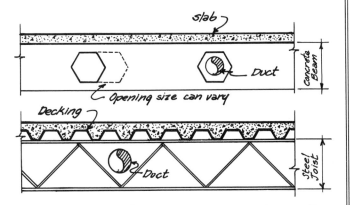

slab

Duct

Opening size can vary

Concrete Beam

Decking

Duct

Steel Joist

Ducts may penetrate openings provided in the beams or joists, thus running across the grain of the framing without reducing the headroom of the space below.

F.

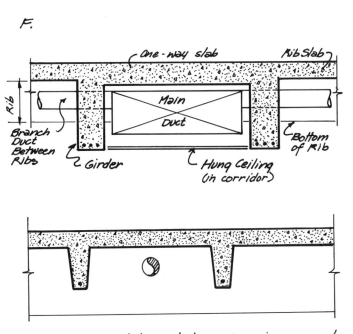

One-way slab

Rib Slab

Rib

Main Duct

Branch Duct Between Ribs

Girder

Hung Ceiling (in corridor)

Bottom of Rib

The area around large duct openings in a concrete framing member is reinforced by the addition of extra steel bars imbedded in the concrete; steel angles or plates reinforce the openings in the webs of steel framing members.

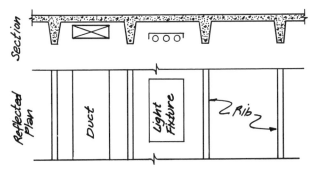

Section

Reflected Plan

Duct

Light Fixture

Rib

Supply and return ducts can run between the ribs of pre-cast joists (or any other one-way system).

A simple beam spans between only two supports.

A continuous beam spans over several supports. Deflection occurs between the supports.

+ = compression
− = tension

top
middle
bottom

ℓ

No load on beam:
Length is constant at top, middle and bottom of beam.

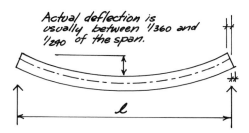

Actual deflection is usually between 1/360 and 1/240 of the span.

ℓ

Loaded Beam
Length at the bottom exceeds length at middle and at top.

HORIZONTAL FRAMING MEMBERS

A beam is subject to two common stresses: bending and shear. When a beam deflects under its load, it is subject to bending stress, often called *flexture* by engineers. The tendency for a beam to drop vertically between its supports causes shearing stresses. Torsion and buckling are less commonly induced stresses.

Bending

In order to see the kinds of stresses that a beam is subjected to when a uniformly distributed load is placed on it, let's exaggerate what happens to it. The load will make the beam sag and curve downward in the center. In an unloaded beam (a beam is actually never totally unloaded because it must always support its own weight), the length at the top, middle, and bottom of the beam are all equal. When a beam is loaded, however, this is no longer the case. To see what happens, look at the accompanying sketches. The sag curve caused by the load has been exaggerated and shown as an arc of a circle. It is now obvious that the top of the beam is the arc of a circle that possesses a shorter circumference than the circle whose arc goes through the center of the beam. By the same token, the beam's bottom is now longer than its center.

Since the top, middle, and bottom all started out having the same length, it follows that when a beam bends from the force of its load, the top is trying to become shorter than it was in its initial position and is therefore being compressed. Since the beam's bottom edge is trying to become longer, because it is being stretched, it is being put into tension. If a beam's top is in compression, and its bottom is in tension, then somewhere as the force goes from the compression stresses at the top to the tension stresses at the bottom, it must pass through a point of zero force, and it does. This point is called the *neutral plane* or *axis*. In beams constructed out of one uniform material, it is located at the center.

A beam is subjected to the greatest bending stresses at the top and bottom; the forces are equal and opposite. This has ramifications for the shape of a beam. Ideally, most of a beam's material would be placed at the top and bottom, and there would be very little material in the middle. That is how engineers shape beams whenever it is practical, such as when manufacturing steel sections. Wood beams are cut to a rectangular shape because the sawing process for any other shape would be very expensive, and would not produce a better beam or a by-product of any value.

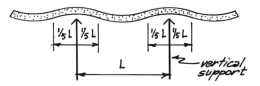

A beam subjected to bending tends to either tear apart at the bottom or crush at the top depending on whether the material inherently can resist tension or compression forces better.

The forces in a continuous beam change from tension at the top over a support to tension at the bottom between supports. This change occurs at approximately 1/5 the distance between supports.

The point at which the flexural stresses change from the top of the beam to the bottom of the beam is the inflection point. It is here that the magnitude of the forces is zero. Consequently for continuous beams, the best place to splice the member is at the inflection point (1/5th point of the span).

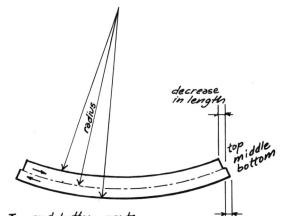

Top and bottom parts want to slide past each other. This tendency is called horizontal shear.

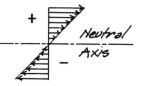

In a beam composed entirely of one material (homogenous), all the forces due to bending above the Neutral Axis will be compressive while all the forces below the Neutral Axis will be tensile.

load = w pounds per linear foot

A _simple beam_ (supported at each end) carrying a uniformly distributed load.

$$M = \frac{wl^2}{8}$$

Diagram showing the change in magnitude of the bending forces of the beam above. Note that the forces are zero at the ends and are maximum at the center.

A _continuous beam_ carrying a uniformly distributed load.

$+\frac{1}{16} wl^2$ $\frac{1}{5}l$ $+\frac{1}{16} wl^2$

Neutral Axis

$-\frac{1}{10} wl^2$ $-\frac{1}{10} wl^2$ $-\frac{1}{10} wl^2$

In a continuous beam, note that the magnitude of the bending forces changes from positive between the supports to negative at the supports. This change occurs at the fifth points of the span.

(NOTE: $+\frac{1}{16} wl^2$ and $-\frac{1}{10} wl^2$ are maximum allowable design forces. The actual forces would be $+\frac{1}{24} wl^2$ and $-\frac{1}{12} wl^2$ respectively).

In concrete beams, steel reinforcement is placed near the bottom between supports in order to resist the tension force, and the concrete above the neutral axis is used to resist the compression. Because of the different stress values of concrete and steel, the neutral axis is not located at the geometric center between the top and bottom of reinforced concrete beams.

Steel beam sections place the maximum amount of material at the top and bottom where the tension and compression forces are maximum, and put just enough material in the web between to handle the shear stress. The web also serves the necessary requirement of connecting the top and bottom flanges so that they act in unison.

The larger the resisting moment of a beam (the distance between the resulting tension and the compression forces), the greater its capacity to take loads. That is why increasing a beam's depth increases its strength at a much faster rate than increasing its width.

Shear

The second of the two most common stresses placed on horizontal framing members is called *direct* or *vertical shear*. Maximum shear stress usually occurs at the ends of beams and girders where they are connected to columns or other vertical supports. Vertical shear is the tendency for one part of a beam to slide vertically in relation to an adjacent part. This type of stress can be especially critical when a column does not line up vertically with the one below it.

Trusses

Trusses can be a logical choice for a horizontal framing member when the span, or occasionally the load-carrying requirements of the situation, exceeds the capacity of standard-size or built-up girders. Compared to a beam or girder, a truss is very deep. The distance between the top and bottom edges of a truss consists of a pattern of connecting compression and tension stress-carrying members, rather than a solid piece of web material. One major advantage of a truss over a girder is that its greater depth gives it added strength and allows it to span longer distances. The pattern of struts and ties that make up the web of a truss permits most of the truss's depth to be open space, and these voids greatly decrease the weight of the truss as compared to the weight of standard or built-up girders, which have solid webs. Therefore a truss will weigh considerably less than a girder carrying the same load over the same span. Another advantage of a truss is that the voids in the web area

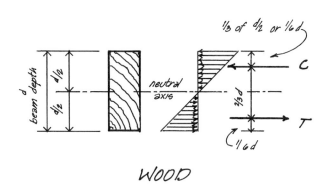

WOOD

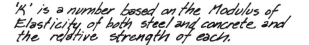

'K' is a number based on the Modulus of Elasticity of both steel and concrete and the relative strength of each.

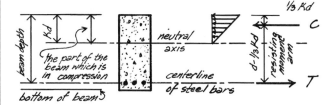

CONCRETE

The concrete material located below the neutral axis is used primarily to separate the area of the compressive stresses from the center of the tensile stresses. The greater this distance is, the larger the capacity of the beam. The added depth also increases the capacity of the beam to resist shear.

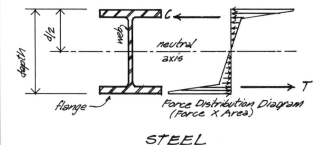

Force Distribution Diagram
(Force × Area)

STEEL

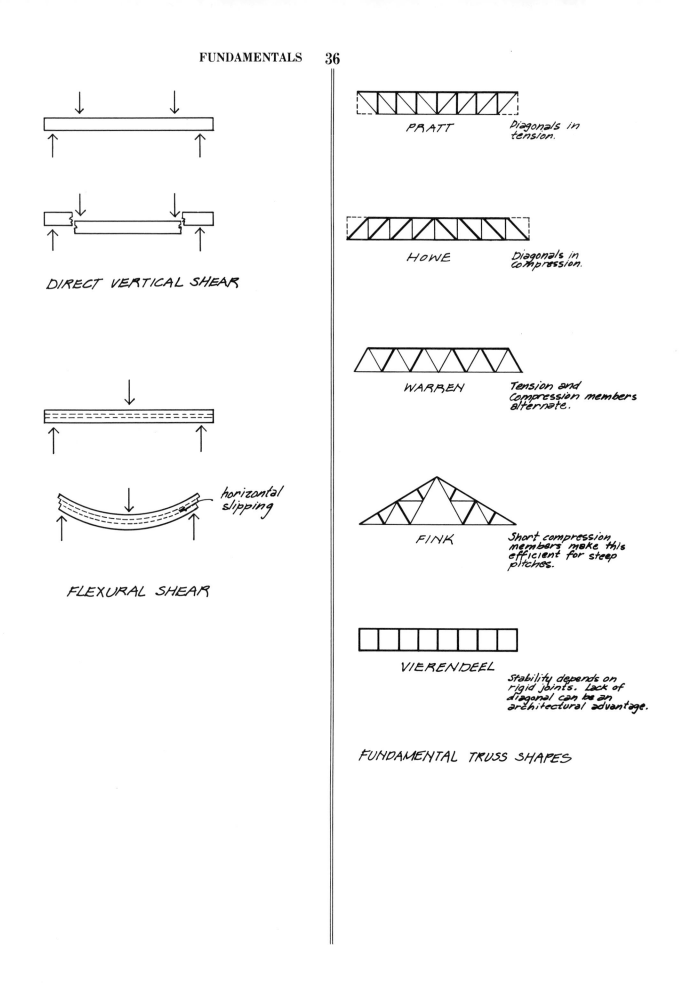

DIRECT VERTICAL SHEAR

FLEXURAL SHEAR

horizontal slipping

PRATT — Diagonals in tension.

HOWE — Diagonals in compression.

WARREN — Tension and compression members alternate.

FINK — Short compression members make this efficient for steep pitches.

VIERENDEEL — Stability depends on rigid joints. Lack of diagonal can be an architectural advantage.

FUNDAMENTAL TRUSS SHAPES

can be used to accommodate large ducts. A girder's considerably shallower depth is a positive attribute in certain circumstances where headroom is a problem. Visually, trusses present an entirely different image than girders do.

VERTICAL COMPONENTS

Columns, and walls in low-rise buildings, are the usual vertical framing members in a building. These vertical elements receive and then transfer down to the foundations, and through them into the ground, all the loads of the structure and its occupants.

Stresses on Vertical Framing Members

Under axial loads, columns have a large capacity to resist failure by crushing, but they are far more susceptible to failure by buckling. This circumstance affects the shape of a column and therefore its final appearance. If columns did not have a tendency to buckle, then the major criteria necessary to determine a column's strength would be its cross-sectional area, and the compressive-strength capacity of the material of which it is made. It is only theoretically possible to obtain a purely concentric axial load. In practice, there is always some imbalance. Therefore, all columns must be designed to resist buckling.

When a column is designed to resist buckling, the shape of the column's cross-section becomes a factor. A column's ability to resist buckling stress is related to the manner in which the column's material is distributed around the vertical axis, through the column's center of gravity. The farther a column's material is from its vertical axis, the more the material will contribute to the column's moment of inertia, or ability to resist buckling. A column will buckle in the direction of its least stability. Therefore, for axial loads, a symmetrical shape is logical because it is equally strong in all directions.

A square has a slightly larger moment of inertia than a circle of equal area, making a square a more stable cross-sectional shape than a circle for a column. A square with the same cross-sectional area as a circle will have a side dimension or width somewhat smaller than the circle's diameter and, therefore, will appear to be smaller. If a square has the same side dimension as a circle's diameter, then the circle and the square will tend to have the same visual impact, but the area

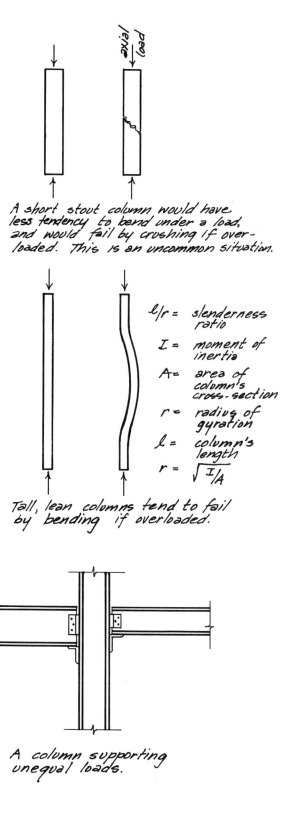

A short stout column would have less tendency to bend under a load, and would fail by crushing if overloaded. This is an uncommon situation.

l/r = slenderness ratio

I = moment of inertia

A = area of column's cross-section

r = radius of gyration

l = column's length

$r = \sqrt{I/A}$

Tall, lean columns tend to fail by bending if overloaded.

A column supporting unequal loads.

AREA: $\pi r^2 = 3.14 \times 6^2$ A = 113.09 in²

MOMENT OF INERTIA:
$I = \frac{\pi r^4}{4} = \frac{(3.14 \times 6^4)}{4}$ I = 1017.36 in⁴

RADIUS OF GYRATION:
$r = \sqrt{I/A} = \sqrt{1017.36/113.09}$ r = 3.00 in

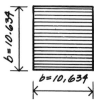

AREA: $b^2 = (10.634)^2$ A = 113.0 in²

MOMENT OF INERTIA:
$I = b^4/12 = \frac{(10.634)^4}{12}$ I = 1065.78 in⁴

RADIUS OF GYRATION:
$r = \sqrt{I/A} = \sqrt{1065.8/113.08}$ r = 3.07 in

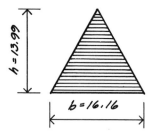

AREA:
$A = \frac{bh}{2} = \frac{16.16 \times 13.99}{2}$ A = 113.04 in²

MOMENT OF INERTIA:
$I = \frac{bh^3}{36} = \frac{16.16 \times (13.99)^3}{36}$ I = 1226.8 in⁴

RADIUS OF GYRATION:
$r = \sqrt{I/A} = \sqrt{1226.8/113}$ r = 3.29 in

If area is constant, I and r
will vary with shape; overall
dimension will also vary.

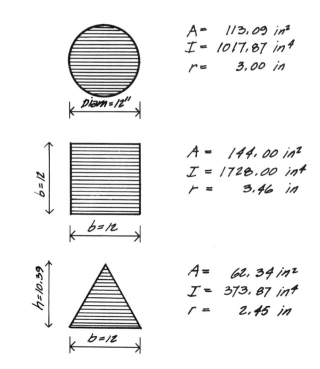

A = 113.09 in²
I = 1017.87 in⁴
r = 3.00 in

A = 144.00 in²
I = 1728.00 in⁴
r = 3.46 in

A = 62.34 in²
I = 373.87 in⁴
r = 2.45 in

Given a constant overall dimension,
a square has the greatest capacity.

and the ability to resist buckling will be significantly larger in the square than in the circle. Therefore, although a round column is an efficient column shape, it is not quite as efficient as a square of the same area, and it is much less efficient than a square of the same size. Round wood or steel columns are not often used in buildings even when the loads are symmetrical, because of the physical and aesthetic difficulty of connecting beams with straight ends to a round column. Another difficulty with round columns occurs when a structure such as an office building or apartment house is divided into rooms. Problems arise in deciding how the partitions should intersect or bypass the columns and what to do with furniture placed next to the columns. The final selection of a column's shape and location depends on the individual building. For example, in a one-story structure, the beams can be placed on top of a round column, because this is a simple connection to execute; in buildings such as warehouses, there are no partitions to worry about.

The outer or exterior row of columns in a building can only be loaded from a maximum of three sides, and under some circumstances it is loaded from only one side. This asymmetrical loading requires that added resisting material be placed within the column in the direction of the greater load. In addition, the column must be placed in the structure so that its shape can best resist all the loads it receives. This means, for example, that a rectangular column would be located along the exterior of a building with its greatest cross-sectional dimension at right angles to the building's facade. This would put the greater amount of its material in opposition to resist the asymmetrical vertical loads, and also at right angles to the horizontal winds, another force that must be resisted.

A general point about columns is that they are almost always continuous from floor to floor, with the beams and girders framing into them. If the beams were placed under the columns at each floor, they would tend to be crushed by the column, since beams are generally designed to take more or less uniformly distributed loads, not the heavily concentrated compression load that a column would impose.

The way columns are framed through the floors depends upon the material that is used to construct them. Concrete columns are poured at the same time as the floor above them is poured. Continuity is obtained by extending the reinforcing bars up from the lower column so that they overlap the bars of the column waiting to be poured above. Wood and steel columns are usually spliced above the floor line in order to simplify construction and to keep the splice away from the point where the beams and girders are connected to the column.

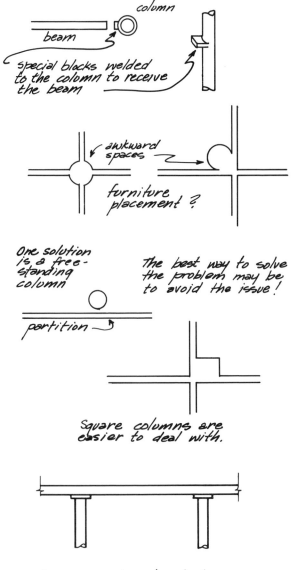

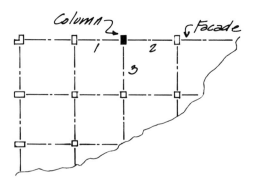

the loads placed on the column by spandrel beams one (1) and two (2) are equal. Therefore, the column load parallel to the facade is symmetrical.

There is no beam available to balance out the load transmitted by beam three (3); thus the load perpendicular to the facade is not symmetrical.

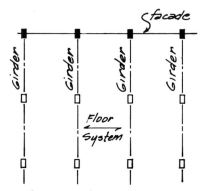

The facade columns are loaded in only one direction. The floor system spans from girder to girder.

Exterior columns are usually placed with their web perpendicular to the facade, in the most efficient position to resist wind loads.

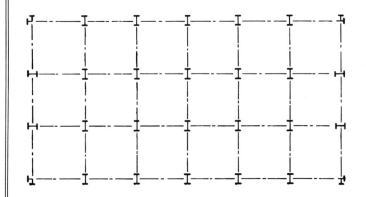

Interior columns are usually placed with their web parallel to the narrow side of the building, since this direction has less mass to resist wind loads.

CORRECT

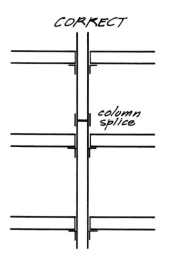

column
splice

Columns must have the
right-of-way.
Most columns are
two-stories high.

INCORRECT

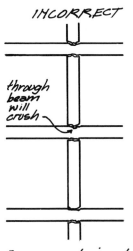

through
beam
will
crush

Beams are designed
to take bending and
shear stress --
not crushing.

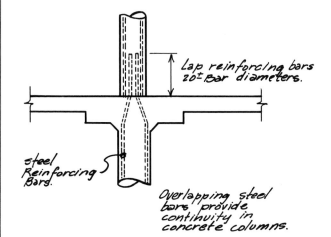

Lap reinforcing bars
20± bar diameters.

steel
Reinforcing
Bars.

Overlapping steel
bars provide
continuity in
concrete columns.

TIED

SPIRAL

Between 1% and 8% of a column's cross-sectional area is vertical steel rods. These vertical rods are held in place with tie bars.

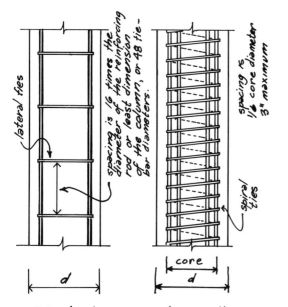

lateral ties

spacing is 16 times the reinforcing rod or least dimension of the column, or 48 tie-bar diameters.

spiral ties

spacing is 1/6 core diameter 3" maximum

d

core

d

Spiral columns are stronger than tied columns having the same cross-sectional area and amount of vertical steel.

The compression under an axial load causes expansion perpendicular to the column's vertical axis. This is better resisted by spiral reinforcing which is actually a helix.

COLUMN SHAPES

Concrete Columns

Shape is easy to determine when using concrete, and round, square, and rectangular concrete columns are common. Although in theory a square column is slightly stronger in its ability to resist and axial load than a round column of equal area, round concrete columns are usually reinforced with spiral ties, which are more closely spaced than the lateral ties used in square or rectangular columns. As a result of this type of reinforcement, a spiral column has a higher load-carrying capacity than a tied column of equal area. Square columns, however, are visually compatible with the rectangular columns that are required when the loads are not axial.

In industrial buildings and garages, for example, where partitioning is not an issue, an architect can use the most efficient structural shape—on balance, usually the round column. Giant cardboard tubes are available as forms, and since the concrete is poured into the forms at the same time that the girders and floor above the columns are poured, the problem of making a joint between a round column and the end of a beam is solved by the continuity of the material. Structures such as office and apartment buildings tend to have square columns, if the loads on them are symmetrical, and rectangular columns proportioned so that their longer side is aligned in the direction of the greater load when the load is not symmetrical.

Steel Columns

If square and round columns are logical engineering shapes, then one might expect to see solid square or round steel columns. Instead, steel columns are usually standard H-shaped sections or built-up members of hollow shapes. There are several reasons for this. First, since steel is about 10 times stronger than concrete in compression, very little cross-sectional area of material is needed to support a load. Except for the fact that a very slender solid column would quickly fail by buckling, steel columns could be very small in width or diameter. In order to make a solid column stable enough to resist the tendency to buckle, its diameter or width would have to be increased so much that a great deal of additional material would be required to construct the column, which would cause its weight and cost to increase. A hollow column can place its material symmetrically about its vertical axis. The farther the column's material is located from its central axis, the more stable the column will be and the more capable it will be of resisting buckling. A hollow column

A1

Even though this column has the same cross-sectional area as the ones below, it is more slender and will therefore be less stable. Beam-to-column connections for such rod-like shapes tend to be more difficult.

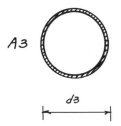

A2

If the cross-sectional areas of two columns are the same, the column with the larger diameter will be more stable. Both columns will have the same ability to withstand pure axial crushing because capacity to resist axial compression is based on area. Since virtually all columns must resist compression and bending, <u>distribution of area</u> is critical.

A3

All three columns have the same area (shown as shaded portions):

$$A1 = A2 = A3$$

However, distribution of area varies as a function of each column's diameter:

$$d_3 > d_2 > d_1$$

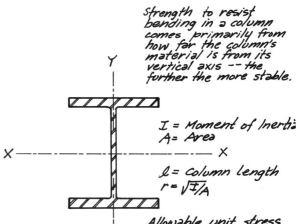

Strength to resist bending in a column comes primarily from how far the column's material is from its vertical axis -- the further the more stable.

I = Moment of Inertia
A = Area

ℓ = Column Length
$r = \sqrt{I/A}$

Allowable unit stress is based on ℓ/r ratio

COLUMN

Column shapes are heavier in cross-section and more compact than beam shapes.

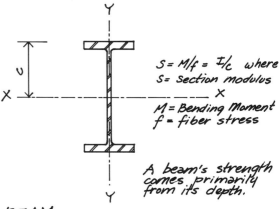

$S = M/f = I/c$ where
S = Section modulus

M = Bending Moment
f = fiber stress

A beam's strength comes primarily from its depth.

BEAM

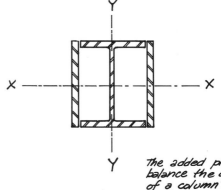

The added plates can balance the distribution of a column's cross-sectional area about its X-X and Y-Y axis.

BUILT-UP COLUMN

Extra stability can be provided in a particular direction when needed, such as when required to resist wind loads.

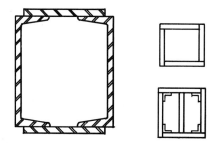

Hollow columns can be fabricated in a variety of different ways.

Extruded square and rectangular columns are not available in sizes large enough to be used in high-rise buildings.

thus reduces the cost and amount of material that is required. The reasoning process that leads architects to hollow steel columns is very similar to the theory that a beam needs the bulk of its material at the top and bottom, not in the middle.

Although round, hollow steel columns are efficient, they are not commonly used because of the problems of connecting beams to them. In an *H*-shaped column, the bulk of the material is farther away from the column's center in one direction than in the other. The weak axis must be strong enough to resist buckling from the axial load. The advantage of having one axis stronger than the other is that the column can be balanced efficiently where there are eccentric loads along one axis that do not exist along the other.

Hollow square and rectangular columns are also efficient, but they are fabricated by welding plates and angles together. The cost of this often exceeds the cost of overdesigning an *H*-shaped column so that its weak axis is adequate to resist buckling, or adding extra plates to an *H*-shaped column to balance its moment of inertia.

The location and proportions of columns are major factors in the appearance of many buildings. Even the decision not to express a column makes a kind of aesthetic statement. For example, the fact that the columns are placed outside the plane of the facade in the Chase Manhattan Tower gives the building a wholly different look from that of the Westcoast Transmission Company Tower, which has no columns at all. Whether a column is round, square, or *H*-shaped may be related to the stresses that will be placed on it, but the shape of a column undeniably influences the visual statement.

COLUMN LOCATION AND SPACING

An inherent give-and-take relationship exists between the appearance of a column and what that column is called upon to do technically. Depending on the design philosophy of the architect, a column can express its function, disguise it, or exaggerate it. There are enough variables so that an architect can load the dice, so to speak, in order to justify a variety of expressions.

The width or diameter of a column is an important design factor when the column is exposed on the building's facade, but width is also important even when the column is not visible. The overall size of a column is affected by such elements as the loads it must support, the mechanical systems it must accommodate, the spacing of the columns, and even whether a column must be fireproofed or not. For example, a steel column that is fireproofed by a layer of insulation will be larger than one that is not fireproofed. How a column is fireproofed is only one of the decisions that the architect makes affecting the aesthetics of a column. The other three—expressing loads, accommodating mechanical systems, and optimum spacing—present more options to the architect. Furthermore, unless a decision is made to express a building's columns on its facade, the treatment of columns, particularly any changes in the columns' size, is not visually apparent. Changes in the size of interior columns is usually based entirely on structural considerations.

EXPRESSING COLUMN LOADS

The influence of the loads on column size depends on such elements as how much accumulated floor area must be supported by the column, what the dead and live load is per square foot, and how many floors must be supported by a column.

Columns on the lower floors of a building support more of a load than the ones located on a higher floor. Starting at the top floor, the columns support only the roof, but on each succeeding lower floor, the columns support one more floor than the columns above. This phenomenon of a progressive change in the load-carrying capacity of a column as a function of its height presents the architect with a variety of alternatives regarding how or even whether to express the column as an aesthetic statement. Unless the decision is made to express a building's columns on its facade, any changes in progressive column size will not be visually apparent. A slight or even a considerable cross-sectional difference in column size would rarely be sensed as one traveled from floor to floor, but would easily be observed if a building's overall facade were viewed.

When composing a building's facade, the architect must decide whether or not to utilize the variations in column width as a design element. Visual consistency can be maintained by keeping a constant cross-section through the column's entire height. This approach simplifies window detailing, and is, therefore, usually the least expensive. Should the architect choose to express the changes in the column size required by variations in the load capacity, then other decisions must be made—for example, whether to decrease the column size gradually at each floor or abruptly every several floors.

As a purely structural, nonvisual, problem, the need to change the load-carrying capacity of a column can be handled in several ways, but when the goal is

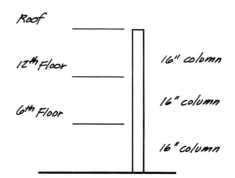

UNIFORM COLUMN SIZE

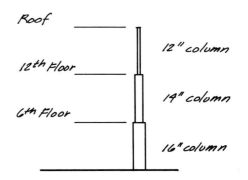

CHANGE IN COLUMN SIZE WITH INCREASE IN LOADS

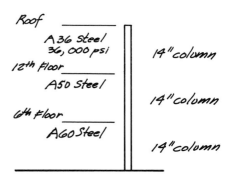

UNIFORM COLUMN SIZE (WITH INCREASE IN STRENGTH OF THE STEEL)

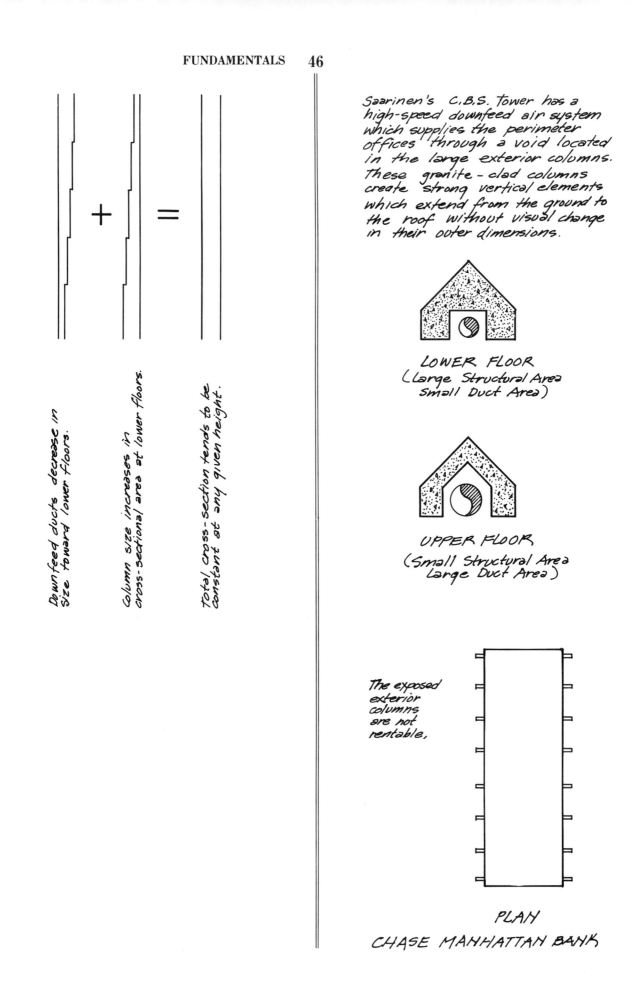

Downfeed ducts decrease in size toward lower floors.

Column size increases in cross-sectional area at lower floors.

Total cross-section tends to be constant at any given height.

Saarinen's C.B.S. Tower has a high-speed downfeed air system which supplies the perimeter offices through a void located in the large exterior columns. These granite-clad columns create strong vertical elements which extend from the ground to the roof without visual change in their outer dimensions.

LOWER FLOOR
(Large Structural Area Small Duct Area)

UPPER FLOOR
(Small Structural Area Large Duct Area)

The exposed exterior columns are not rentable,

PLAN
CHASE MANHATTAN BANK

to keep a constant cross-sectional size throughout the full height of the column, the strength of the material out of which the column is constructed can be varied as the load changes. Structural steel is available, for example, in a variety of strengths that range from 36,000 psi to over 100,000 psi. Thus, several changes in the strength of the column steel can—and often are—made in a tall building. When the framing material is reinforced concrete, the architect has an opportunity to vary both the strength of the concrete mix and the amount of steel reinforcement within the columns.

Another approach is to use a hollow or partially hollow column shape. The hollow or void in the column can be used to contain vertical pipes and the small, high-velocity air ducts that serve the perimeter heating and cooling units. The thickness of the column wall can be decreased as the height of the building increases—due to the decrease in the accumulated load it must support.

If a hollow column is used when the mechanical distribution system is fed down from the roof, an interesting symbiosis occurs. The farther down from the roof a duct goes, the smaller it becomes, since the accumulated amount of air it must deliver drops off with each succeeding floor. At the same time, the column's shell becomes thinner as it rises from the ground, and the net result is more or less constant visual cross section.

There are other ramifications to exposing columns. Most real-estate regulations and standard business practice permit landlords to charge rent for the floor space, including the space occupied by columns, up to the exterior glass line. If the column is placed beyond the building line, the space it occupies cannot be rented, whereas if the column is placed on the interior side of the glass, the space it occupies can produce income even though the tenant cannot use the column except for hanging pictures. If a column is located beyond the building line, lateral bracing becomes a problem because, in order to prevent buckling, a column must then be braced parallel to the building face as well as perpendicular to the facade.

INSULATION

When columns are placed outside the building envelope, insulation is required to keep the exterior columns at approximately the same temperature as the interior columns. If this were not done, the expansion of the heated interior columns of a high-rise building would make the columns several inches longer than

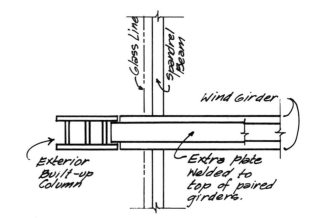

PLAN AT COLUMN

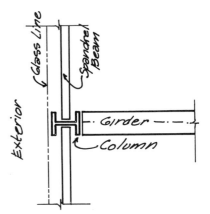

PLAN — TYPICAL SPANDREL
intersects column at
right angle to girder

SECTION THROUGH WIND GIRDER,
CHASE MANHATTAN BANK

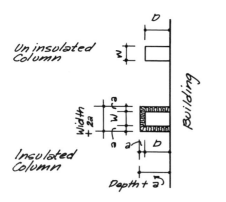

Un insulated
Column

Insulated
Column

Building

Width + 2a

Depth + a

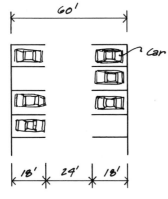

60'

Car

18' 24' 18'

the exterior columns, with drastic results. Insulation affects the proportions of the column and even the overall scale of the building as perceived from the street, because insulation must be added to both sides of the column's width but only once to its depth.

A column's visual width or diameter will be affected by whether the column needs to be large enough to accommodate pipes or ducts. The thickness of the insulation required to protect ducts or pipes located within column enclosures along the exterior walls will also increase the overall column size.

COLUMN SPACING

The distance between columns is one of the more important decisions that ultimately affects a building's exterior pattern. The use to which a building will be put by its occupants usually determines the distance that will be required between columns. For example, a garage usually has approximately 60-foot-wide bays (that is, the columns are spaced every 60 feet) because of the rhythm created by an 18-foot car, a 24-foot driving lane, and another 18-foot car, all of which yield a total of 60 feet.

Architects sometimes design facades from the outside in. A client will come to them already owning a piece of land that has unique physical dimensions. The zoning code may impose further restrictions, most notably by requiring that the building be set back from the property line. An architect faced with an overall maximum building dimension will tend to divide whatever that dimension is into an even number of structural bays along the facade. Unfortunately, this apparently logical decision often leads to aesthetic confusion because the number of bays based on such a formal subdivision of the facade may bear no relationship whatsoever to the interior function of the building.

MULLIONS

The placement of mullions, the vertical separations between one window and an adjacent window, is also related to the spacing of columns. The mullion also serve as a stiffening member by taking the wind load from the glass and curtain wall panels and transferring it to the building's structural frame.

Usually the spacing of mullions is based on a subdivision of the column bay. Sometimes the columns are placed close enough together so that a subdivision of

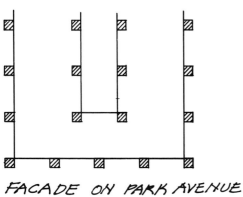

FACADE ON PARK AVENUE
399 PARK AVENUE
NEW YORK CITY

This composition creates a 'confusion' of columns when viewed from the street since the interior columns are fully visible and do not align with the exterior columns.

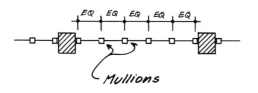

Mullions

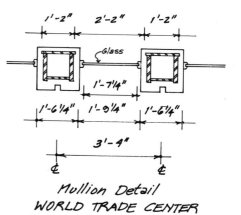

Mullion Detail
WORLD TRADE CENTER

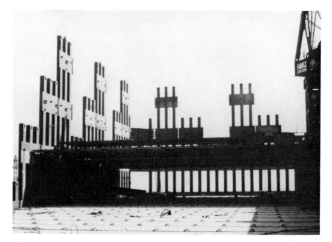

World Trade Center under construction. Columns were installed in groups of three, tied together with a spandrel panel. Each column then was insulated and covered.

Window washing rig poised over the edge of the C.B.S Tower.

the space between them is not necessary, and the column doubles as a mullion.

In high-rise buildings, mullions or columns usually have tracks built into them to guide window-washing equipment. The wheels of the scaffolding run in these vertical guides, much as a train runs along its tracks.

The development of silicon has permitted glass to be joined without mullions. The glass is supported structurally at the top and bottom, and the joint between the adjacent pieces is caulked with this colorless translucent material. Glass joined in this manner must be thick enough not to deflect between the top and bottom under severe winds, because silicon lacks the bracing strength that is usually supplied by mullions.

Chapter 4

CORNERS, CORES, AND WIND BRACING

The ways in which structural components are used to create corners, cores, and wind-bracing systems have a tremendous visual impact on a building.

CORNERS

To understand what is structurally possible, as well as the aesthetic options that are available to an architect who is considering how a building should turn a corner, it is necessary to examine why the load placed on some columns—in particular, on the corner columns—is different from the loads placed on columns in other locations.

Even when columns are regularly placed on a regimented grid throughout a building, they are not all called upon to support identical loads. The type and amount of load varies with individual columns. Because of this, the architect is presented with a design tool that can be used to make an aesthetic statement about the structural nature of corners.

Columns located at the corner of a building constitute one of the more common special cases. To understand how corner columns are different, let's look at how the load-carrying function varies in a typical exterior and a typical interior column. A column will generally support loads placed on the floor around it, collecting the loads to a point halfway over to the next column. A typical interior column needs to support twice the contributing amount of floor area that an exterior or facade column does, and four times the area that a corner column is required to support. Therefore, given even spacing of columns and assuming only vertical loads, it follows that exterior columns could have a smaller cross-sectional dimension than interior columns made of the same material.

Corner columns could have even smaller cross-sections than facade columns. Curiously, though, this relative size relationship is seldom used by architects as a form-giver or design element. In fact, the size of the corner columns has often been exaggerated by twentieth-century architects such as Mies van der Rohe and Eero Saarinen in order to express their visual sense of a corner. Apparently the principal concern was that all columns appear to be uniform, even when turning a corner.

An example of how an architect handles the aesthetic problem of turning a building corner can be seen by looking at two buildings that are examined in the case studies of Part Two. Both buildings have the same basic framing system consisting of a central core sur-

John Hancock Tower, Chicago, Illinois.

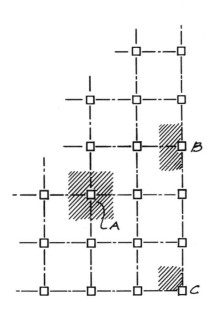

A   TYPICAL INTERIOR COLUMN
     Area of Floor Supported
     1 x 1 = 1 unit

B   TYPICAL FACADE COLUMN
     Area of Floor Supported
     1 x 1/2 = 1/2 unit

C   TYPICAL CORNER COLUMN
     Area of Floor Supported
     1/2 x 1/2 = 1/4 unit.

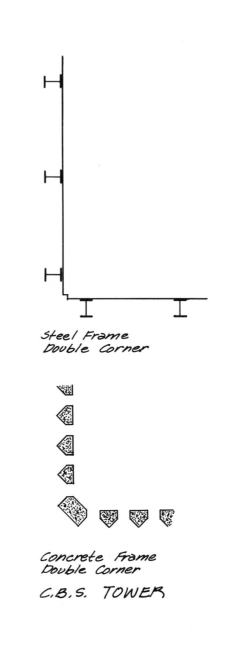

Steel Frame
Double Corner

Concrete Frame
Double Corner

C.B.S. TOWER

rounded by a row of closely spaced exterior columns. In the case of the 38-story CBS office tower in New York, the exaggeration of the corner statement has been carried to an extreme. An intriguing construction photograph (included in the Part Two case study of this building) shows the building structure completed, even though the entire section of the corner column between the second and third floors is missing. This piece of column was omitted in order to permit the hoisting of mechanical equipment directly from the street into the second-floor mechanical-equipment room.

Due to the two-way rib framing of the floor, the column at the corner was called upon to support such a small vertical load that it could be safely omitted. Despite this, the building's design called for the corner columns to be double the visual size of all the other columns.

In contrast, in One Shell Plaza in Houston, the architect used variations in the load-carrying needs of the exterior columns, including the corner ones, to produce an undulating facade that expresses the variation in load that each column is called upon to support.

The load at the end of each individual rib in a one-way rib system is half the total floor load that the rib is called upon to carry. The load at the end of a rib in a two-directional floor system is also half of the load on the rib. But since there are now two ribs (one in each direction) sharing the floor load, the load on each rib is one-half the load on the floor. Therefore, the load on the end of each rib will be one-half of one-half of the load, or one-quarter of the floor load. The diagram shows that one end of each of the corner bay ribs terminates into another rib at right angles to it. This rib acts as a girder and must pick up all the loads of the ribs bearing on it, and so its total load will vastly exceed the load on a typical rib that has no other ribs framing into it. This means that the load transferred to each end of this rib-girder is greater than at the end of any other rib and thus, in turn, the column under this rib girder must carry a greater load, which is expressed by providing a larger cross-section for that column.

The undulating facade is also made possible by the fact that, in nature, stresses do not start and stop abruptly at a given point. Instead, they gradually ease off and disperse, especially when the material is continuous (as is the case with the concrete of One Shell Plaza). The loads that are transferred to the columns adjacent to the major load carrier are larger than the loads transferred to columns located farther away. These loads gradually diminish to a typical load of one-half the load placed on the rib. It is this gradual change in load from the typical column along the sides of the building to the maximum load of the rib girder, and

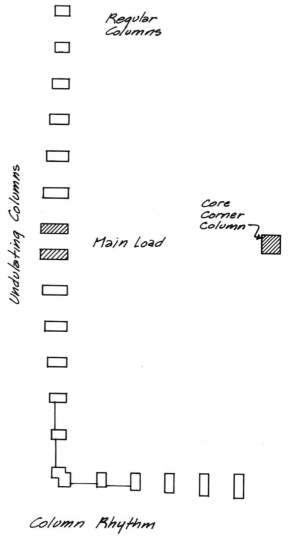

Column Rhythm
ONE SHELL PLAZA

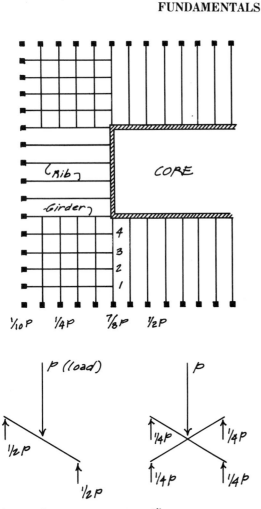

then the diminishing of the load down to the corner, that permits the changes in column size and the subtle undulations of One Shell Plaza.

Most large buildings present more than one face to public view, thereby creating the dual problems of facade continuity and directional change. The facade treatment may vary from face to face or be identical on all sides. The handling of a corner can reflect this as continuity or change. The means employed to turn a corner may be chosen for purely aesthetic reasons or may be a reflection of the particular framing system that is used. Often an architect selects a framing system that creates the desired facade and corner situation for his or her visual statement. In such cases, the load pattern can become a form giver.

CORES AND WIND BRACING

The core of a building is the area reserved for elevators, stairs, mechanical equipment, and the vertical shafts that are necessary for ducts, pipes, and wires. In addition, the core contains washrooms and some public corridor space. The walls of the cores are also the most common location for the vertical wind bracing. By locating the wind bracing within the core walls, an architect is able to make use of a wall that is required for other purposes, for example, to enclose stairs or elevator shaft. This dual use eliminates the need to create an additional wall that could interfere with the use of the building.

Cores

Typically, building cores are centrally located, but architects locate cores in a wide variety of other places. They can be placed eccentrically within the building, at remote ends, and sometimes even in one or more corners. The location is usually chosen for a particular overriding reason or for a combination of reasons, and the final selection of the core location often carries with it an accompanying visual impact. This visual statement can be particularly dramatic if the core is located at the building's exterior. It may be dominating if the core is placed outside the structure's general envelope. In some buildings, the core is split into two or more clusters rather than being massed in a single location.

Several factors influence the location of the core, particularly in high-rise buildings. The primary consideration is the use and circulation patterns of the people who will occupy the building. Second, when the walls of the various vertical shafts are called upon to perform the additional task of providing the wind-brac-

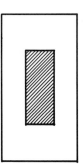

TYPICAL CORE
located approximately at building's center

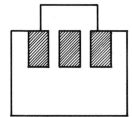

OFF-CENTER CORE
provides more useable office area

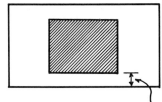

OFF-CENTER CORE
this dimension can become too small to be practical

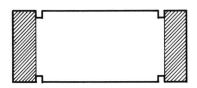

END CORES

Variations in column depth create undulating ripples in the facade. One Shell Plaza, Houston.

Here, the eccentric core required use of an additional 'mini-core' for mechanical equipment shafts to service the more remote ends of the building.

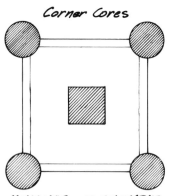

KNIGHTS OF COLUMBUS

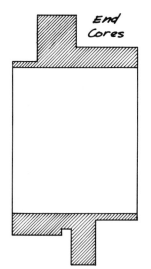

AMERICAN LIFE INSURANCE

ing system, the core shafts must be located in the proper place to stiffen the building as a whole. The taller the structure, the more critical the core location becomes. Third, those shafts containing ducts and other mechanical equipment must be located in a manner that will permit a logical horizontal distribution of the heating, ventilating, electric and other systems at each floor level. Finally, vertical shafts containing the exit stairs must be located in such a way as to conform to the maximum travel distances required for safe exiting of the building in an emergency.

There are other influences and restraints on the placement of the core, but even from this abbreviated list, one can sense the various combinations that are possible when combining the different elements that constitute the building core. For example, an architect could locate stairs at the ends of a building and centrally place the elevators. Or he or she might want to express the mechanical shafts separately from the elevator shafts and stairs. Some architects place shafts on the exterior to serve as form givers. The possibilities are endless, but in the hands of a creative architect, the core can become one of the major form givers.

Wind Bracing

Modern technology has brought about major changes in wind-bracing systems. Early high-rise steel frame buildings had closely spaced columns and weighed considerably more than today's structures. For example, the columns of the Empire State Building are spaced approximately 19 feet apart, and the weight of the steel framing comes to over 42 pounds per square foot. Today, high-rise steel frame buildings are constructed with much greater distances between columns, and with a total structure often weighing one-half or less than their counterparts of the 1930s. This decrease in framing weight is primarily due to more sophisticated bracing systems, which require less material than older buildings did, and to the development of stronger grades of steel, which can carry greater stresses and span larger distances than earlier framing members of the same cross-section were able to.

The ability of steel to span greater distances, which means that the distances between columns can be greater, permits far more flexibility in the subdivision and use of interior space. At the same time usability is increased by the new technology, costs are being reduced. The price of steel is directly related to its weight, so decreases in weight result in cost savings. (In addition, any savings in the weight of the framing system also result in another saving—a smaller foundation can be used to support the structure.) This search for weight-saving methods of construction motivated the research that produced stronger grades of steel, as well as new bracing and joining methods.

Advances in technology, while producing lighter, and more cost-effective buildings, have also made them more willowy. Modern buildings tend to bend in the wind much as trees do. Of course, if a building really bent as much as a tree in a storm, its occupants would soon have motion sickness, so, although buildings can safely bend a great deal, this is not a practical solution, because partitions, ceilings, walls, and people's psyches would all crack. Therefore, engineers have had to devise a number of ingenious ways to stiffen today's lighter buildings and often the methods used to stiffen buildings have been used to make a design statement. This can be done most dramatically when bracing is placed on the exterior facade. When this happens, the bracing becomes the major visual statement of the entire building.

The concept of expressing structure on the exterior is not a new one. Gothic cathedrals, in fact, are clear articulations of loads and stresses that are transmitted through a structure to the ground. In addition to their highly functional nature, flying buttresses constitute a major statement about the building's aesthetics.

The wind-bracing system is often incorporated into the core. The walls that enclose elevator shafts, stairways, and duct shafts in high-rise buildings can usually provide an unobtrusive and structurally sound place to locate the wind bracing. In some buildings, these core walls, which are functionally required, turn out to possess adequate stiffness to resist the wind loads, and in many moderate-rise buildings, relatively inexpensive reinforcement or bracing can be incorporated within the core walls. When the wind bracing is incorporated into the core walls, the location of the core becomes an important factor for that reason, too. Most often, though, the core walls are used for the wind bracing because the bracing does not interfere with circulation, and is usually the most cost-effective system. Core bracing is sometimes combined with the more dramatic exterior bracing in very tall buildings, forming what is called a *tube-within-a-tube* system of bracing.

While some architects like the visual impact of exterior bracing on buildings, others feel that the diagonal lines of the bracing destroy the views from the interior. Building cores tend to be located at or near the center of the building because this location can usually accommodate all the requirements of the mechanical distribution system, as well as the system of circulating people. In addition, a central core serves to maximize the amount of naturally lighted perimeter spaces. Unless a building is exceptionally tall, the walls of a centrally located core will provide an adequate

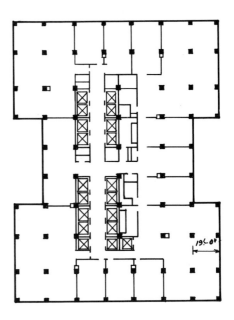

EMPIRE STATE BUILDING

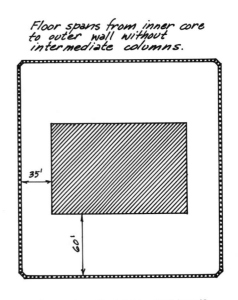

Floor spans from inner core to outer wall without intermediate columns.

WORLD TRADE CENTER

Exterior wind-bracing pattern. John Hancock Tower, Chicago. Skidmore Owings and Merrill, Architects.

The wind-bracing pattern in the outer wall has a major visual impact on the interior space.

space and a functional location for the wind bracing. Additionally, a central core leaves the exterior unencumbered and therefore free to contain as much glass as the views and heat loss will justify.

In some imaginative buildings the cores and wind-bracing systems are expressed with great visual impact. The average client and architect do not always search for creative solutions to problems. The constraints of budget often do not permit it, and there is the ever-present danger that in less than competent hands the search for creativity will degenerate into creating something different just for the sake of being different. Most architects will have enough to do manipulating the proportions and textures of the facade to create varied and excellent designs without also manipulating the cores and wind-bracing systems as design tools. Still, the possibility of manipulating the core remains another strong design option, as does the possibility of working with an exterior bracing system. In the latter instance, this may not only be a design option, but actually may be, under certain circumstances, the optimum engineering choice.

Schematic Core Diagrams

The accompanying schematic diagrams illustrate a variety of ways a core can be located within a building plan.

Sometimes the function and massing of the building are the overriding considerations, and the wind-bracing system must be accommodated in the locations available. In this type of situation, which is the more common, the type of wind-bracing is selected in order to be compatible with its location within the structure.

In other instances, the wind-bracing system itself will be the dominating form giver, and will determine the location of the core and shaft.

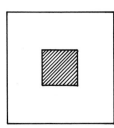

WESTCOAST TRANSMISSION CO.

WESTCOAST TRANSMISSION CO.

Square Central Core

acts as a wind bracing inner tube.

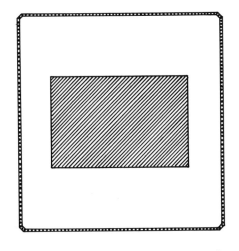

WORLD TRADE CENTER

WORLD TRADE CENTER

Central Steel Core

contributes to wind bracing. The major wind bracing is provided by closely-spaced (3'-4") columns which act together to form an exterior rigid bracing tube.

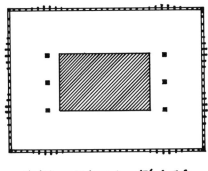

ONE SHELL PLAZA

ONE SHELL PLAZA

Central Concrete Core

Walls act as inner tube; closely-spaced columns act as outer tube. Resulting effect is tube-within-a-tube wind bracing solution.

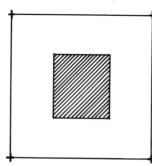

BOSTON COMPANY

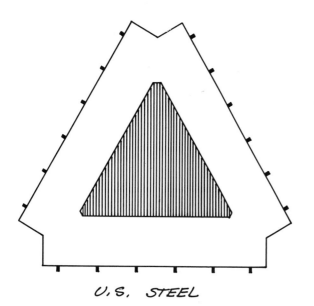

U.S. STEEL

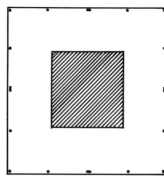

CITICORP

BOSTON COMPANY

Square Central Core

contains some wind bracing.
Exterior walls express
diagonal steel bracing.

U.S. STEEL HEADQUARTERS

Triangular Central Core

Wind bracing is provided
by a combination of core
wall bracing, hinged joints
between secondary floors
and columns, and a cap truss
at the top.

CITICORP TOWER

Central Core

Diagonal bracing in the
core is supplemented by
diagonal chevrons on the
exterior walls and a
400-ton concrete weight
(tuned mass damper) at
the top which slides
horizontally in opposition
to wind-caused sway.

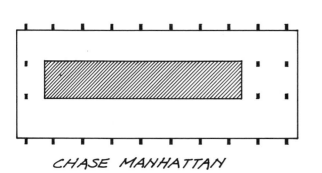

CHASE MANHATTAN

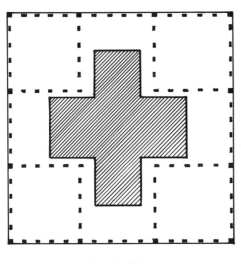

ONE LIBERTY PLAZA

SEARS

CHASE MANHATTAN BANK

Rectangular Core

is offset to provide two different office space depths.

One-story K-bracing in core walls is supplemented with 3'-0" deep wind girders.

ONE LIBERTY PLAZA

Rectangular Core

provides a central corridor.

Two-story K-bracing in core wall is more efficient than the more common one-story K-brace. The extra-wide core makes this arrangement feasible.

SEARS TOWER

Five-part Multi-Core

Building is divided into nine square structural tubes which terminate at different heights.

Wind bracing uses a combination of all individual tubes, resulting in a bundle-tube system.

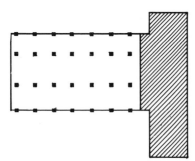

PHILADELPHIA SAVINGS FUND (PSFS)

PHILADELPHIA SAVINGS FUND SOCIETY

End Core

Poor exiting pattern because of common path to stairs.

Wind bracing provided by knee braces at beam-to-column connections. Modest height and heavy dead loads minimize wind problem.

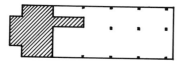
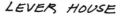

LEVER HOUSE

LEVER HOUSE

End Core

with questionable exiting pattern.

Wind bracing in core walls with additional transverse rigid frames in column bays past core area.

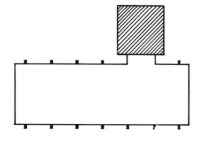

INLAND STEEL

INLAND STEEL HEADQUARTERS

Offset Core

presents a concentration of exit locations.

Wind bracing is provided by rigid steel wind girders which span entire width.

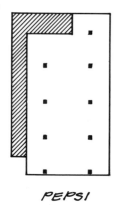

PEPSI

PEPSI HEADQUARTERS

Angle Core

provides remote stair location and frees open space for maximum use.

Wind bracing requirements are modest (11 floors) and are provided by rigid beam-to-column connections and core wall bracing.

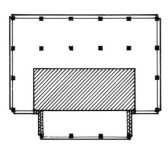

SEAGRAM

SEAGRAM BUILDING

Eccentric Core

permits adequate depth for office space.

Shear walls in the core extend beyond the core into the exterior walls.

M.I.T. EARTH SCIENCE

M.I.T. EARTH SCIENCE LAB

End Cores

provides excellent exiting paths from all areas as it eliminates dead ends.

Concrete cores are connected longitudinally at both top and bottom to provide needed wind bracing.

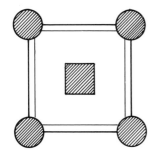

KNIGHTS OF COLUMBUS

KNIGHTS OF COLUMBUS

Corner Cores

have similar exiting advantages as end cores.

The five monolithic cores each act as a separate wind bracing tube.

CORNELL AGRONOMY

CORNELL AGRONOMY LAB

Perimeter Core System

provides mechanical spaces on east and west sides while north and south ends house stairs.

Perimeter shear walls stiffen concrete frame skeleton.

BRACED BAYS

1

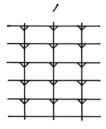

PORTAL
FRAME

2

DEEP
KNEE BRACE

3

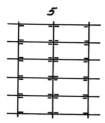

DIAGONAL
BRACE

4

K - BRACE
(K = 木)

5

WELDED
RIGID JOINTS

6

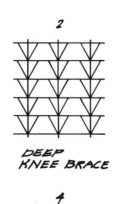

DOUBLE HEIGHT
K - BRACE

A braced bay is a line of columns
tied together by a bracing
system which causes them
to act in unison.

BRACING PLANS

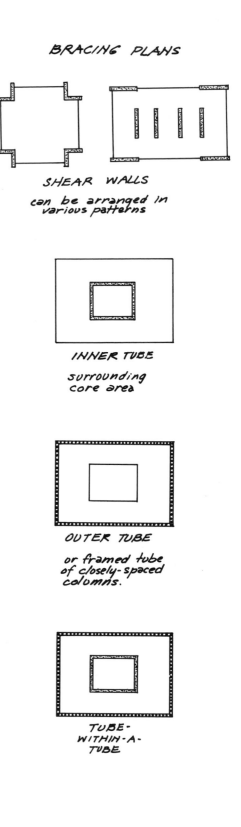

SHEAR WALLS

can be arranged in
various patterns

INNER TUBE

surrounding
core area

OUTER TUBE

or framed tube
of closely-spaced
columns.

TUBE-
WITHIN-A-
TUBE

BRACING SECTIONS

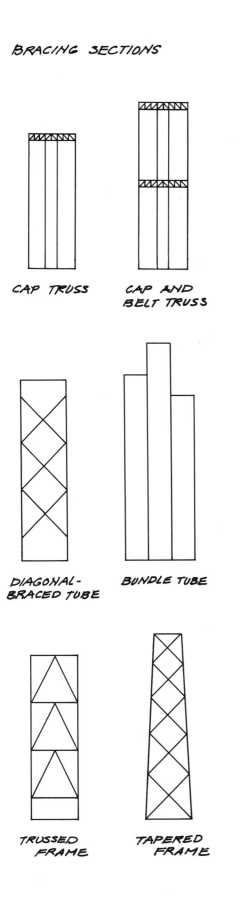

CAP TRUSS   CAP AND
                   BELT TRUSS

DIAGONAL-   BUNDLE TUBE
BRACED TUBE

TRUSSED   TAPERED
FRAME   FRAME

Chapter 5

LOCATION OF MECHANICAL EQUIPMENT

The mechanical systems that provide the sophisticated comfort controls people have come to expect require a great deal of space. Some architects choose to express the space required for a building's mechanical equipment, but the majority either suppress or disguise it. When an architect does choose to make a visual statement with the mechanical equipment, it becomes an element of the building's design.

Furnaces, cooling towers, and most other bulky equipment can be easily hidden away in cellars, or put on rooftops, where they will have little obvious visual impact, but the grilles of an air-supply-and-exhaust system are not easily tucked away in one place. It is the air handling parts of the mechanical systems that have the greatest potential visual impact on architecture and that present the major architectural challenge, as the grilles must be on the building's exterior and the distribution and return systems are ubiquitous.

In buildings that are places of work or recreation (called *occupied spaces*), the air supply is usually provided entirely by mechanical means. In places where people live (called *habitable spaces*), the building codes specify that a structure must have windows for direct fresh air supply. Architects often supplement natural ventilation with mechanical systems such as air conditioning. Any heating or cooling system using treated air must have one set of grilles and louvers to control the intake air and another set to provide for exhausting air. These grilles must be placed on the building's exterior and, as such, can become an important design expression. In addition, the distribution system of ducts and pipes required to transport air and fluids to and from mechanical-equipment spaces can be contained relatively inconspicuously within a building or they can be turned into a form-generating tool of architectural expression. Imagine what a Gothic cathedral would have looked like had its designers had to provide for air-conditioning ducts.

Supply-and-return pipes and ducts for the various environmental systems can reach a typical floor from a mechanical area located on another floor by following either an exterior or an interior path. The most common solution is to place the ducts and pipes in vertical shafts located within the building core. The exterior distribution methods either provide vertical distribution within the columns along the facade, or create special separate vertical shafts for mechanical needs on the building's exterior. Wherever the ducts and pipes are placed, the design possibilities are great. The shafts can be hidden in the interior; they can be dis-

Cornell University Agronomy Laboratory, Ithaca, New York.

67

Mt. Sinai Hospital, New York City, S.O.M. Architects
What appears to be large exterior columns are actually
hollow shafts for pipes and ducts.

Blue Cross Building, Boston, Paul Rudolph architect
Mullions above "Y" support columns are 1/2 load bearing
and 1/2 air supply. Mullions between "Y's" are return air
shafts.

guised within the columns, thus creating an image of massive structural support; or when they are expressed as separate elements on either the exterior or interior of the buildings, they themselves become design elements.

Whatever technical trade-off must be made often depends on the overall geometry of the building. Should a designer choose to run vertical shafts within the building core, then horizontal branches to the exterior of the building must be included at each floor level. Should the shafts be located on the exterior, then they must be insulated. If the structural columns are to serve a double function and also be used as shafts, then many small shafts will be created in lieu of several larger ones—another technical trade-off. When vertical mechanical distribution shafts are placed on a building's exterior, they run the risk of conveying the impression of being structural members, rather than being perceived as the mechanical shafts they actually are. When this occurs they may be considered aesthetically dishonest by some architects.

Large buildings usually have two main horizontal areas for environmental control: an exterior zone along the outer walls and an interior zone. The heat loss and gain in an exterior zone is far greater than in an interior zone simply because the exterior zone is adjacent to an outside wall that receives the impact of a full range of outdoor temperatures in all seasons. The interior areas of a building are subject to heat buildup from a variety of sources: Each person using the building acts like a radiator set at 98.6 degrees F. Heat is generated by lights and electrical equipment, especially large computers. When combined, these factors may make the deep, inner spaces uncomfortably warm, especially during the winter heating season. This phenomenon has led architects, in an energy-conserving approach, to devise systems that will take warm air from the interior zones and move it to the cooler exterior zones. However, in the majority of buildings the interior versus exterior zones question is solved by creating a separate system of ducts for the interior and another for the exterior.

The interior zone is almost always served by shafts located in the core of the building, while the exterior zone can either be served by risers at the exterior or, by branches at each floor leading out from vertical ducts located in the core.

In some buildings, such as research laboratories, a high percentage of their volume is devoted to mechanical equipment. This is due primarily to the need to exhaust all the used air, which may be contaminated, rather than recycle it. In the hands of a talented architect, the expression of the many exhausts and other mechanical distribution systems in buildings like

Only when viewed from adjacent buildings can the thin slot of louvers be seen above the spandrel beam on the middle floor of the photo. 88 Pine St., New York City.

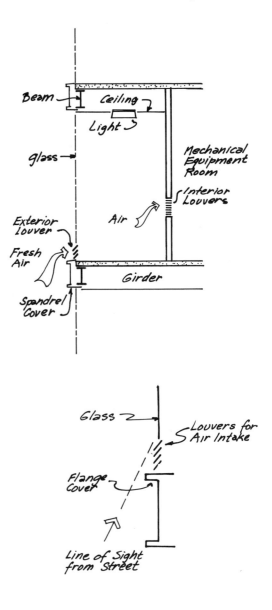

University of Pennsylvania Biology Laboratory, Louis Kahn architect
Exhaust shafts and stair towers alternate as dominant forms on the exterior.

these can become the form givers for the basic building mass and expression.

As noted earlier, architects can use various design elements to suppress or disguise the mechanical systems. An interesting case in point is the office tower at 88 Pine Street in New York, where the architect used some unusual methods to disguise the exterior louvers used to admit and exhaust the air needed for the building. The visually exaggerated flanges on the spandrel girders of this building place the louvers out of the line of sight of a person looking up at the building from the street level, with the result that the mechanical floor areas look the same to passers-by as a typical office space.

A corridor was built along the perimeter of the actual mechanical equipment space so that when people looked through the glass of the facade they would not see equipment. The disguise was furthered by the installation of lights in the corridor ceiling, which could be turned on at night so that the space would appear to be an occupied space.

Depending on the philosophy of an individual architect, the mechanical system of a building can be treated in one of three basic ways, all of which are presented in the case studies of Part Two. It can constitute a design opportunity as seen in Kahn's Richards Medical Laboratories building at the University of Pennsylvania, or it can be handled simply and forthrightly as seen in such examples as the U.S. Steel and Chase Manhattan Bank corporate headquarters. The third alternative is to subordinate the mechanical system to an overall building design concept, expressing it in one location and disguising it in another. An example of this can be seen in the Seagram building.

Chapter 6

LIFE SAFETY

In the last few decades, life safety requirements have exerted an increased influence on the design of buildings. In part, this has come from a growing awareness of the necessity to protect life and property, but it has also occurred because of the availability of new materials and improved methods of combating the problems of smoke and fire.

SHAFTS

The location and height of shafts is an important element in fire safety. Fire generates heat, and heat rises. One of the primary controls imposed by building codes, therefore, is the requirement that no more than two floors be connected by open wells or shafts. Enclosed shafts and shafts with openings protected by self-closing doors (i.e. exit stairs) or self-closing dampers (i.e. air conditioning ducts) can rise as high as necessary, provided their walls are constructed out of appropriate fire rated material. This requirement is intended to limit the rapid spread of fire from one floor to the next. One result of this restriction is that an architect may be prevented from designing a monumental staircase that rises three or more floors in an open well—that is, he will be prevented from doing this unless he can provide a satisfactory way of keeping a potential fire from rising in the well.

STRUCTURAL MATERIALS

The ability of structural materials to keep their integrity during a fire is a key element of fire safety. Some materials lose their strength more quickly than others when exposed to heat; some burn; some give off poisonous gases. Thus, the choice of a building's framing material is critical to the nature of fire protection. Failure of the structural material can cause the building to collapse.

Since wood burns, its use is limited to relatively small buildings. There is, however, a gradation in the degree of wood framing's combustibility, which is dependent on the cross-sectional size of the wood-framing members. As anyone who has tried to light a log with a match knows, smaller pieces of wood catch fire more easily than large pieces.

While steel does not burn (it melts at approximately 2600 degrees Fahrenheit), it starts to lose its

Endo Laboratory, Garden City, New York.

71

strength between 700 and 1000 degrees Fahrenheit, so it must be "fireproofed" in order to prevent this from happening. Depending on the size and the use of the building, different types and amounts of fireproofing are required. The various methods of fireproofing can have a large impact on the final appearance of a building.

Concrete disintegrates under prolonged high temperatures. Fundamentally, however, it not only is inherently fireproof but also serves as protection for the steel reinforcement rods placed within it. In fact, when concrete is used as the flooring material for a steel-framed building, it is often used to encase the steel framing members to fireproof them.

No material, of course, is truly fireproof. The most that building codes can do is rate the required amount of fire protection needed by the various parts of the building, depending on its size and use, and assign to each particular part of the building a specific minimum number of hours that it must retain its integrity during a fire. The purpose of a time rating is to permit everyone to leave the building safely, and to provide time for firefighters to combat the fire. The rating requirements vary from a maximum of 4 hours, for the columns of a large building, to permitting flammable wood construction in small buildings such as single-family houses. Even in a so-called "fireproof" building with a 4-hour fire resistance rating (often referred to as a "4-hour" structure), not all the parts of the building are rated at 4 hours. The more critical parts, such as columns, might be rated at 4 hours, but other, less critical parts require (and receive) less protection. For example, the floor construction might be required to have a 3-hour resistance rating and the roof only a 2-hour rating.

FIRE PROTECTION OF STRUCTURAL STEEL

Fire safety can be divided into two parts. One part is concerned with the problem of physically removing people from a structure in a quick and logical method in the shortest possible amount of time. This problem is basically addressed by the building codes in terms of door, stair, and exit requirements. The second part is the nature of the materials with which a building is actually constructed and the impact they have on a building's design.

In selecting a framing material for a high-rise building or any major structure, an architect is basically limited to either concrete or steel. Wood framing is generally restricted to structures that are of a modest height and area and can be easily and quickly exited.

Concrete, unless it is used in very thin sections,

will not disintegrate or lose its strength before the required time period for exiting the building and combating the fire has ended. Almost invariably, the dimensions of the framing members necessitated by the loads that they must carry vastly exceed the minimum dimensions needed to resist a fire. For example, a 6-inch-thick reinforced concrete wall would receive a 4-hour rating, which is the highest rating that the buildings codes impose on any framing members. Steel, as noted, loses its strength at a relatively low temperature, but methods can be devised to prevent the steel framing from reaching unsafe temperatures. The most common method used to protect the steel is to insulate it with some other material. Other methods of protecting it include cooling, shielding, and isolating it from a source of flames.

Insulation

Several different materials are used to insulate steel. Concrete, plaster, and sprayed-on fibers are the most commonly used substances. A host of other materials, such as gypsum board and a variety of masonry materials, are also used. Special paints have been developed that foam when heated and thus are able to provide some insulation. The thickness of the material used varies with the amount of protection required, which, in turn, depends on the type of structure and the function of the particular member being protected. Concrete is a common fireproofing material simply because it is usually the material used for floor surfaces, and thus is readily available for surrounding the beams and columns.

One of the major aesthetic results of insulating a steel framing member is that the insulation, as well as any cover over it, drastically changes the visual proportions of the member. The effect is especially deceiving when a steel member is covered with insulation and then wrapped in thin sheet metal. This method protects the underlying framing member, but its overall proportions become much heavier, and the effect is more massive than the uncovered framing member alone would convey. The untrained eye sees what appears to be a large exposed steel framing member. The trained architectural eye knows better. Whether this type of proportion change distorts the steel's scale, or whether it reinforces the visual statement by exaggerating the framing member, is a matter of interpretation that varies with the particular architect. The fact remains that when one sees what appears to be exposed structural steel in a high-rise building, something else is occurring because no building code or responsible architect would permit a situation so fraught with potential danger.

Examples of the fire-insulating values of a few of the more commonly used materials appear below.

Thickness	Material	Protection
Wall		
6 inches	reinforced concrete	4 hours
8 inches	solid brick	4 hours
12 inches	hollow block	4 hours
Floor		
5 inches	concrete slab	4 hours
Steel Beams and Columns		
2 inches	concrete with wire mesh	4 hours
2½ inches	gypsum plaster and metal lath	4 hours
1 inch	vermiculite-gypsum plaster on metal lath	4 hours
1¼ inch	sprayed on mineral fiber on beams	4 hours
2¼ inches	sprayed on mineral fiber on small columns	4 hours

Flame Shielding

Flame shielding, which is a relatively new concept, is a method of deflecting a flame away from a critical structural member. It is more commonly used for the protection of horizontal members, and affects the design of a building because its presence increases the apparent size of the beam or girder.

Flame shielding works on the concept that the shape, size, and position of the shield will combine to deflect flames away from the structural member it is protecting, thus preventing the structural member from reaching an unsafe temperature. This approach is mostly limited to beams because a hierarchy of safety prevents its use on columns. If a vertical support fails, then all the levels above that point are destroyed. If a horizontal member fails, then only that particular layer is damaged. (This is why the codes assign a higher protection rating to a column than to a beam, and in turn, a lower rating to a floor than to a beam. The repercussions of a failure are limited in this way.) Another concept, that of size, is also involved: a large member can dissipate the heat applied to part of it more easily than a small beam. Flame shielding was used to protect the exposed webs of the spandrel beams at One Liberty Plaza in New York.

Isolation

Isolation works on the theory that when a structural member is placed in a position where it cannot be

SPRAY-ON FIBERS

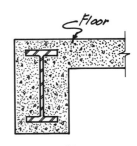

CONCRETE

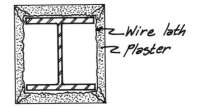

WIRE MESH LATH TO SUPPORT PLASTER

INSULATION

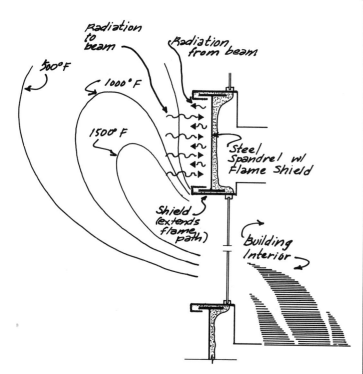

FLAME SHIELDING

The schematic above demonstrates how exterior heat radiation temperature is distributed when there is a fire inside a building that has a flame-shielded exposed steel spandrel girder

Concrete towers support isolated exposed structural steel. Knights of Columbus, New Haven, Conn.

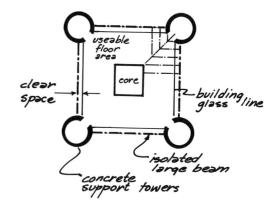

ISOLATION

endangered by flames it will remain structurally sound during a fire. The best way to isolate a framing member is to place it outside the occupied part of a building. The specific distance that is safe or even adequate is a matter of judgment, and is sometimes a difficult decision. Safe distance is usually determined by fire tests conducted on a full-scale mock-up of a portion of the building. The geometric configuration between the framing member that is being isolated and the source of the flame, as well as the dimensions of the framing member itself, are the controlling design factors. A large structural member can more easily dissipate the heat applied to it than a small member can, because the large member has greater surface area.

The architects of the Knights of Columbus building used the principle of isolation to protect the fully exposed spandrel beams. Concrete towers supported the very large spandrel beams located outside the building's glass line. These horizontal supports are thus removed and isolated from the flammable contents of the building.

Cooling

Sprinklers can be an effective way of dousing a flame, but tend to be of limited value in protecting a building's framing system. If more combustible material is present as a fuel source than the sprinklers can handle, and if the sprinklers are the only system available to protect the steel, the steel is in effect unprotected and structural failure can occur. Sprinklers are often used to supplement other types of fire-protection methods such as insulation. The use of sprinklers can permit longer travel distances to building exits, and larger amounts of floor area. Unfortunately, there is always a possibility that a water main will burst so enough fail-safe time to exit the building must be provided. If the part of the building that is protected by the sprinkler system is not receiving a cumulative load from other floors, then the sprinklers may be able to provide the needed protection. An example of this would be a structure which had its exposed steel beams protected by a sprinkler system and its columns (which are subject to cumulative loads from other floors) protected by fire-resistant insulation in addition to the sprinklers.

Another cooling technique is to create hollow framing members, which are then filled with water. The framing members are interconnected with a series of loops, and the water contained inside this system is free to circulate. A fire causes the steel to become heated, which, in turn, causes the water encased within the columns or other framing members to heat up. Since hot water rises by gravity, and the columns are all cross-connected to form closed loops, the heat of

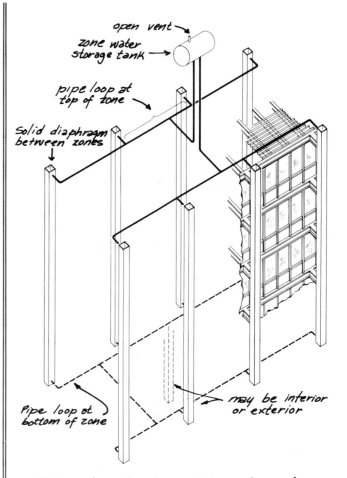

Schematic of a liquid-filled column fire protection system

COOLING

A smoke barrier surrounds the opening between floors, and a row of sprinkler heads ring the barrier.

Sprinkler
heads
6 ft o.c.

Smoke barrier on
all sides of opening
between floors

fire will cause the water to circulate and thus bring cool water to the initial area of heat source, cooling the steel and keeping it structurally sound. The water contained in the hollow framing members is treated with antifreeze and rust-inhibiting additives in much the same way that a car radiator is. This system is more effective for columns than for horizontal beams. The exterior columns of the U.S. Steel Building in Pittsburgh are protected in this manner.

EXITS

Both the number and the location of stairs and exits are critical parts of a life-safety system. Elevators are not considered legal exits in a fire emergency because they might fail to operate and can actually become lethal devices by delivering people to the wrong floor or trapping them. Moreover, elevator shaft doors cannot close tightly and the elevator shafts, which connect the floor containing the fire to the rest of the building, often contain smoke.

Moving stairs usually can be counted as a means of egress, as long as they consist of no more than one-half of the required total number of stairs. When moving stairs connect more than two levels, the open shaft they create becomes a problem, and the shafts must be designed so they do not act as flues. In older buildings, the openings for moving stairs were protected by concealed steel shutters that were balanced in place on counterweights. The heat generated by a fire will melt a fusible link connected to the counterweights, allowing the shutters to close. Naturally, a moving stair protected in this manner could not serve as an exit. In new buildings, smoke curtains and banks of sprinklers leave moving stairs accessible as escape routes.

Exit requirements are discussed in more detail in Chapter 7.

SPRINKLER SYSTEMS

Most codes require commercial buildings over five floors in height to have a sprinkler system. Usually, these buildings have an acoustic ceiling, which is hung below the structural ceiling. This ceiling conceals the ducts, pipes, and electric conduits, and it can easily be used to conceal horizontal sprinkler piping.

The pattern of the sprinkler heads on the ceiling is a design consideration for the architect, who will have to integrate them with the light-fixture pattern, the air supply-and-return grilles, and in some cases, the speaker system. Additionally, the building design must include vertical shaft spaces to contain the sprinkler riser piping that goes from floor to floor.

STANDPIPE SYSTEMS

Standpipe systems were the forerunners of sprinklers. A standpipe system is a network of empty pipes that usually are placed in stair halls. They connect at the bottom to an outlet (called a *siamese connection*) in the street that permits firefighters to fasten a hose from a fire hydrant to the pipe system. Each floor has a required number of hose cabinets, each one containing a long length of hose that is attached to the standpipe. Without a standpipe system, firefighters would have to carry fire hoses up the numerous flights of a skyscraper. Most high-rise buildings contain both sprinkler and standpipe systems.

WATER TOWERS AND PUMPS

In order to provide enough water at the proper pressure throughout the sprinkler and standpipe systems installed in high-rise buildings, large tanks (usually constructed of redwood because it swells and therefore stays amazingly watertight, and because it does not rot) are placed on the building's roof. These tanks are filled slowly by small pumps when there is no emergency. The tanks feed the sprinklers and standpipes by gravity during a crisis. The biggest drawback to the tanks is their limited capacity, usually not much more than 20 to 30 minutes of water flow.

These tanks often were an aesthetic problem for architects because they created large, awkward lumps on the roofline. Powerful pumps are now available; located in cellars, they are capable of providing adequate water pressure for most high-rise buildings. Very tall buildings can be zoned into several vertical layers, with pumps serving the lower zones and tanks the higher zones. Whenever pumps are used, a standby pump and emergency power are also provided.

Fire trucks are furnished with pumps powered from their engines and capable of supplying water from a street hydrant to the top of most tall buildings. These pumps can be connected by a fire hose to the sprinkler and/or standpipe system if there is a power failure or a mechanical breakdown of the building pump.

ACCOMMODATIONS FOR THE HANDICAPPED

An awareness of the difficulties many physically handicapped people have in getting into and using buildings has resulted in the building codes' preventing the cre-

A hose cabinet, appropriately located, eliminates the need for firefighters to carry hose.

Siamese Connection. Located outside of the building, it provides a means of connecting fire hoses. They can be either free-standing or flush with the building face.

A redwood water reserve tank atop a high rise building.

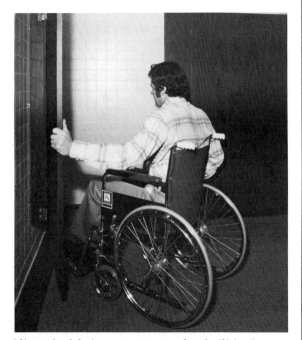

Providing wheelchair access to everyday facilities is easy in the planning stage, but is difficult once the building is finished.

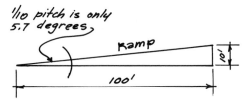

¹/₁₀ pitch is only 5.7 degrees

Ramp

10'

100'

Pitch is limited to ratio of one foot in ten feet (¹/₁₀) for most ramps. (Some codes require ¹/₁₂).

ation of physical obstacles and providing for the wheelchair-bound, amenities that most people take for granted. Access to facilities such as telephone booths, drinking fountains, and toilets are now mandated.

Major life-safety situations such as exiting a building by wheelchair or crutches during a fire make ramps a necessity in lieu of, or in addition to, steps. Ramps can become a major design factor because they occupy a large amount of space, especially compared to stairs. Ramps are not required as a means of exit from the floors of high-rise buildings served by elevators, as the amount of space they would occupy would be excessive. Wheelchair-bound individuals must be evacuated by firefighters who have access to key-controlled elevators.

Perhaps the major architectural impact of accommodating the handicapped is that public buildings are seldom set up on pedestals, with monumental steps rising to them. Instead, they now sit sedately on the ground and have grade-level access.

Most requirements for the handicapped are simply common sense and are based on the premise that a way must be provided for handicapped people to reach all parts and facilities of a building. Designing water coolers and toilet facilities so that they are available to the wheelchair-bound alters very little architecturally, yet it radically affects the lives of those who benefit from these adjustments.

DETECTION AND CONTROL

Building codes require many additional kinds of life-safety equipment. Some of the more significant include elevator-recall systems, a voice-communication system between stair halls and a fire-command station in the lobby, smoke detectors in ducts and mechanical areas, and alarm systems activated by the various detectors. These items do much to ensure the safety of a building's occupants, and their visual impact is invariably minimal. Often, the devices are hidden from the view of everyone but the maintenance crews.

Controls can be built into mechanical ventilation systems that will automatically shut them down when smoke is detected. Air supply fans can be reversed to exhaust smoke, and stairways can be pressurized to prevent smoke from entering them when a stair door is opened.

Codes can offer only a minimum set of standards. Nothing prevents owners or architects from exercising prudent judgment to provide additional safeguards.

Chapter 7

BUILDING CODES AND ZONING ORDINANCES

In a complex society, regulation is one of the facts of life. The buildings in which people live, work, and play are subject to many controls. Local and regional government agencies have been established to protect the public and the environment from dangerous and undesirable conditions that sometimes occur when manmade structures are erected, and the result is innumerable building codes and zoning ordinances. In the United States, these rules and regulations can vary from community to community, but all are based on fundamental construction methods necessary to protect public safety and welfare.

BUILDING CODES

Building codes not only affect the selection of the materials that an architect uses to build a structure; they can influence the size and shape of the building as well. For example, depending upon how fire-resistant the selected construction materials are, the codes will permit different maximum areas per floor and different total numbers of floors for the building.

The impact of the relationship between building materials and the size of a building can be most easily demonstrated by an example. Assume that an architect is planning to design a resort. He wishes to use exposed, laminated-wood beams and other wood construction in order to create a rustic atmosphere. Chart 1, reproduced from the National Building Code, known as BOCA, lists hotels under the use-group R-1. When R-1 is intersected with construction type 4 (heavy timber), the chart shows that the maximum height permitted for a structure of this type is 4 stories or 50 feet, whichever is greater. The chart also indicates that no more than 14,400 square feet of space is permitted on each floor. If the client's needs can be accommodated within these height and area limitations, then all is fine. If not, a different type of framing system will have to be considered—one that permits either more height or more area.

Chart 2 provides specific information regarding the amount of fire protection that is required for each particular part of a building. The information differs based on the variations in construction types listed in Chart 1. The building code can also be referred to for further explanation, and indeed the chart often refers the reader to the code. For example, under type 4 construction, Chart 2 shows that bearing walls require a two-hour rating (see 1 under Structure Element).

Park Avenue, New York, New York.

CHART 1

Table 501
HEIGHT AND AREA LIMITATIONS OF BUILDINGS
Height limitations of buildings (shown in upper figure as stories and feet above grade), and area limitations of one or two story buildings facing on one street or public space not less than 30 feet wide (shown in lower figure as area in square feet per floor). See Note a.

NP — Not permitted
NL — Not limited

Use Group		Type 1 Protected Note b 1A	Type 1 Protected Note b 1B	Type 2 Protected 2A	Type 2 Protected 2B	Type 2 Unprotected 2C	Type 3 Protected 3A	Type 3 Unprotected 3B	Type 4 Heavy timber 4	Type 5 Protected 5A	Type 5 Unprotected 5B
A-1 Assembly, theaters		NL	NL	5 St. 65' 19,950	3 St. 40' 13,125	2 St. 30' 8,400	3 St. 40' 11,550	2 St. 30' 8,400	3 St. 40' 12,600	1 St. 20' 8,925	1 St. 20' 4,200
A-2 Assembly, nightclubs and similar uses		NL	NL 7,200	3 St. 40' 5,700	2 St. 30' 3,750	1 St. 20' 2,400	2 St. 30' 3,300	1 St. 20' 2,400	2 St. 30' 3,600	1 St. 20' 2,550	1 St. 20' 1,200
A-3 Assembly — Lecture halls, recreation centers, terminals, restaurants other than night clubs		NL	NL	5 St. 65' 19,950	3 St. 40' 13,125	2 St. 30' 8,400	3 St. 40' 11,550	2 St. 30' 8,400	3 St. 40' 12,600	1 St. 20' 8,925	1 St. 20' 4,200
A-4 Assembly, churches	Note d	NL	NL	5 St. 65' 34,200	3 St. 40' 22,500	2 St. 30' 14,400	3 St. 40' 19,800	2 St. 30' 14,400	3 St. 40' 21,600	1 St. 20' 15,300	1 St. 20' 7,200
B Business		NL	NL	7 St. 85' 34,200	5 St. 65' 22,500	3 St. 40' 14,400	4 St. 50' 19,800	3 St. 40' 14,400	5 St. 65' 21,600	3 St. 40' 15,300	2 St. 30' 7,200
E Educational	Note c,d	NL	NL	5 St. 65' 34,200	3 St. 40' 22,500	2 St. 30' 14,400	3 St. 40' 19,800	2 St. 30' 14,400	3 St. 40' 21,600	1 St. 20' 15,300 Note e	1 St. 20' 7,200 Note e
F-1 Factory and industrial, moderate	Note i	NL	NL	6 St. 75' 22,800	4 St. 50' 15,000	2 St. 30' 9,600	3 St. 40' 13,200	2 St. 30' 9,600	4 St. 50' 14,400	3 St. 40' 10,200	2 St. 30' 4,800
F-2 Factory and industrial, low	Note i	NL	NL	7 St. 85' 34,200	5 St. 65' 22,500	3 St. 40' 14,400	4 St. 50' 19,800	3 St. 40' 14,400	5 St. 65' 21,600	3 St. 40' 15,300	2 St. 30' 7,200
H High hazard	Note f	5 St. 65' 16,800	3 St. 40' 14,400	3 St. 40' 11,400	2 St. 30' 7,500	1 St. 20' 4,800	2 St. 30' 6,600	1 St. 20' 4,800	2 St. 30' 7,200	1 St. 20' 5,100	NP
I-1 Institutional, residential care		NL	NL	9 St. 100' 19,950	4 St. 50' 13,125	3 St. 40' 8,400	4 St. 50' 11,550	3 St. 40' 8,400	4 St. 50' 12,600	3 St. 40' 8,925	2 St. 35' 4,200
I-2 Institutional, incapacitated		NL	8 St. 90' 21,600	4 St. 50' 17,100	2 St. 30' 11,250	1 St. 20' 7,200	1 St. 20' 9,900	NP	1 St. 20' 10,800	1 St. 20' 7,650	NP
I-3 Institutional, restrained		NL	6 St. 75' 18,000	4 St. 50' 14,250	2 St. 30' 9,375	1 St. 20' 6,000	2 St. 30' 8,250	1 St. 20' 6,000	2 St. 30' 9,000	1 St. 20' 6,375	NP
M Mercantile		NL	NL	6 St. 75' 22,800	4 St. 50' 15,000	2 St. 30' 9,600	3 St. 40' 13,200	2 St. 30' 9,600	4 St. 50' 14,400	2 St. 30' 10,200	1 St. 20' 4,800
R-1 Residential, hotels		NL	NL	9 St. 100' 22,800	4 St. 50' 15,000	3 St. 40' 9,600	4 St. 50' 13,200	3 St. 40' 9,600	4 St. 50' 14,400	3 St. 40' 10,200	2 St. 35' 4,800
R-2 Residential, multiple-family		NL	NL	9 St. 100' 22,800	4 St. 50' 15,000 Note g	3 St. 40' 9,600	4 St. 50' 13,200 Note g	3 St. 40' 9,600	4 St. 50' 14,400	3 St. 40' 10,200	2 St. 35' 4,800
R-3 Residential, one- and two-family		NL	NL	4 St. 50' 22,800	4 St. 50' 15,000	3 St. 40' 9,600	4 St. 50' 13,200	3 St. 40' 9,600	4 St. 50' 14,400	3 St. 40' 10,200	2 St. 35' 4,800
S-1 Storage, moderate		NL	NL	5 St. 65' 19,950	3 St. 40' 13,125	2 St. 30' 8,400	3 St. 40' 11,550	2 St. 30' 8,400	3 St. 40' 12,600	2 St. 30' 8,925	1 St. 20' 4,200
S-2 Storage, low	Note h	NL	NL	7 St. 85' 34,200	5 St. 65' 22,500	3 St. 40' 14,400	4 St. 50' 19,800	3 St. 40' 14,400	5 St. 65' 21,600	3 St. 40' 15,300	2 St. 30' 7,200
U Utility, miscellaneous		NL	NL								

Note a. See the following sections for general exceptions to Table 501:
  Section 501.4 Allowable area reduction for multistory buildings.
  Section 502.2 Allowable area increase due to street frontage.
  Section 502.3 Allowable area increase due to automatic sprinkler system installation.
  Section 503.1 Allowable height increase due to automatic sprinkler system installation.
  Section 504.0 Unlimited area one-story buildings.
Note b. Buildings of Type 1 construction permitted to be of unlimited tabular heights and areas are not subject to special requirements that allow increased heights and areas for other types of construction (see Section 501.5).
Note c. For tabular area increase in buildings of Use Group E, see Section 502.4.
Note d. For height exceptions for auditoriums in buildings of Use Groups A-4 and E, see Section 503.2.
Note e. For height exceptions for day care centers of Type 5 construction, see Section 503.3.
Note f. For exceptions to height and area limitations for buildings of Use Group H, see Article 6 governing the specific use. For other special fireresistive requirements governing specific uses, see Section 904.0.
Note g. For exceptions to height of buildings for Use Group R-2 of Types 2B and 3A construction, see Section 904.2.
Note h. For height and area exceptions for open parking structures, see Section 607.0.
Note i. For exceptions to height and area limitations for special industrial uses, see Section 501.1.1.
Note j. 1 foot = 304.8 mm; 1 square foot = 0.093 m^2.

CHART 2

Table 401
FIRERESISTANCE RATINGS OF STRUCTURE ELEMENTS (IN HOURS)

Structure element Note a		Type 1 Section 402.0 Protected 1A	1B	Type 2 Section 403.0 Protected 2A	2B	Unprotected 2C	Type 3 Section 404.0 Protected 3A	Unprotected 3B	Type 4 Section 405.0 Heavy timber Note c 4	Type 5 Section 406.0 Protected 5A	Unprotected 5B
1 Exterior walls	Loadbearing	4	3	2	1	0	2	2	2	1	0
		← Not less than the rating based on fire separation distance (see Section 905.2) →									
	Nonloadbearing	← Not less than the rating based on fire separation distance (see Section 905.2) →									
2 Fire walls and party walls (Section 907.0)		4	3	2	2	2	2	2	2	2	2
		← Not less than the rating required by Table 907.1 →									
3 Fire separation assemblies (Section 909.0)	Fire enclosure of exits (Sections 817.11, 909.0 and Note b)	2	2	2	2	2	2	2	2	2	2
	Shafts (other than exits) and elevator hoistways (Sections 909.0, 915.0 and Note b)	2	2	2	2	2	2	2	2	1	1
	Mixed use separation (Section 313.0)	← Fireresistance rating corresponding to the rating required by Table 313.1.2 →									
	Other separation assemblies (Note i)	1	1	1	1	1 (Note d)	1	1	1	1	1
4 Fire partitions (Section 910.0)	Exit access corridors (Notes f, g)	1	1	1	1	1 (Note d)	1	1	1	1	1
	Tenant spaces separations (Note f)	1	1	1	1	0 (Note d)	1	0	1	1	0
5 Dwelling unit separations (Sections 910.0, 913.0 and Notes f and j)		1	1	1	1	1 (Note d)	1	1	1	1	1
6 Smoke barriers (Section 911.0 and Note g)		1	1	1	1	1	1	1	1	1	1
7 Other nonbearing partitions		0	0	0	0	0 (Note d)	0	0	0	0	0
8 Interior bearing walls, bearing partitions, columns, girders, trusses (other than roof trusses) and framing (Section 912.0)	Supporting more than one floor	4	3	2	1	0	1	0	see Sec. 405.0	1	0
	Supporting one floor only or a roof only	3	2	1½	1	0	1	0	see Sec. 405.0	1	0
9 Structural members supporting wall (Section 912.0 and Note g)		3	2	1½	1	0	1	0	1	1	0
		← Not less than fireresistance rating of wall supported →									
10 Floor construction including beams (Section 913.0 and Note h)		3	2	1½	1	0	1	0	see Sec. 405.0 Note c	1	0
11 Roof construction, including beams, trusses and framing, arches and roof deck (Section 914.0 and Notes e, i)	15' or less in height to lowest member	2	1½	1	1	0 (Note d)	1	0	see Sec. 405.0 Note c	1	0
	More than 15' but less than 20' in height to lowest member	1	1	1	0	0 (Note d)	0	0	see Sec. 405.0	1	0
	20' or more in height to lowest member	0	0	0	0	0 (Note d)	0	0	see Sec. 405.0	0	0

Note a. For fireresistance rating requirements for structural members and assemblies which support other fireresistance rated members or assemblies, see Section 912.1.
Note b. For reductions in the required fireresistance rating of exit and shaft enclosures, see Sections 817.11 and 915.3.
Note c. For substitution of other structural materials for timber in Type 4 construction, see Section 1703.1.1.
Note d. Fireretardant-treated wood permitted, see Sections 904.3 and 1702.4.
Note e. For permitted uses of heavy timber in roof construction in buildings of Types 1 and 2 construction, see Section 914.4.
Note f. For reductions in required fireresistance ratings of exit access corridors, tenant separations and dwelling unit separations, see Section 810.4 and 810.4.1.
Note g. For exceptions to the required fireresistance rating of construction supporting exit access corridor walls, tenant separation walls in covered mall buildings, and smoke barriers, see Sections 911.4 and 912.2.
Note h. For buildings having habitable or occupiable stories or basements below grade, see Section 807.3.1.
Note i. Not less than the rating required by code.
Note j. For Use Group R-3, see Section 309.4.
Note k. 1 foot = 304.8 mm.

Upon further investigation, to determine the required fire rating for columns supporting more than one floor (intersect line 8 under Structure Element with Type 4 construction), Chart 2 refers the reader to the building code because the information is too detailed to be included in a chart. The text of the code under that section states that columns supporting floor loads cannot be less than 8 inches by 8 inches in cross-section or less than 6 inches by 8 inches when supporting roofs.

Building codes are concerned with innumerable items and often run to hundreds and even thousands of pages. Every section of the code obviously has some impact on a building, but not every section has a major impact of a form-giving nature. The list that follows notes code items that often affect a building's overall design. The list is selective; individual architects might include different items or omit some of the items on this list.

1. Total permitted area as a function of construction materials.

2. Total permitted height as a function of construction materials.

3. Number and location of required stairs and exits.

4. Required amount of natural and/or artificial light.

5. Required amount of natural and/or artificial ventilation.

6. Required number and types of plumbing fixtures (for washrooms).

7. Pipe spaces required for plumbing and storm-drainage systems.

8. Heating equipment.

9. Air-conditioning equipment.

10. Elevator machine rooms and shafts.

11. Electric-equipment spaces and shafts.

12. Fire-protection systems.

13. Fire-extinguishing equipment.

14. Total building size as a function of building use.

ZONING ORDINANCES

While building codes tend to tell an architect how a structure can be built, zoning regulations tell him or her where the structure can be built and how bulky it can be. They define the areas of a community in which buildings intended for certain specific uses can be constructed. For example, manufacturing is often allowed only in a particular area, which is usually some distance from residential areas. Zoning ordinances can also limit the overall bulk of buildings and the percentage of the ground they can cover. In addition, they may mandate such things as how many parking spaces must be provided; the amount of open space; yards and plaza sizes; and, in major cities, the type of vertical setbacks that are required.

Among the major items covered by most zoning ordinances are the following:

1. Building use permitted in each area of the community.

2. Lot-area regulations.

3. Yard-size regulations.

4. Building height and setback requirements.

5. Distances between buildings.

6. Parking and truck-dock requirements.

7. Ratio of floor area to total building size.

8. Ratio of open space on the ground to the maximum height of the structure.

RELATIONSHIP BETWEEN CODES AND ZONING ORDINANCES

Apparent jurisdictional overlap may occur between zoning ordinances and building codes. For example, they could conflict over minimum side-yard requirements. A zoning ordinance may specify the size of a yard or set back from a property line that must be provided for a particular type of building, while the building code may establish a minimum yard dimension that is required in order to provide adequate light and ventilation for a window facing onto a yard. Often these requirements are not the same, and since both requirements must be met, the stricter of the two prevails.

Another type of conflict can occur when a building code does not limit a building's height provided proper fire rated materials are used in its construction, but the town zoning ordinance states that no building can be more than, for example, eight stories high. Or the reverse situation might apply: that is, a town zoning ordinance might permit an eight-story hotel while the building code specifies that hotels may not be more than four stories high if they are of heavy-timber construction. In either case, a solution must be found that satisfies all requirements, and the decisions that result from such conflicts inevitably influence the design of the building.

Apart from building codes and zoning ordinances, the requirements of special-interest agencies can also affect a building. For example, the Board of Health sets up rules for restaurants and hospitals, and the Department of Labor has requirements to protect workers such as mandating guardrails or window ledges to protect window washers. Many of these types of rules will affect the design of buildings. The list of special-interest requirements is enormous, but fortunately their effect on the design of a building is relatively minor, especially when compared with the requirements of the building codes and zoning ordinances. Occasionally, though, a special-interest agency regulation does influence the design of a building.

EXIT REQUIREMENTS

One of the decisive form-givers in any major building is the location of its required means of egress. This is a separate problem from the location of decorative or ceremonial stairs, which codes refer to as "convenient" or "ornamental" stairs.

Although building codes go into minute detail describing exit requirements and the way in which exiting enclosures must be constructed, the five points that follow have a major impact on the overall building design.

1. Use of the building, for example, as an office, store, or school.

2. Total number of people in the building as a determinant of the required number of separate exits.

3. Limitations on the maximum travel distance permitted to reach an exit enclosure.

4. Provision for a choice of paths to an exit, and a choice of exits in case one exit is blocked.

5. Provision that exits must lead the occupants to a safe area.

Items 1, 2, and 5 are an automatic spellout of the codes. Items 3 and 4 require proper proportioning and shaping of spaces by the architect in order to comply with a specific maximum travel distance and a specific maximum dead-end corridor length. This proportioning can have a dramatic effect on the overall shape of the building. For example, most codes will not permit any dead end corridors in a hospital; therefore, the stairs must be located at the ends of the building.

Elevators can make a major design contribution or be part of a nondescript core, but in either case they may not count as a means of exiting as they could fail during an emergency. Hyatt Regency Hotel, Atlanta, Georgia.

Location of Stair Cores as Affected by Building Codes

EXAMPLES OF CODE INFLUENCE ON EXIT STAIRS

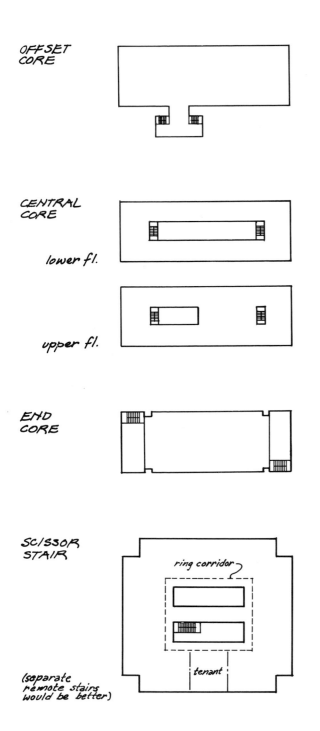

OFFSET CORE

CENTRAL CORE

lower fl.

upper fl.

END CORE

SCISSOR STAIR

ring corridor

tenant

(separate remote stairs would be better)

Offset core creates large travel distance to exits, therefore should not be used in large buildings and violates common-sense definition of remote exits.

Central core remote ends are used for stair location. Good code compliance but creates some problems when the elevator core drops off in upper floors, as one stair will tend to float.

End cores have no dead end corridors created by stair locations. Perhaps the safest solution. An additional advantage is that elevator lobbies can have a window. The main drawback is the loss of exterior office space.

Scissor stairs make sense only when floor areas need not be subdivided, or in a very small building. The problem is threefold in a large building with multiple tenants. First, the exits are not remote by any common-sense definition; second, the maximum travel distance to the stair becomes excessive; third, the maximum dead-end corridor length becomes excessive. The creation of a ring corridor around the core solves the dead-end problem, but creates a real estate agent's nightmare in terms of lost rentable space.

No dead-end corridor.

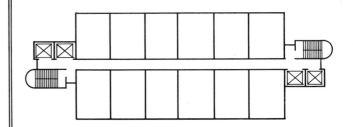

Dead-end corridor conforms to most major codes (40-foot maximum). Occupants in apartment "A" are blocked from both stairs if there is a fire in the corridor between their door and the first stair. Occupants in apartment "B" have a choice of direction in case of a fire.

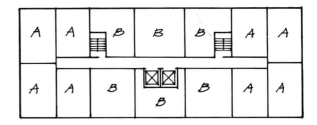

The architect has certain obligations regarding his design regardless of whether the prevailing code sets a maximum dead-end corridor, permits no dead end, or allows any length corridor.

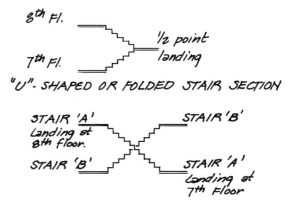

8th Fl.

7th Fl.

½ point landing

"U"- SHAPED OR FOLDED STAIR SECTION

STAIR 'A'
Landing at
8th floor.

STAIR 'B'

STAIR 'B'

STAIR 'A'
Landing at
7th floor

SCISSOR- STAIR SECTION

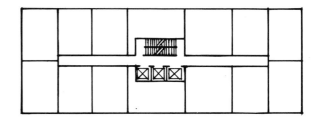

A 'scissor-stair' does not fold on itself at a landing halfway between floors. Rather, it's a straight run from floor to floor. Two such straight-run stairs can be placed in one shaft at a considerable cost advantage.

MAJOR STEPS IN DESIGNING A STAIR TO MEET CODE REQUIREMENTS

(Code excerpts courtesy of the BOCA Basic/National Building Code, 1990)

1. Determine the use group of the building, construction type, and total area. (See Charts 1 and 2)

2. Determine the floor area per person from a chart giving the area for each occupancy group. (Chart 3)

3. Determine the total building code population by dividing the net square footage of the floor area by the area per person.

4. Determine the minimum number of exits required. Check locations where one exit is permitted. Check locations having public assembly use. (Chart 4)

5. Check maximum travel distance from the most remote point to an exit enclosure. This number will depend on such items as whether the building is sprinklered and whether the floor is above, on, or below grade. *Note:* The total maximum travel distance includes travel through both rooms and corridors. (Chart 5)

6. Check dead-end corridor requirements. This does not count travel within a room or space before going to the corridor.

7. Check termination requirements. Can stairs exit through a lobby? Must they go to the roof? In general, stairs must lead to "legal" open space.

8. Set basic size of stairway. Usually based on the number of people per 22 inches of width. Use chart such as BOCA table 808.2 in combination with fixed minimums as BOCA 810.3.

This still leaves a large number of other requirements that the architect must comply with, such as door sizes, handrail heights, treads, and risers. But the gist of the stair has been set and a schematic design of the building can be realistically developed.

CHART 3

Table 806.1.2
MAXIMUM FLOOR AREA ALLOWANCES PER OCCUPANT

Use	Floor area in square feet per occupant
Assembly with fixed seats	See Section 806.1.6
Assembly without fixed seats	
Concentrated (chairs only—not fixed)	7 net
Standing space	3 net
Unconcentrated (tables and chairs)	15 net
Bowling centers, allow 5 persons for each lane including 15 feet of runway, and for additional areas	7 net
Business areas	100 gross
Courtrooms—other than fixed seating areas	
Educational	
Classroom area	20 net
Shops and other vocational room areas	50 net
Industrial areas	100 gross
Institutional areas	
Inpatient treatment areas	240 gross
Outpatient areas	100 gross
Sleeping areas	120 gross
Library	
Reading rooms	50 net
Stack area	100 gross
Mercantile, basement and grade floor areas	30 gross
Areas on other floors	60 gross
Storage, stock, shipping areas	300 gross
Parking garages	200 gross
Residential	200 gross
Storage areas, mechanical equipment room	300 gross

Note a. 1 foot = 304.8 mm; 1 square foot = 0.093 m^2.

CHART 4

Table 809.2
MINIMUM NUMBER OF EXITS FOR OCCUPANT LOAD

Occupant load	Minimum number of exits
500 or less	2
501–1,000	3
over 1,000	4

807.5 Length of travel: All *exits* shall be so located that the maximum length of *exit access* travel, measured from the most remote point to an approved *exit* along the natural and unobstructed line of travel, shall not exceed the distances given in Table 807.5.

CHART 5

Table 807.5
LENGTH OF EXIT ACCESS TRAVEL [in feet[c]][a]

Use Group	Without sprinkler system	With sprinkler system[b]
A, B, E, F-1, I-1, M, R, S-1	200	250
F-2, S-2	300	400
H	—	75
I-2, I-3	150	200

Note a. See the following sections for modifications to travel distance requirements.
Section 601.4.1: For the exit access travel distance limitation in malls.
Section 603.1.4: For the exit access travel distance limitation in HPM use facilities.
Section 606.7: For the exit access travel distance limitation through an atrium space.
Section 624.9: For the exit access travel distance limitation in temporary structures.
Section 807.5.1: For increased limitation in Use Groups F-1 and S-1.
Section 807.5.2: For increased limitation in Use Group A-5.
Section 809.3: For buildings with one exit.
Note b. Buildings equipped throughout with an automatic sprinkler system in accordance with Section 1004.2.1 or 1004.2.2.
Note c. 1 foot = 304.8 mm.

812.1 Passageways: Every required interior and exterior *exit* element which does not adjoin a *public way* shall be directly connected to the *public way* or to an open *court* leading to the *public way* by an enclosed passageway at the level of *exit discharge* or other unobstructed *exit* element constructed as provided for in this section. *Building areas* below the level of *exit discharge* shall be separated from the passageway in accordance with the requirements for the enclosure of *exits*.

812.3 Lobby: Where an *exit* discharges into an interior *lobby* located at the level of *exit discharge*, such *lobby* shall be provided with an *automatic fire suppression system*, and any other portion of the floor with access to the *lobby* shall be provided with an *automatic fire suppression system* or shall be separated therefrom in accordance with the requirements for the enclosure of *exits*.

813.2 Number of doorways: Each occupant of a room or space shall have access to at least two *exits* or *exit access* doors from the room or space where the occupant load of the space exceeds that listed in Table 813.2, or where the travel distance from any point within the space to an *exit* or *exit access* door exceeds that listed in Table 813.2.

818.1 By stairway or ladder: In buildings more than three stories in *height*, except those with a roof slope greater than four units vertical in 12 units horizontal (4:12), access to the roof shall be provided by means of a *stairway*, an *alternating tread stair* in accordance with Section 817.6.5 or a ladder and trap door. The ladder shall not be on the exterior of the building. Where the roof is used as a roof garden or for other habitable purposes, sufficient *stairways* shall extend to the roof to provide the necessary *exit* facilities from the roof as required for such occupancy. Roof trap doors shall be constructed to comply with Section 927.2.

CHART 6

Table 808.2
EGRESS WIDTH PER OCCUPANT

Use group	Without sprinkler system (inches per person)[b]		With sprinkler system[a] (inches per person)[b]	
	Stairways	Doors, ramps and corridors	Stairways	Doors, ramps and corridors
A, B, E,F, M, R, S	0.3	0.2	0.2	0.15
H	—	—	0.3	0.2
I-1	0.4	0.2	0.2	0.2
I-2	1.0	0.7	0.6	0.5
I-3	0.3	0.2	0.3	0.2

Note a. Buildings equipped throughout with an automatic sprinkler system in accordance with Section 1004.2.1 or 1004.2.2.
Note b. 1 inch = 25.4 mm.

Part Two

CASE STUDIES

CBS Tower, New York, N.Y.

*T*his part consists of an analysis of eighteen buildings, half of which are framed with concrete and half with steel. In each case study, emphasis is placed on the ways that various technical and legal requirements have contributed to the final architectural image. Decisions related to the structural and mechanical systems, to the detailing of a building, and also to the need to comply with building codes and zoning ordinances all must be integrated with the architect's aesthetic orientation and client needs in order to create a building that will, one hopes, be worthy of being considered architecture.

The case studies are, in part, a personal interpretation of the building's aesthetic statement, with particular emphasis on the technical aspects that contribute to or detract from the overall design statement.

A significant additional use of these case studies is to illustrate actual examples and solutions to some of the issues that were discussed in Part One.

All of the plans in this part are drawn at a constant scale (1 inch equals 40 feet) regardless of actual building size, in order to permit an accurate graphic comparison of the buildings. Sections taken through the buildings are also drawn at the same scale where page size permits. Some tall structures had to be drawn at a smaller scale (1 inch equals 80 feet) and very tall buildings at a third scale (1 inch equals 100 feet) in order to fit within the page size.

In each of the case histories, at least one photograph of the building is provided along with the following diagrammatic materials:

1.   A ground-floor plan showing how the building accommodates itself to its site.

2.   A typical architectural floor plan showing how the space is used.

3.   A framing diagram of a typical floor.

4.   A diagram indicating the pattern of significant vertical wind-bracing systems.

5.   Schematic mechanical system diagrams indicating the fresh-air intakes, the location of major mechanical equipment spaces, the general path of supply and return air, and the location of the air exhaust.

Intelligent comparison requires the use of common criteria. All buildings consist of certain fundamental elements such as structural, mechanical, and cladding systems. The proportional amount of space required for each of these various systems is an important function in determining the basic geometric layout a building will have.

The total floor area that must be provided in a building is determined by assessing and combining the amount of space needed by the users and the amount of space needed for support functions. An architect must be able to estimate how much additional space a building must contain over and above that required for occupant use. One of an architect's first tasks is to establish the space-ratio requirements between the various functions and uses of the building.

The buildings included in this section have all been analyzed in order to determine a series of significant ratios regarding the amount of space or area required for a series of technical and support functions, such as the relationship between usable and gross areas and the amount of space required for mechanical shafts, exit patterns, and structural framing. The chart provided at the end of this section offers a means of instantly comparing key data items for all the buildings analyzed.

The data for all the case studies in this book are based on original working drawings.

Although to make a definitive statement about the relationship between design and technology would require many more case studies than are presented here, it is hoped that these will prove a modest beginning.

SEAGRAM BUILDING

THE Seagram Building holds a unique place in the evolution of modern American architecture. It has been argued that its purity, its proportions, and the placement of its podium make it as much a piece of sculpture as architecture. In this sense it can be compared to the classical Greek buildings, which were placed on their sites in a way that enabled the viewer to behold them from all sides.

It is necessary, however, to look beyond the clean, seemingly pure lines that Mies van der Rohe created in order to see the price that the architects of record, Kahn and Jacobs of New York City, were forced to pay in order to achieve the final illusion of sophistication that this building has come to represent. Indeed, one of the principal reasons that critics have admired the main facade is its clean, uninterrupted lines. But where are the louvers for the fresh-air intakes and exhaust? The height of the building precludes any reasonable assumption that the louvers expressed at the top can serve the entire 38-story building. Unfortunately, the answer to this question is not so pure as we might like. Mies van der Rohe very cleverly sculpted two boxes that were placed on the sides of the building's core at the main lobby level. These boxes are outside the enclosed part of the lobby and remain consistent with Miesian design theory in that they do not touch (and therefore violate) the underside of the building mass above them. It is on top of these story-high boxes that the air-intake louvers are cleverly hidden. He constructed a very neat system that restores logic to the original assumption that the Seagram Building was too tall not to have a mechanical zone in the lower part of the building. In light of Mies' emphasis on purity, it is at least an odd, if not a controversial decision, for him to conceal or disguise this lower zone, as well as to hide the air exhaust at the rear of the building.

Structurally the building must have some type of wind bracing. In the Seagram Building, the overall proportions of the building required that the core be set off from the center in order to provide meaningful contiguous office space on each floor. The need to do this severely limited the availability of places for the engineer to locate the wind bracing. As a result, some of the bracing had to be placed along a pair of exterior walls. Rather than express the wind bracing as a different, special function, the exact opposite was done. Solid concrete walls were covered with exactly the same window frames as the rest of the building. The window spaces were then glazed with green marble. This material was chosen because it mimicked the effect of the tinted glass windows. To give the devil his due, this has proved to be a fairly clever fake, because from a relatively short distance away, one cannot tell the real windows from the marble ones. But fake they are, and this is more than a bit disillusioning to consider, especially when weighed against Mies van der Rohe's many comments on purity of form and expression.

Despite all of the efforts to disguise the mechanical and structural requirements of the building, what remains is a meticulously articulated form, carefully placed on its site—something like a beautiful woman who is helped by clever make-up to disguise some unfortunate scars.

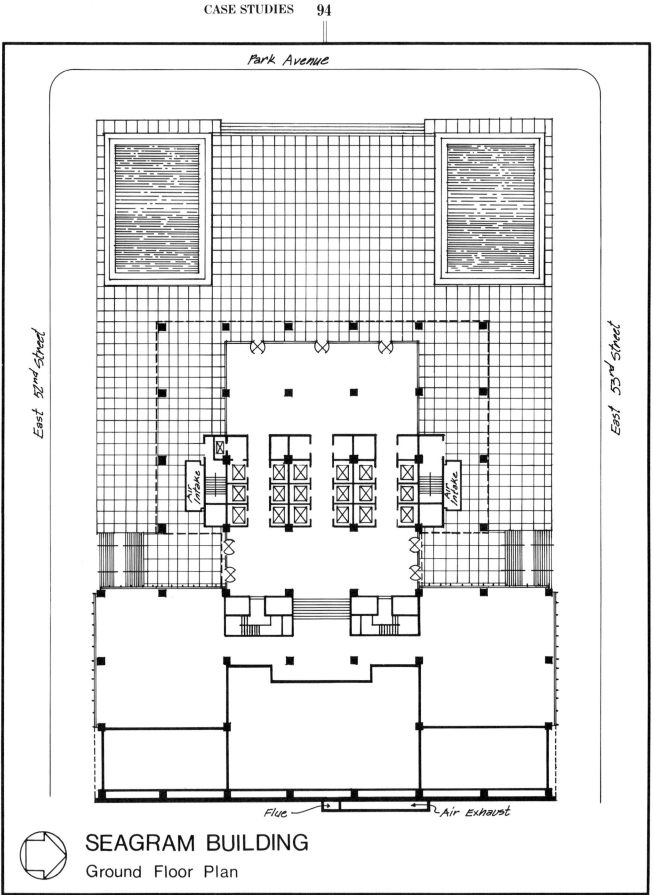

SEAGRAM BUILDING
Ground Floor Plan

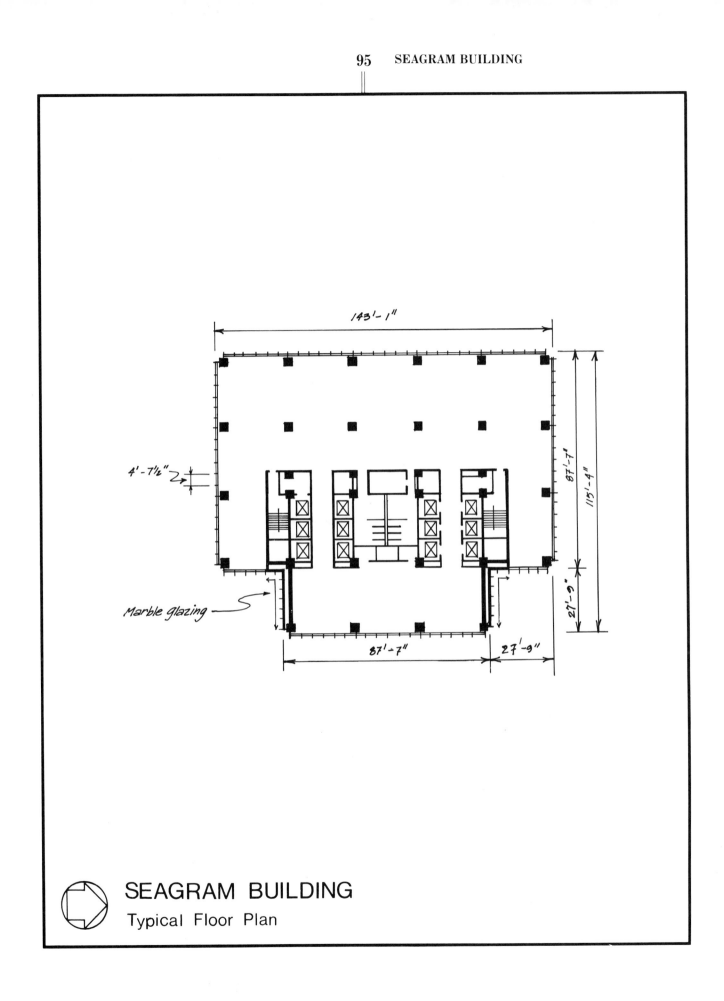

SEAGRAM BUILDING
Typical Floor Plan

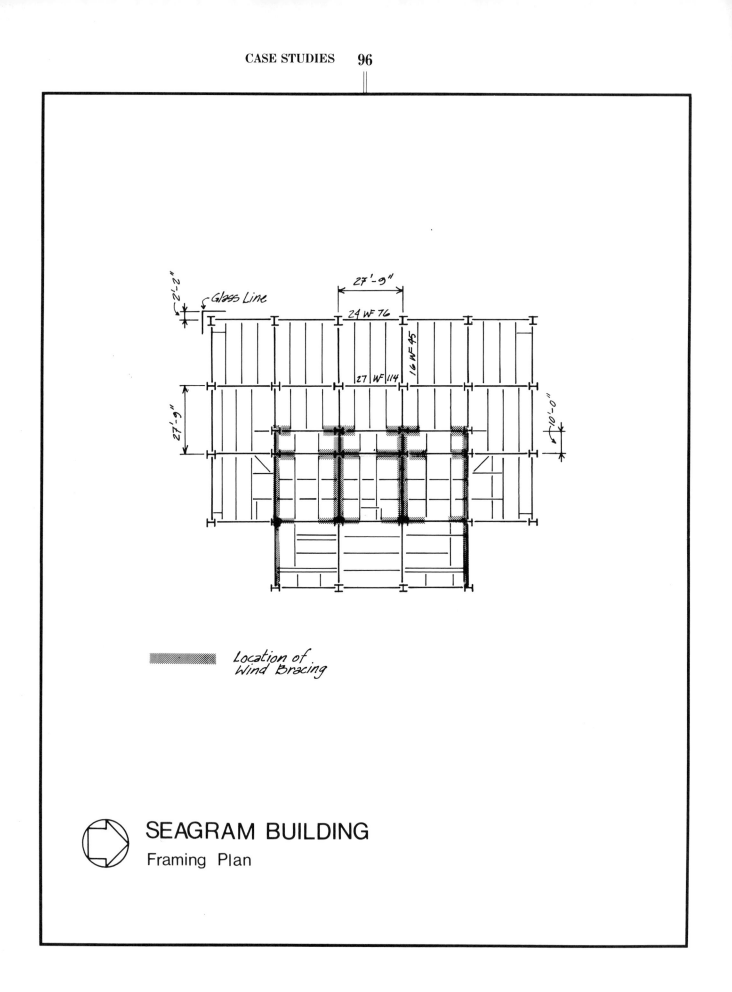

Location of
Wind Bracing

SEAGRAM BUILDING
Framing Plan

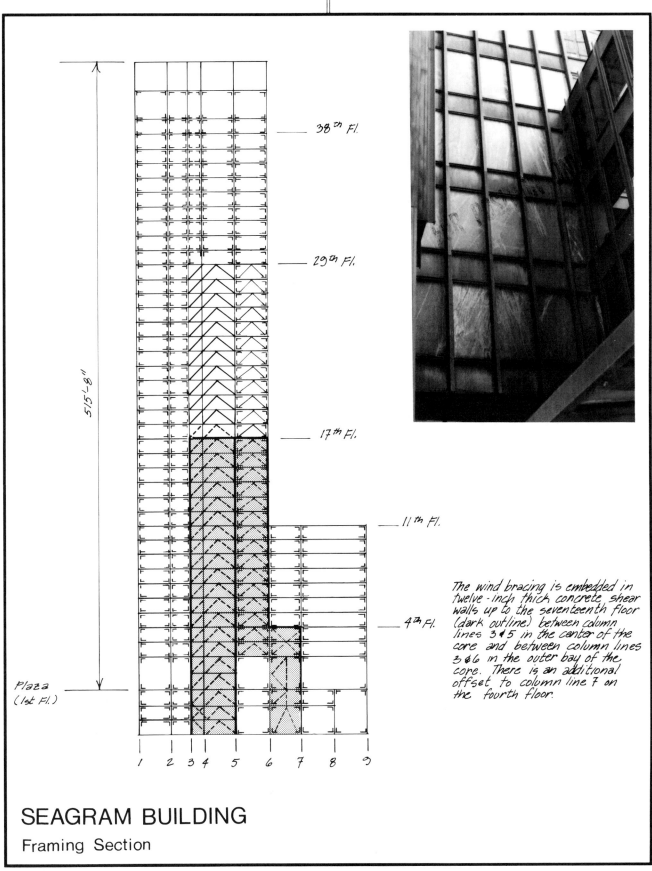

515'-8"

38th Fl.

29th Fl.

17th Fl.

11th Fl.

4th Fl.

Plaza
(1st Fl.)

1 2 3 4 5 6 7 8 9

The wind bracing is embedded in twelve-inch thick concrete shear walls up to the seventeenth floor (dark outline) between column lines 3 & 5 in the center of the core and between column lines 3 & 6 in the outer bay of the core. There is an additional offset to column line 7 on the fourth floor.

SEAGRAM BUILDING
Framing Section

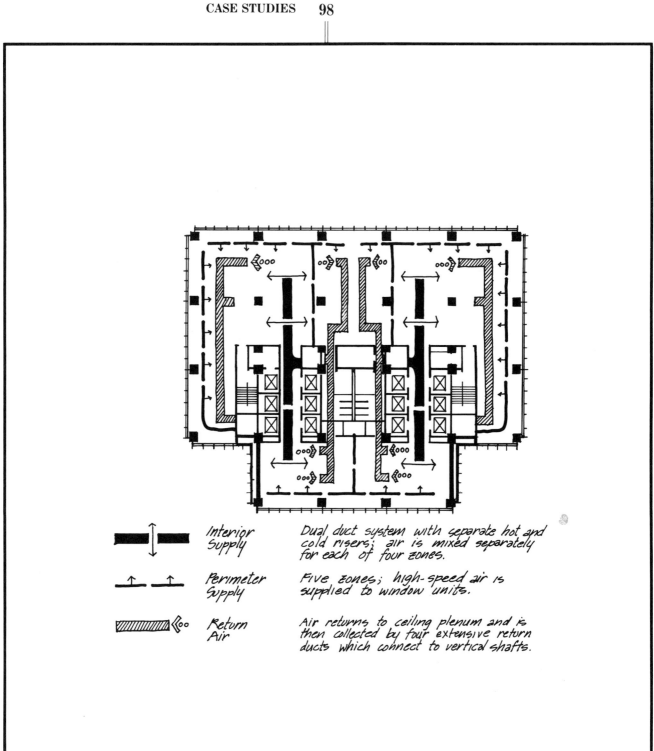

▬▬▬ ↕	Interior Supply	Dual duct system with separate hot and cold risers; air is mixed separately for each of four zones.
↑ ↑	Perimeter Supply	Five zones; high-speed air is supplied to window units.
▨▨▨ ⟨oo	Return Air	Air returns to ceiling plenum and is then collected by four extensive return ducts which connect to vertical shafts.

SEAGRAM BUILDING

Mechanical Plan

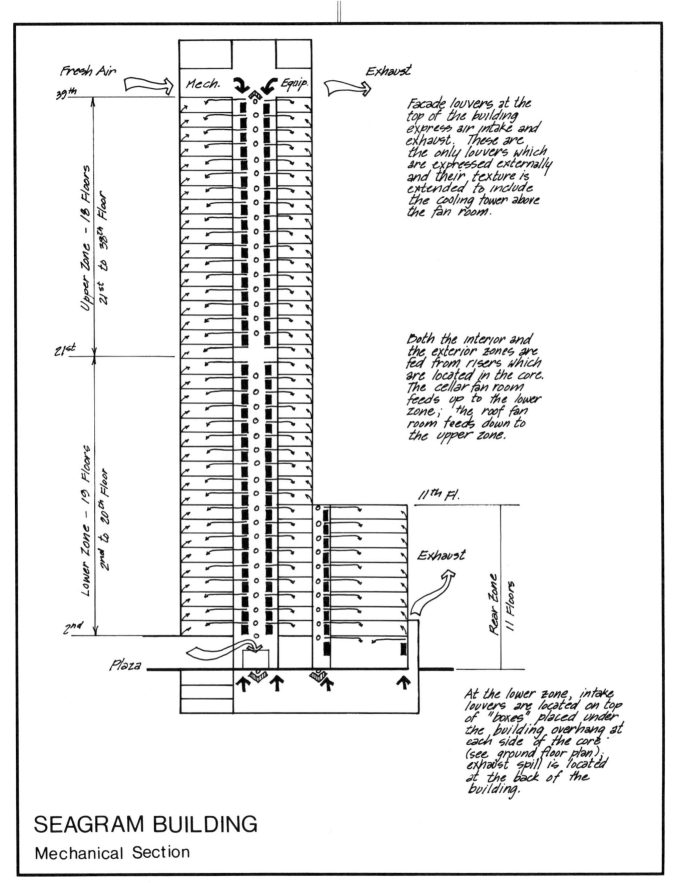

Fresh Air

Exhaust

39th

Mech.   Equip.

Upper Zone - 18 Floors
21st to 38th Floor

21st

Lower Zone - 19 Floors
2nd to 20th Floor

2nd

Plaza

11th Fl.

Exhaust

Rear Zone
11 Floors

Facade louvers at the top of the building express air intake and exhaust. These are the only louvers which are expressed externally and their texture is extended to include the cooling tower above the fan room.

Both the interior and the exterior zones are fed from risers which are located in the core. The cellar fan room feeds up to the lower zone; the roof fan room feeds down to the upper zone.

At the lower zone, intake louvers are located on top of "boxes" placed under the building overhang at each side of the core (see ground floor plan); exhaust spill is located at the back of the building.

SEAGRAM BUILDING
Mechanical Section

KNIGHTS OF COLUMBUS HEAD- QUARTERS BUILDING

THE staid proportions of the Knights of Columbus tower in New Haven, Connecticut, have created an extremely rugged and highly individualistic office tower that can be seen for miles. It is a building that is easy either to hate or to love but very hard to ignore. The analogy to a modern-day castle is inevitable.

Several rather unusual construction methods were used to create this unique architectural statement, and the methods, in turn, reinforced the design.

The core of this building is split into five separate vertical towers. A square center core contains the elevators, and the other four, more visible towers are huge ceramic-covered cylinders placed at each of the corners. Within these twentieth-century turrets are the stairs, the mechanical shafts, and the toilet facilities. These massive, windowless corner towers are connected to each other at each floor by ponderous rust-colored, exposed steel girders. The structure as a whole seems somber, staid, and almost monumental.

The major technological innovation that has an impact on the building's visual statement is the structural use of exposed steel. Heavy, 36-inch-deep girders span the 72 feet between the corner towers and are located 5 feet beyond the exterior side of the tinted glass facade. This exterior location was made possible by a combination of mutually supportive items: (1) the absence of close by adjacent buildings, (2) the heat-dissipating capacity provided by the surface area of the large-scale girders, (3) recognition by the code authorities that each floor acts as an independent unit, because the ends of each girder are supported on the noncombustible concrete mass of the corner cores. This means that damage on any individual floor would not be cumulative and endanger an adjacent floor. These combined factors led to the acceptance of this solution, which permits the use of uncovered, visually exposed steel framing on a high-rise tower.

The interior beams that frame between the inner core wall and the exterior spandrel beams are also exposed structural steel. These beams satisfied the building code officials by being protected by a sprinkler system, as well as being isolated from the adjacent floors by the concrete floor surface they support.

Since all the structure was exposed for design reasons, consistency dictated that the mechanical distribution systems could also become part of the building's visual statement. The perimeter supply air is furnished in risers contained in each corner tower. From there it runs horizontally in an exposed duct along the glass wall. The duct doubles as a guardrail in front of the floor-to-ceiling glass. It is interesting to note that the exterior system supplies most of the air due to the short distance from the outer wall to the core and the partition-free open spaces. The interior office space is supplied by a duct placed between the double diagonal beams that span the distance between each cylindrical tower and the corners of the central elevator core. Return air is simply allowed to flow into recessed openings located above the double doors leading into two of the corner towers. Once inside the tower, the air returns to the mechanical floor. The lighting system is also exposed, forming a fish-skeleton type pattern in conjunction with the beams, as can be seen in the photograph. The light troughs also incorporate the required sprinkler piping.

The top floor serves as the mechanical-equipment room. The exterior of this floor is provided with the identical exterior, clear plate-glass that the tenant floors have, except for two panels on the east facade that are replaced by louvers. At present, there are no other nearby structures tall enough to allow anyone to observe the interestingly color-coded equipment behind the glass windows. If such mechanical spaces could be spotlessly maintained, they could no doubt be laid out in a manner to create their own aesthetics and intrigue. (This was, in fact, done at Kennedy Airport, New York City, in the central mechanical building.) In this building, however, the texture of the glass facade when seen from the street below yields no clue as to what lies behind it.

The Knights of Columbus building clearly articulates several separate functions. The towers express the vertical movement of people and mechanical shafts. The structural steel frame, the lighting, and the ducts all make a major contribution to the texture of the building. The interior space is a difficult space to subdivide freely, but this is a minor issue, one that is

Interior beam and light fixture pattern in ceiling.

happily avoided on most floors, since the span between the center core and the glass facade is only 31 feet and the single-tenant occupancy obviates the need for major subdivision. Subdividing would be a problem because of the difficulty of placing partitions at any location other than up against the underside of the exposed beams, which run only at right angles to the facade. Additionally, the light-fixture pattern and the lack of flexibility in the air supply-and-return systems makes deviations from the open plan difficult to achieve.

The rigid symmetry of the design has also placed equal amounts of glass on all four facades, a problem shared with most buildings, but emphasized in this particular one by horizontal sun shades placed symmetrically on all sides of the building. There is perhaps some rationalization for the shades on other than the south side, where they actually do shield out the sun, since they serve as a working platform for window cleaners. The amount of usable floor area in relation to the core space is very inefficient, and is perhaps the biggest economic price that was paid for the decision to use five separate cores for a building containing fewer than 8,000 square feet of tenant space per floor.

The architects, Roche Dinkeloo, wanted a strong statement. They have produced one that dominates the New Haven skyline. They may have done some things that can be questioned and second-guessed, but they have not been timid. Their tower sits squat and somber, a modern-day fortress that expresses how it was put together and gains its strength by doing so.

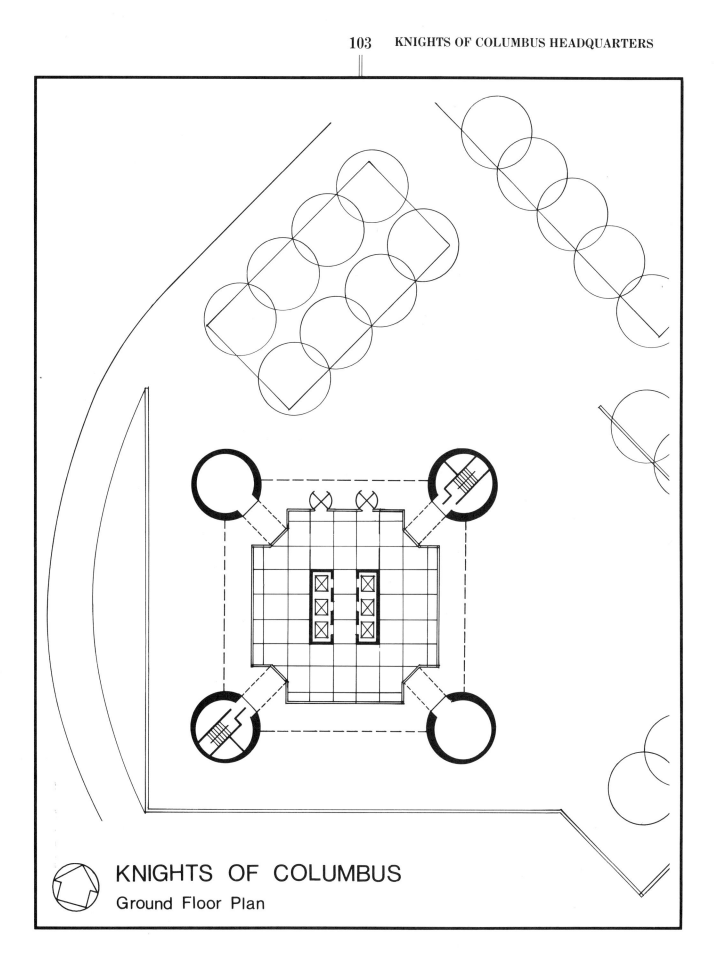

KNIGHTS OF COLUMBUS
Ground Floor Plan

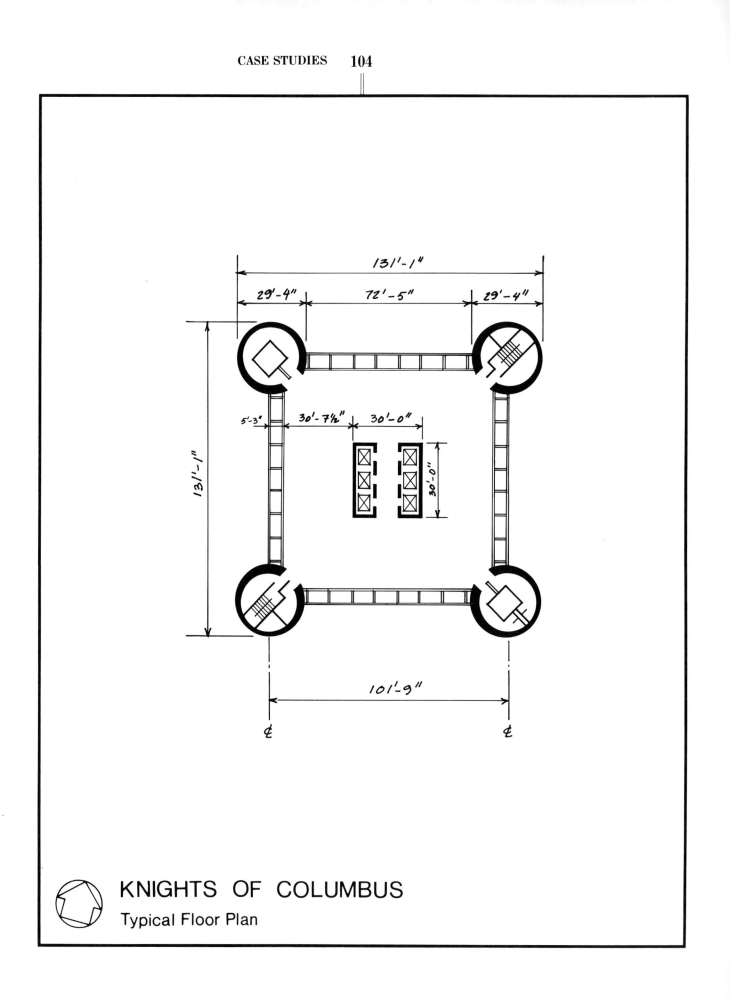

KNIGHTS OF COLUMBUS

Typical Floor Plan

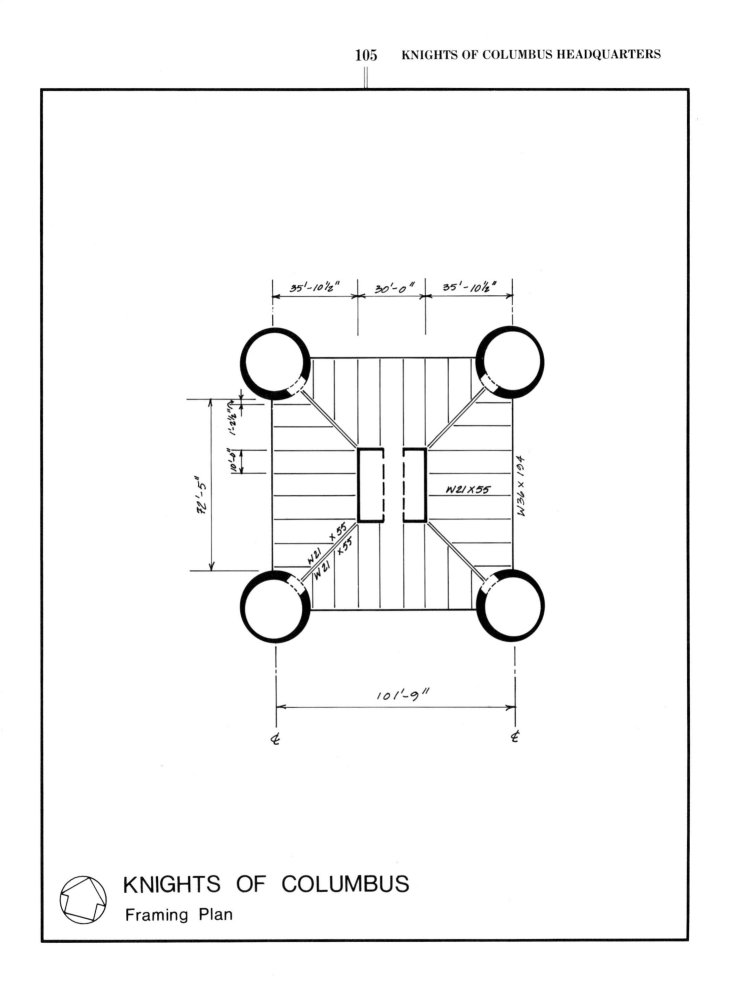

KNIGHTS OF COLUMBUS
Framing Plan

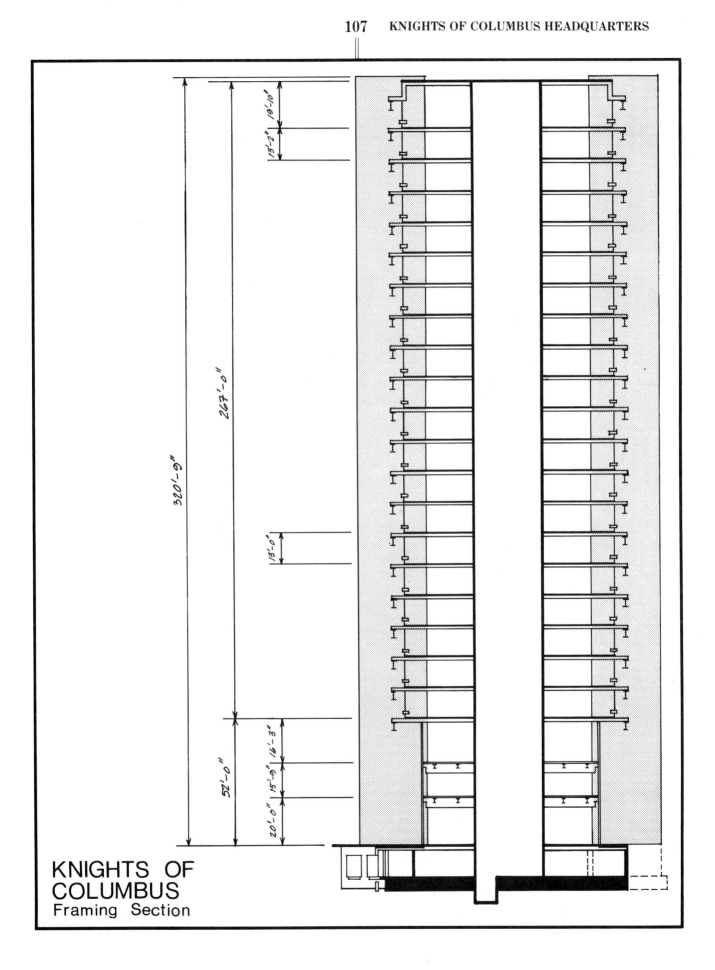

KNIGHTS OF
COLUMBUS
Framing Section

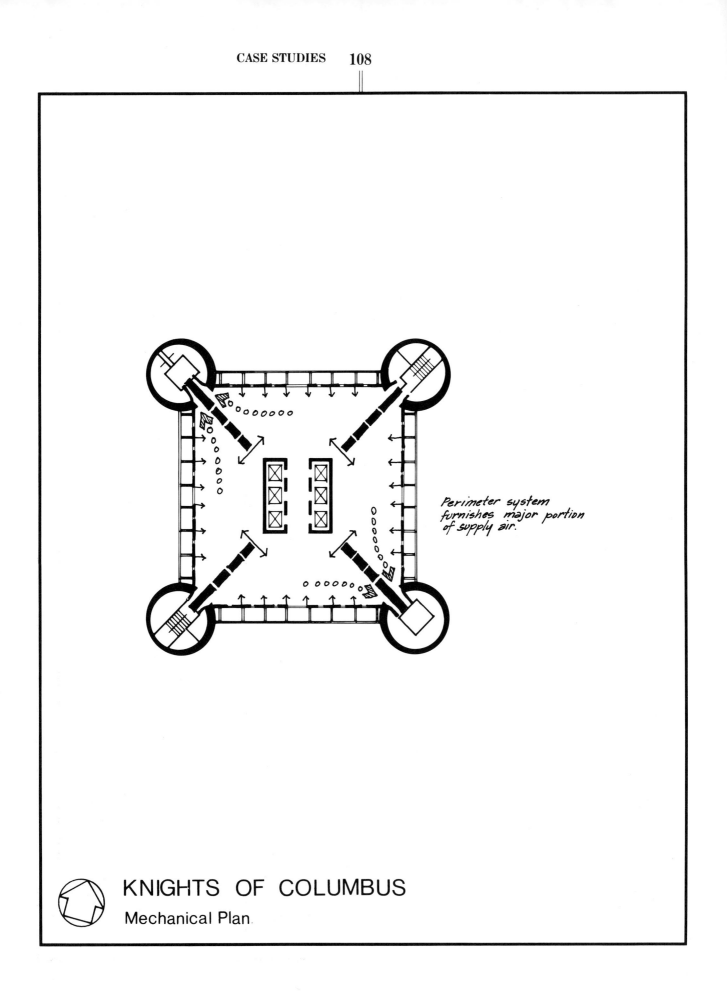

Perimeter system
furnishes major portion
of supply air.

KNIGHTS OF COLUMBUS
Mechanical Plan.

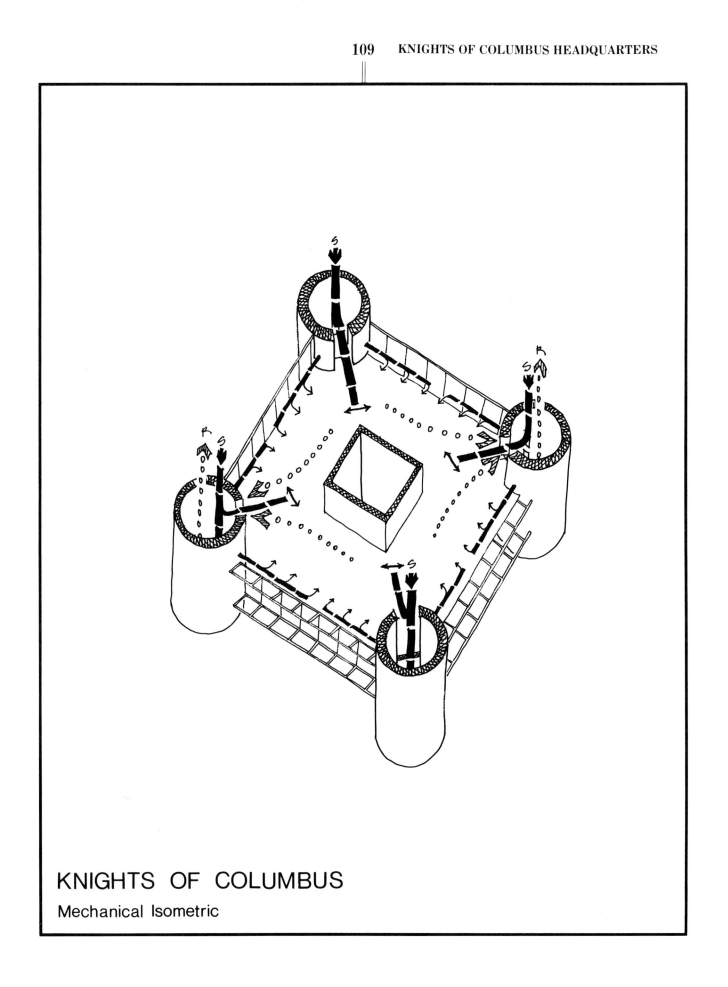

KNIGHTS OF COLUMBUS
Mechanical Isometric

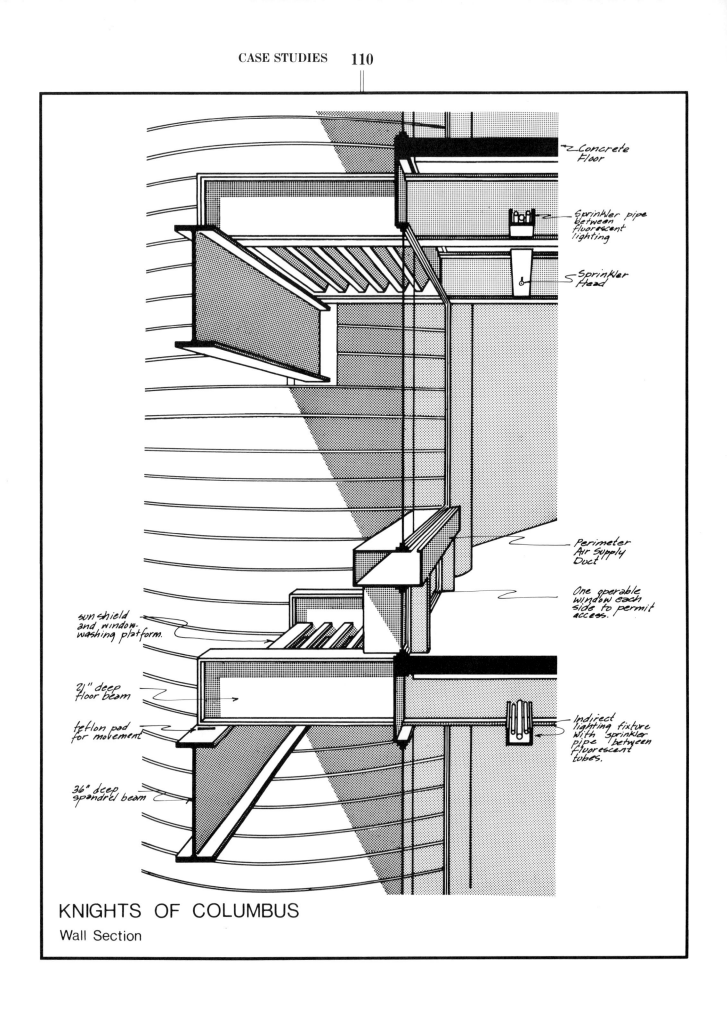

Concrete Floor

Sprinkler pipe between fluorescent lighting

Sprinkler Head

Perimeter Air Supply Duct

One operable window each side to permit access.

sun shield and window-washing platform.

21" deep floor beam

teflon pad for movement

36" deep spandrel beam

Indirect lighting fixture with sprinkler pipe between fluorescent tubes.

KNIGHTS OF COLUMBUS

Wall Section

ONE LIBERTY PLAZA

WITH its clean stark lines and uncluttered details, One Liberty Plaza in New York City represents a second-generation update of the Miesian approach. The structure's underlying skeleton is exposed, but the expression is a bit stylized and exaggerated. Whether the overstatement strengthens or weakens the design is, of course, open to one's personal interpretation and perceptions.

The exterior rectangle obtains its texture from the deep rhythms of what appear to be exposed, naturally rust-colored steel columns and spandrel beams, which alternate with tinted horizontal bands of mullionless glazing. The spandrel beams are 6½ feet deep, just slightly larger than the sheets of tinted glass with which they alternate. Strong repetitive shadow patterns are created by an outer plane of projecting beam-and-column webs. Recessed glazing is placed between the top of one spandrel and the underside of the next, while the broad expanses of the beam and column webs create a third vertical plane of their own. The flanges of the spandrel are exaggerated and protrude 1 foot, 8 inches from the web, creating a strong shadow line and an overstated sense of strength.

The presence of mechanical equipment is clearly and boldly stated by the texture of louvers on the fifteenth and fortieth floors.

The structure makes several more subtle statements about itself. One does not see the actual structurally required size of the load-carrying spandrel beams. Once the basic design decision was made to alternate a spandrel beam with a glass-wall panel, the depth of the spandrel could be tuned to justify the desired and preconceived proportion. For example, if a shallower depth had been desired, the size of the beam flanges could have been increased. In this particular building, the method of protecting the steel from the heat of a fire also had a major effect on the size of the beams. A variety of fire protection methods were combined in order to obtain the fire-rating protection necessary for the steel framing located along the facade.

The way in which the spandrel beam is fireproofed is somewhat involved since it used three separate design concepts. The inside face of the beam's web and the flanges are protected by sprayed-on insulating material. The exterior face of the web is visually exposed and is protected by a flame shield, which is a sheet-metal device that exaggerates the width of the beam's flanges, and therefore can deflect flames that might come out through a window and heat the outside web. Another helpful fire-safety phenomenon that contributed to the acceptance of this solution is the fact that a large surface dissipates heat more quickly than a small one, and the exposed surface of the beam web in this building is extremely large.

The exterior structural columns were sprayed with fireproofing material and then carefully wrapped in sheet steel to simulate their structural shape. The result of all this cleverness is an increase in the visual size of the spandrel beams and columns. In addition, the final shapes convey the impression that you are looking at the actual framing system when, in fact, you are not.

The vertical wind-bracing frame is located in the walls of the central core. A two-story height was required to contain the most structurally desirable slope for the diagonal members of the wind bracing system. Architecturally, the plan of the core is split into two parts; therefore, when the two-story-high bracing section reaches its apex, it occurs over the core's central corridor rather than behind an elevator or stair shaft. The result is that a small part of each diagonal's top penetrates the corridor space on alternate floors. This subtle expression of even a part of the interior wind-bracing system is a rather unique architectural statement.

One Liberty Plaza is not a typical speculative building. Therefore, the architect had the luxury of being able to place the columns outside the glass line and, thus, outside of the rentable area of the building. Had the columns been inside the glass line, the space they occupy could have been rented even though it obviously could not be used.

Mechanically, the building is served from equipment rooms located in the cellar and on the fifteenth and fortieth levels. Vertical air-distribution shafts are located at two separate points within the core for the interior zone, and at four separate locations for the exterior zones. Short horizontal runs lead to the exterior induction units from the shafts in the core. The exterior columns provide just enough space on their interior side to enclose the necessary piping for the induction units.

The floor construction is more standard than the exterior system. Wind girders, (girders that have increased load-carrying capacity in order to take the wind load imposed on the facade, in addition to the floor loads of the building) connect from the exterior columns back to girders in the central core. These girders are, in turn, supported by columns, but the columns in the core do not align with the ones along the exterior of the building.

When all is said and done, the impact that the facade conveys is one of elegance, uncluttered dignity, and the massive solidity of an exposed-steel frame. The educated viewer knows that only a part of what appears to be exposed really is, and that the actual supporting steel is not really so massive as it appears. It is true that the building possesses a more solid scale than a pure statement of load would have required, but fire protection is as much a part of architecture as support. To the architect's credit, the building never comes close to being pompous.

The skillful interplay of scale, the relentless rhythm of glass and steel layers, and the crisp detailing without any clutter combine to create a rich, staid, understated elegance that the architects wished to convey on behalf of their stockbroker clients.

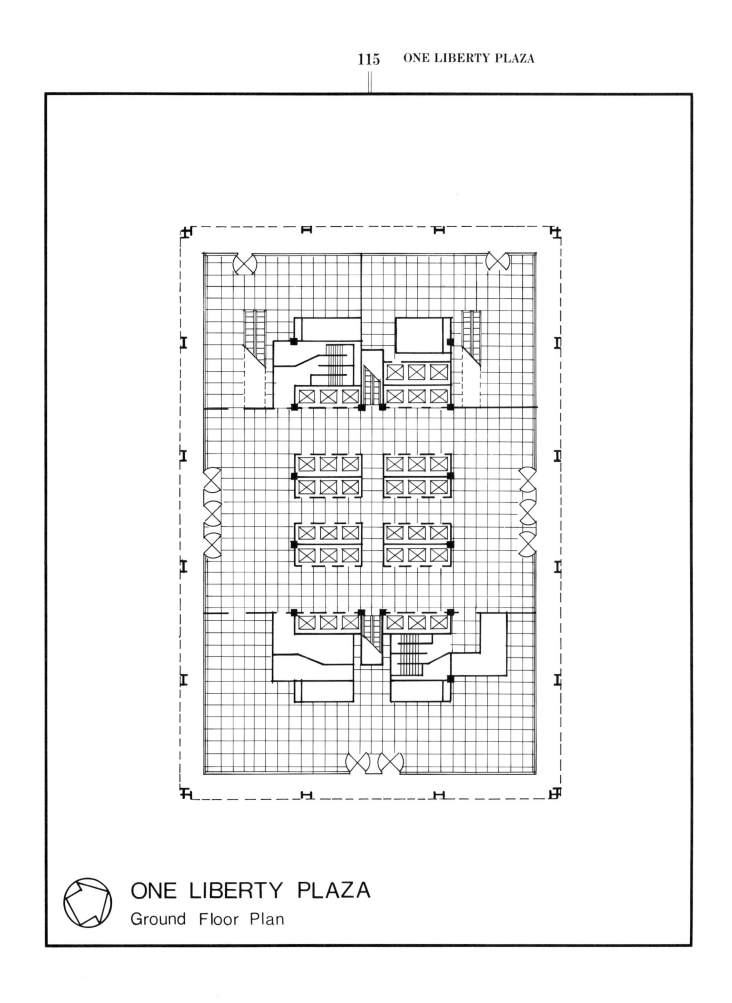

ONE LIBERTY PLAZA
Ground Floor Plan

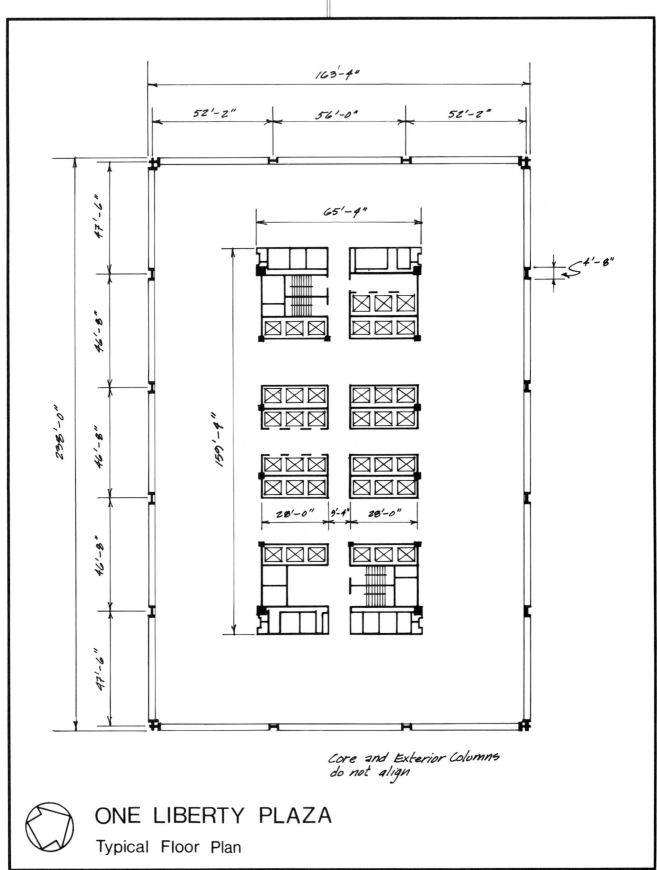

Core and Exterior Columns
do not align

ONE LIBERTY PLAZA

Typical Floor Plan

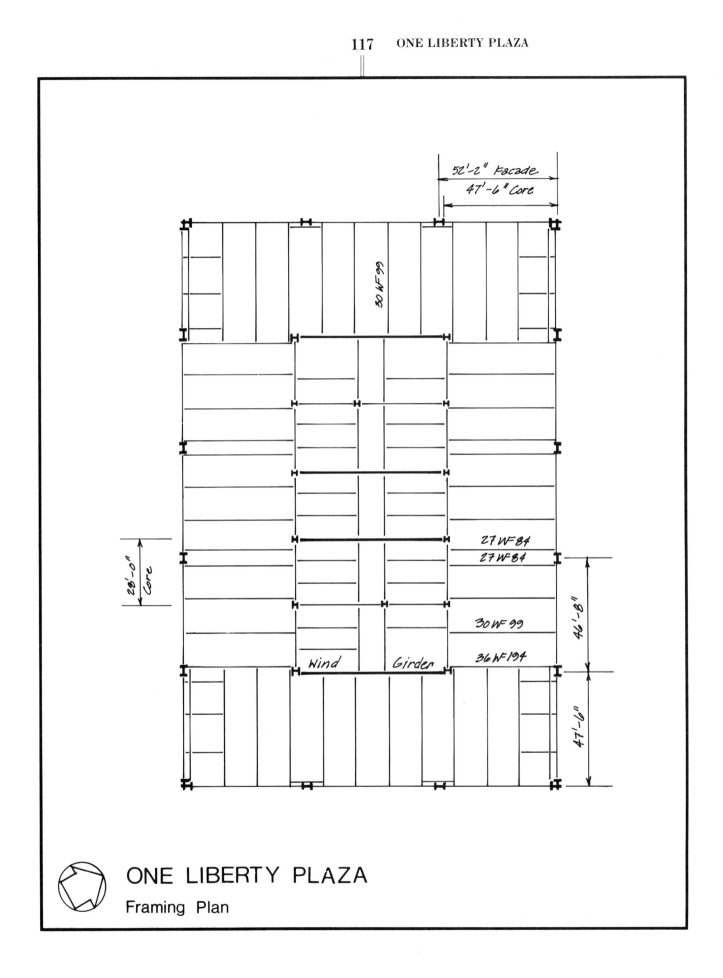

52'-2" Facade
47'-6" Core

30 WF 99

28'-0" Core

27 WF 84
27 WF 84

30 WF 99

36 WF 194

Wind   Girder

46'-8"

47'-6"

ONE LIBERTY PLAZA

Framing Plan

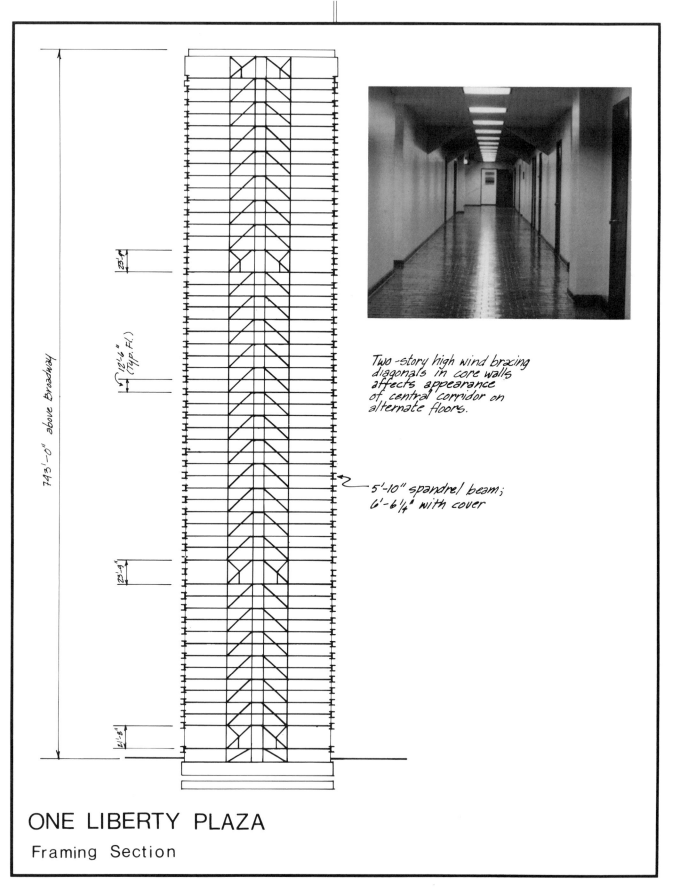

743'-0" above Broadway

25'-9"

10'-6" (Typ. Fl.)

125'-9"

21'-8"

Two-story high wind bracing diagonals in core walls affects appearance of central corridor on alternate floors.

5'-10" spandrel beam; 6'-6¼" with cover

ONE LIBERTY PLAZA

Framing Section

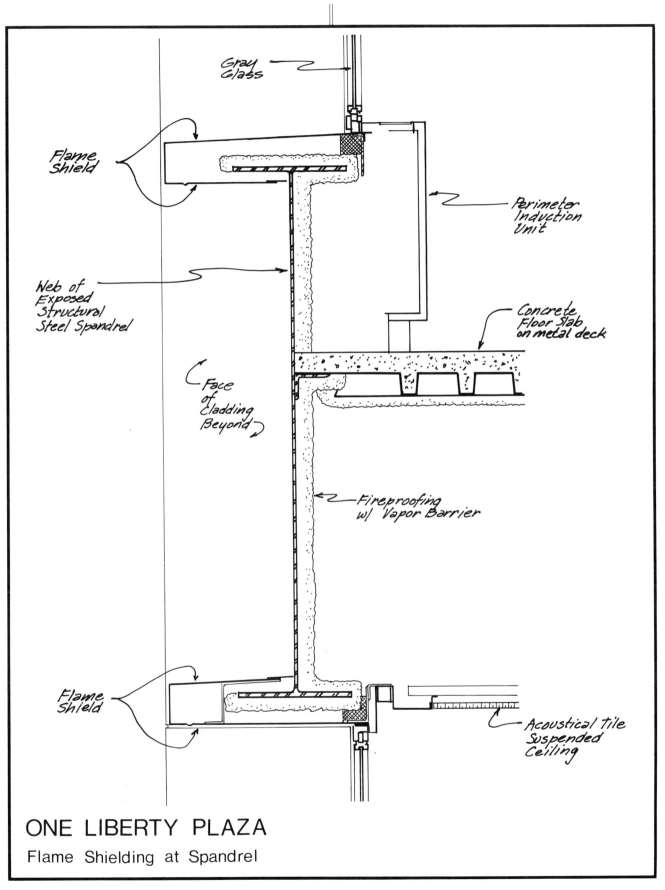

Gray Glass

Flame Shield

Web of Exposed Structural Steel Spandrel

Face of Cladding Beyond

Flame Shield

Perimeter Induction Unit

Concrete Floor Slab on metal deck

Fireproofing w/ Vapor Barrier

Acoustical Tile Suspended Ceiling

ONE LIBERTY PLAZA
Flame Shielding at Spandrel

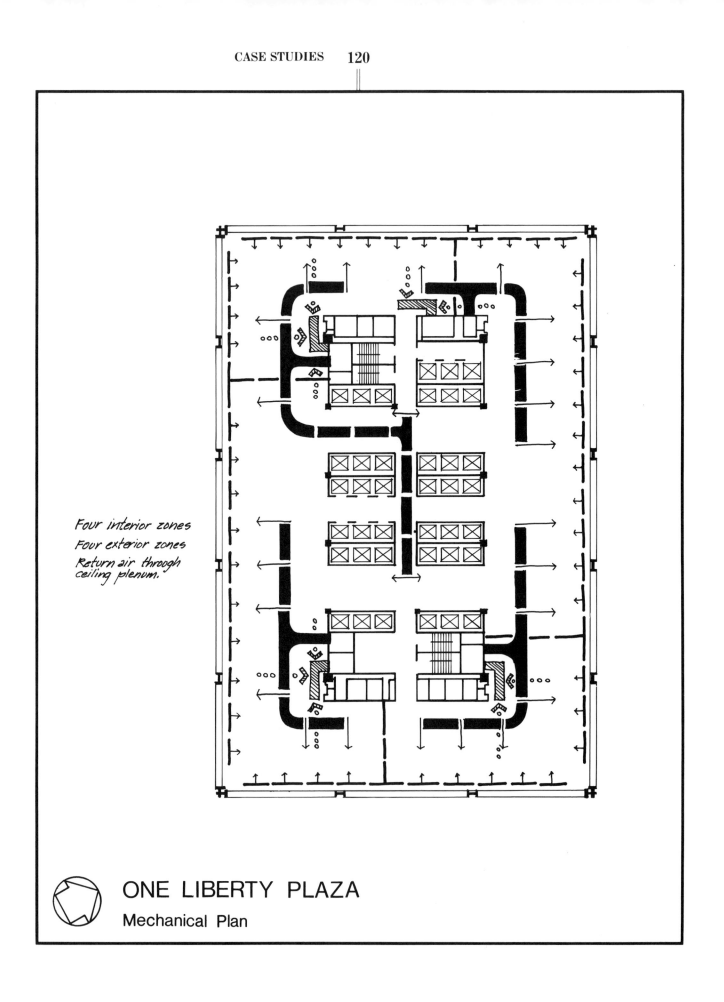

Four interior zones
Four exterior zones
Return air through
ceiling plenum.

ONE LIBERTY PLAZA
Mechanical Plan

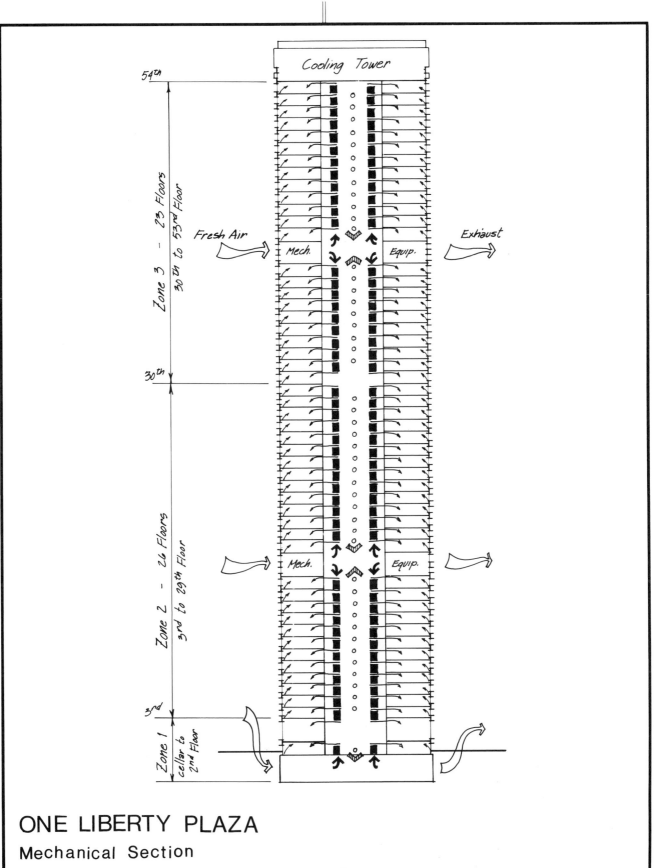

54th

Zone 3 — 23 Floors
30th to 53rd Floor

Cooling Tower

Fresh Air

Mech.   Equip.

Exhaust

30th

3rd

Zone 2 — 26 Floors
3rd to 29th Floor

Mech.   Equip.

Zone 1
cellar to
2nd Floor

ONE LIBERTY PLAZA
Mechanical Section

CHASE MANHATTAN BANK CENTRAL OFFICE BUILDING

SINCE the emergence of the high-rise structure at the turn of the century, one of the classic problems of architecture has been the dilemma over whether to express the verticality of the supporting columns or the horizontal layering of floors. By freeing the columns from the plane of the facade, Skidmore, Owings, and Merrill was able to express both options in the corporate headquarters of the Chase Manhattan Bank.

The rugged columns rise out of the plaza and soar visually undiminished to the sky. Perhaps the most distinguishing feature of this building is the unbroken vertical ribbing of its massive (2'-10″ × 4'-11″) columns rising over 800 feet above the street, but the horizontal bands on each floor are also emphasized by their cantilevered ends. One cannot help but speculate on how much this building owes to Raymond Hood's Philadelphia Savings Fund Society Building, built in 1932. An examination of the floor plan reveals that the column-free dimension between the core and the outer walls is different on each side of the core. This permits greater flexibility in the type of individual office sizes and arrangements.

By placing the columns on the exterior of the structure beyond the plane of the facade, the architect presented the engineer with a technological problem—namely, how to stabilize the columns in the plane parallel to the building's long facade. The spandrel beams that are located within the plane of the facade cannot intersect the column. Thus, the column can only be braced directly by the wind-girder which spans across the building through the core. The solution was to greatly stiffen the girder in the area where it is intersected by the spandrel beam. This was accomplished by using a pair of 3-foot-deep girders and uniting them with a heavy steel top plate where they connect to the column. The girder is stiffened in its horizontal plane by the addition of the plate, and this in turn provides it with the capacity to stabilize the column. This detail also permits the transfer of wind forces from the spandrel beam into the exterior column.

The building's wind-bracing consists of two interacting systems. One is a series of paired, three-foot-deep girders tying opposing exterior columns together across the narrow and more critical dimension of the structure. The second system is a pattern of K-bracing, imbedded with the core walls.

Mechanically, the building is divided into three vertical zones, and the grillwork handled in a clean, no-nonsense manner. The texture of the louvers is visible as a two-story-high horizontal band located at the eleventh, thirty-first, and fifty-first floors, and again as a three-story-textured area at the roof, which conceals the cooling towers. The vertical striping pattern of the window mullions continues across the mechanical levels, integrating the louvers on these parts of the facade into the building's texture without their being disguised.

The methods used for the horizontal distribution of air at each floor are straightforward. Interior and exterior zones are supplied separately from shafts located within the core, and return air flows back through the plenum above the hung, acoustical-tile ceiling to a series of return air ducts that convey it to the return air shafts. The exceptionally deep wind-girders were pierced to permit ducts and return air to move through them. Some of these openings are as large as two feet by seven feet. If ducts had been placed below these girders, the space required above the ceiling to accommodate them would have become impractically deep.

In its use of glass, the building is a product of its time. All facades are treated equally, regardless of orientation. Three-eighths-inch-thick, fixed, plate-glass windows seal out the world. Power failure renders a building of this type unusable, as even hardy souls willing to forego elevators for stairs must still have air to breathe. A dangerous issue is created by the heavy thickness of the glass. It may be too thick for occupants to break in order to vent smoke during a fire.

A major factor that helps to set the Chase Manhattan Bank tower apart from the mundane is the handsome public plaza that was the result of a negotiated trade-off with New York City; the architects agreed to include a public plaza, in order to obtain zoning permission for the building's unbroken vertical height. S.O.M. used this option well. Without this plaza to free the structure from its neighbors, the careful detailing of unbroken columns and the expressive power of the tower's cantilevered ends would have been swallowed up in the canyons of Wall Street.

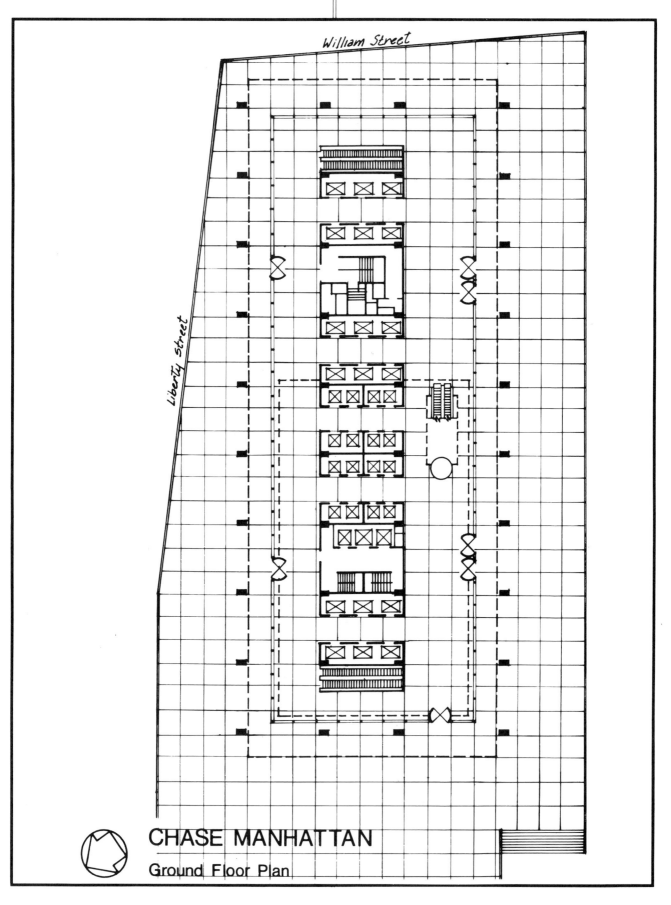

William Street

Liberty Street

CHASE MANHATTAN

Ground Floor Plan

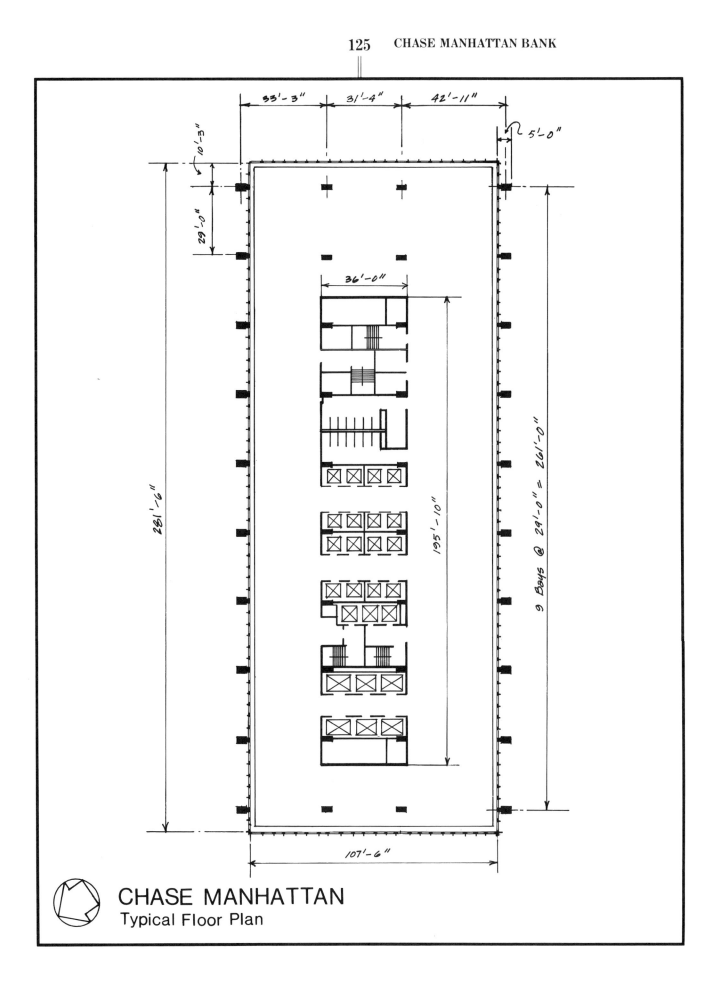

CHASE MANHATTAN
Typical Floor Plan

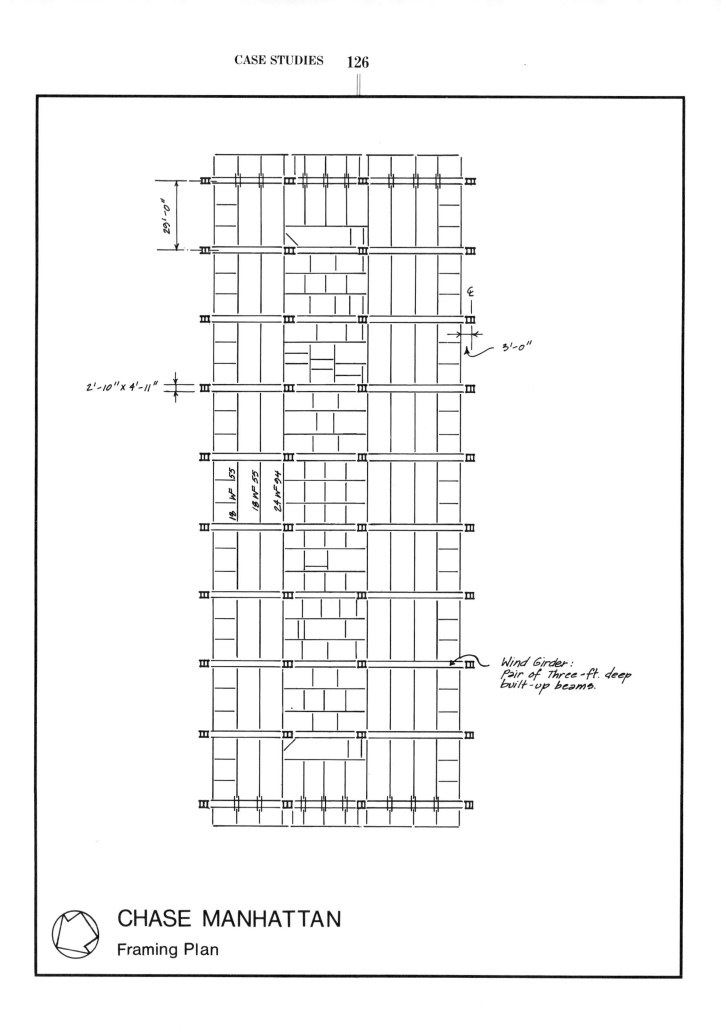

29'-0"

℄

3'-0"

2'-10" X 4'-11"

18 WF 55
18 WF 55
24 WF 94

Wind Girder:
Pair of Three-ft. deep
built-up beams.

CHASE MANHATTAN

Framing Plan

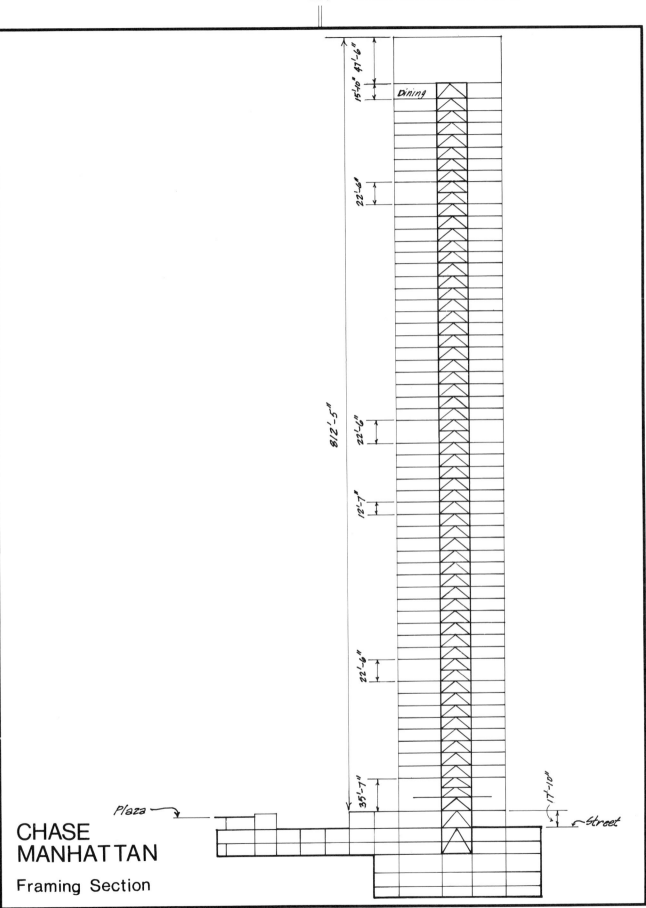

CHASE
MANHATTAN
Framing Section

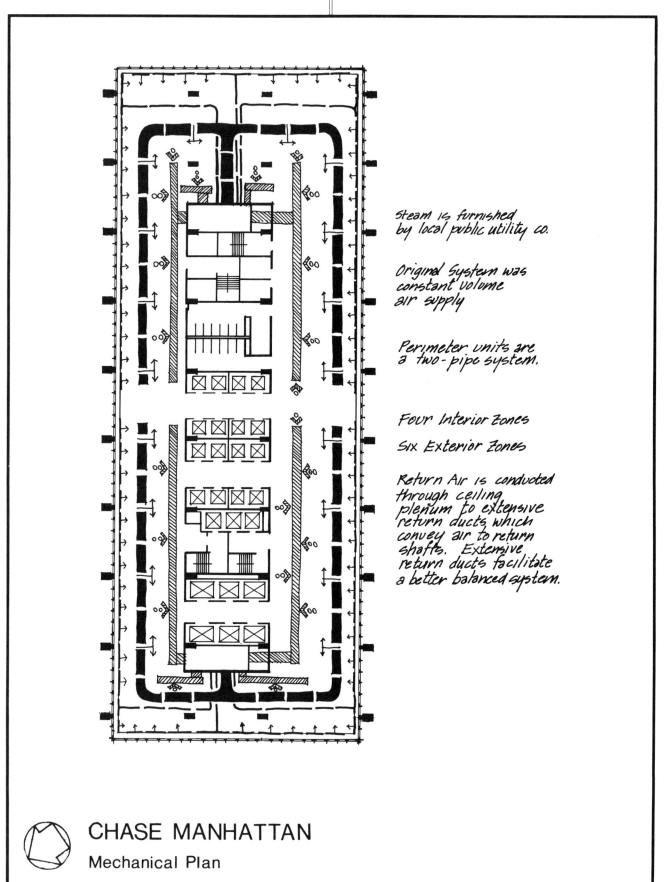

Steam is furnished by local public utility co.

Original System was constant volume air supply

Perimeter units are a two-pipe system.

Four Interior Zones

Six Exterior Zones

Return Air is conducted through ceiling plenum to extensive return ducts, which convey air to return shafts. Extensive return ducts facilitate a better balanced system.

CHASE MANHATTAN

Mechanical Plan

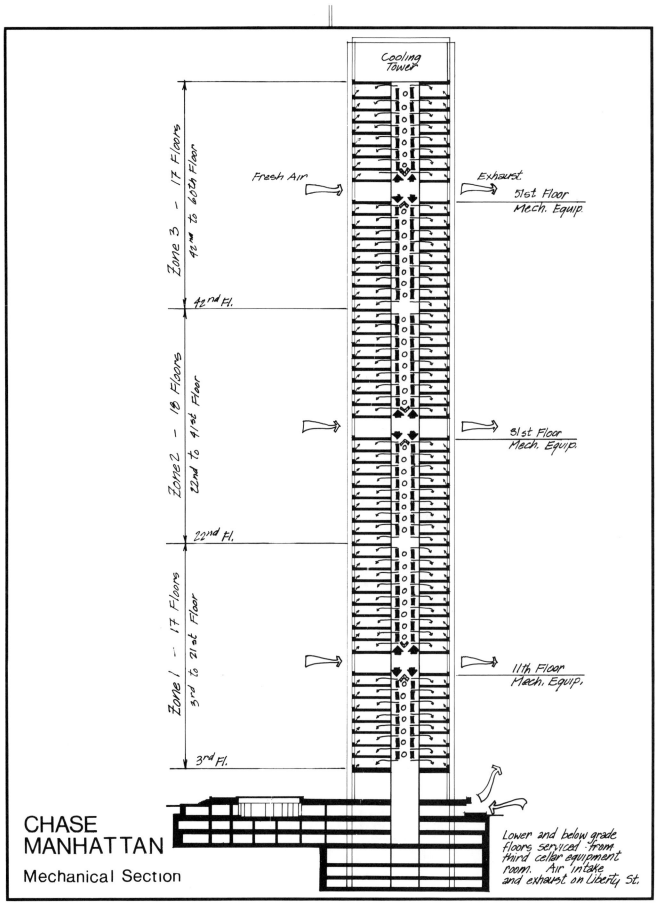

Cooling Tower

Fresh Air

Exhaust.
51st Floor
Mech. Equip.

Zone 3 — 17 Floors
42nd to 60th Floor

42nd Fl.

Zone 2 — 18 Floors
22nd to 41st Floor

31st Floor
Mech. Equip.

22nd Fl.

Zone 1 — 17 Floors
3rd to 21st Floor

11th Floor
Mech. Equip.

3rd Fl.

Lower and below grade
floors serviced from
third cellar equipment
room. Air intake
and exhaust on Liberty St.

CHASE MANHATTAN
Mechanical Section

THE BOSTON COMPANY BUILDING

THE Boston Company Building is a paragon of quiet understatement. This structure avoids falling into the shoe-box stereotype of so many similar buildings. It has dignity and elegance, and is honestly devoid of gimmickry. The building's plan is a simple square within which is contained a centrally located service core. The structure's mass is well proportioned and possesses a life and character that is engendered mostly by its texture. This texture is achieved by a straightforward and yet subtle expression of the diagonal wind-bracing system, which is incorporated within the plane of the facade.

The wind-bracing system is a variation of the tube-within-a-tube bracing method, in which the central service core acts as the inner tube and the repetitive, triangular bracing pattern contained in the plane of the facade acts as the outer tube. The three huge triangles that brace the exterior wall divide its surface into three, horizontal visual blocks.

The diagonal bracing must cross in front of the windows in its path, and where this occurs, each individual rectangular panel of glass that is crossed is replaced by an aluminum panel. This creates a pattern similar to the effect that might be achieved if one were to color in the squares on a chess board to trace the path of a bishop. The material used to block out the pattern of the wind bracing is the same as that used for the spandrel panels between floor levels. The result is a low-keyed statement.

Louvers for supply and exhaust air are placed only where they are needed rather than in a formal, organized pattern. The mechanical equipment, located on the seventeenth and forty-first floors, does not occupy the entire floor area, nor does it require that all of the perimeter of the space it occupies have exterior louvers. The architects simply used whatever surface area was required for louvers, no more, no less. This is in sharp contrast to I.M. Pei's approach in the tower at 88 Pine Street in New York City, where he took elaborate pains to disguise the location and true nature of the necessary, mechanical equipment-room louvers.

Several other important structural details were handled in a refreshing way. The four massive corner columns taper with their increase in height, paying tribute to their cumulative loading. The base of each multi-story, inverted V-brace is tied horizontally with a massive six-foot-deep girder that also accepts loads from the facade columns. Since the typical spandrel beam is only 16-inches deep, this differential is again handled forthrightly by increasing the height of the spandrel panels and decreasing the height of the glass panels in the curtain wall to adjust for the tie-girder's extra depth.

The result of all these slight variations in the size and location of curtain-wall panels is a richness of texture. This combination of rhythmic and random variation is accomplished, somewhat surprisingly, without any loss of clarity or diminution of the overall statement the building makes. This is a refreshing change from the forced, and often faked, "cleanliness" of so much of the International Style.

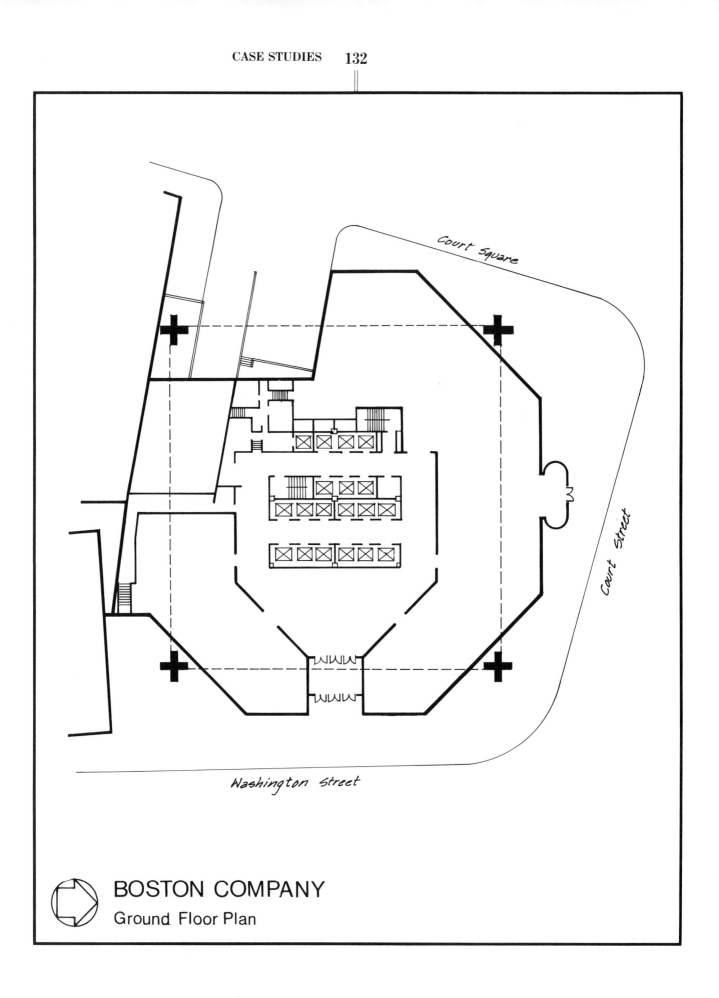

BOSTON COMPANY
Ground Floor Plan

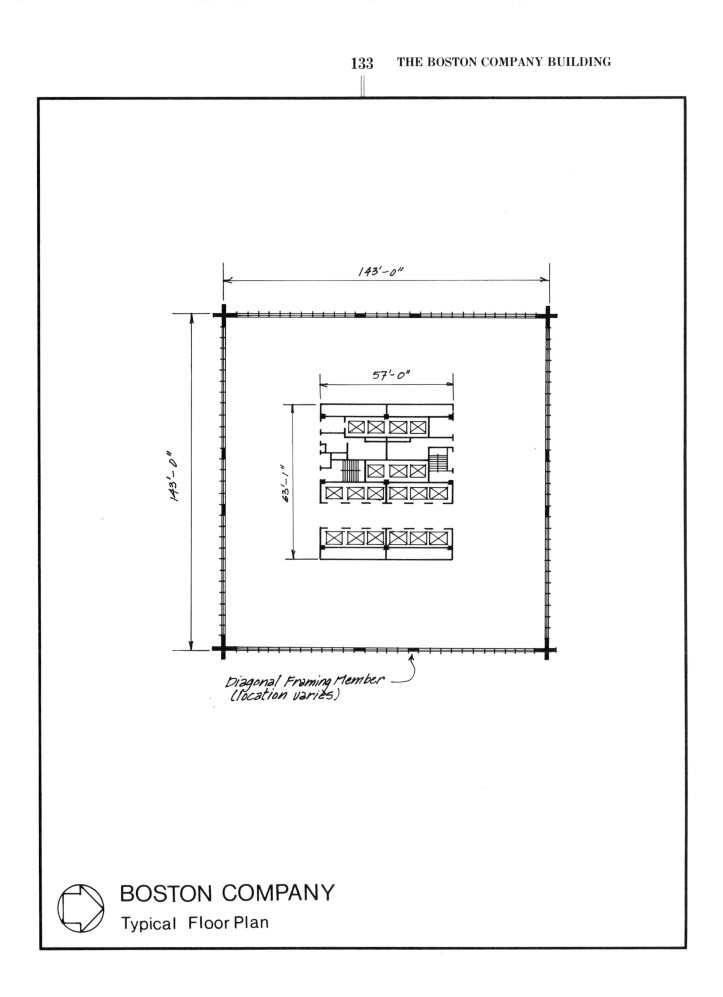

143'-0"

143'-0"

57'-0"

63'-1"

Diagonal Framing Member
(location varies)

BOSTON COMPANY
Typical Floor Plan

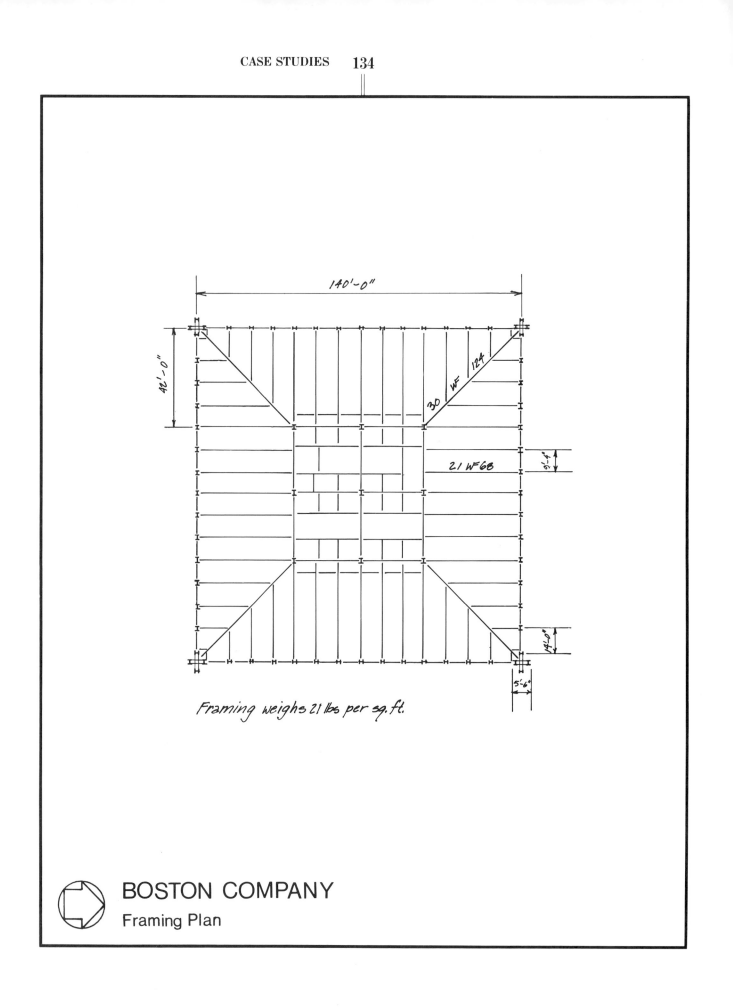

140'-0"

42'-0"

30 WF 124

21 W 68

5'-4"

14'-0"

5'-6"

Framing weighs 21 lbs per sq. ft.

BOSTON COMPANY

Framing Plan

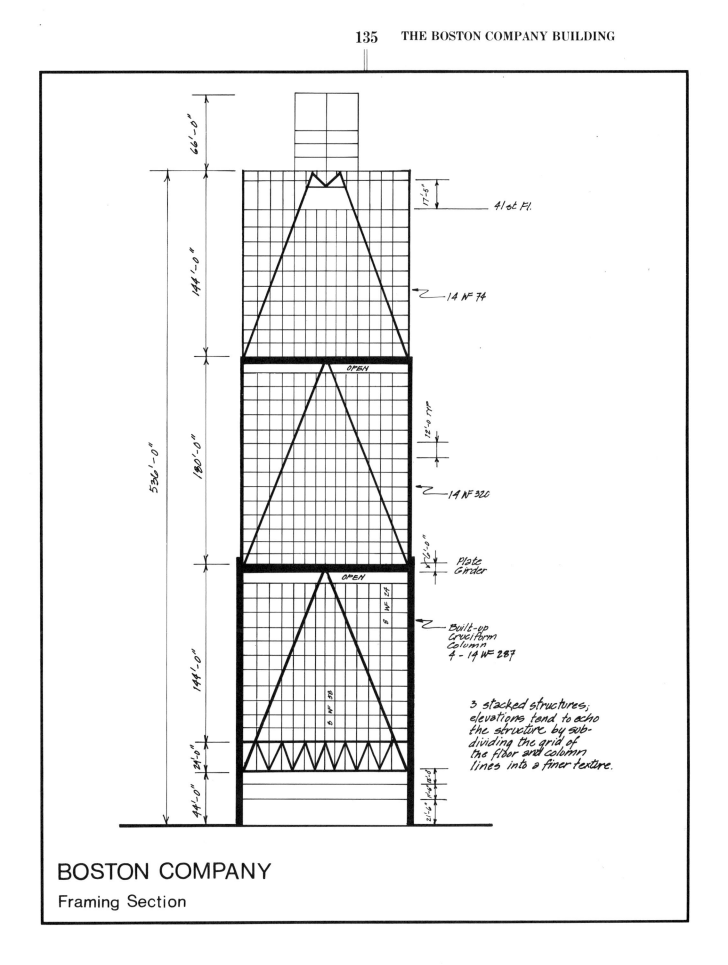

66'-0"

144'-0"

536'-0"

180'-0"

144'-0"

24'-0"

44'-0"

17'-6"

41st Fl.

14 WF 74

12'-0 TYP

14 WF 320

5'-0"

Plate Girder

OPEN

OPEN

8 WF 24

8 WF 58

Built-up Cruciform Column 4 - 14 WF 287

21'-6"   12'-0"

3 stacked structures; elevations tend to echo the structure by sub-dividing the grid of the floor and column lines into a finer texture.

BOSTON COMPANY

Framing Section

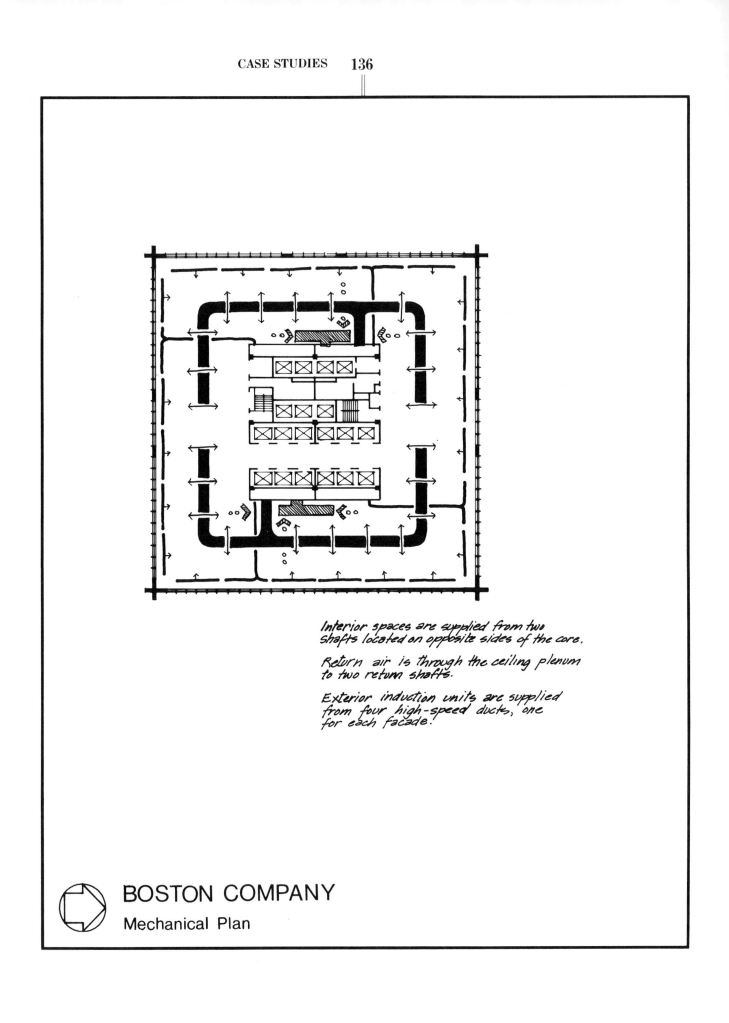

Interior spaces are supplied from two shafts located on opposite sides of the core.

Return air is through the ceiling plenum to two return shafts.

Exterior induction units are supplied from four high-speed ducts, one for each facade.

BOSTON COMPANY
Mechanical Plan

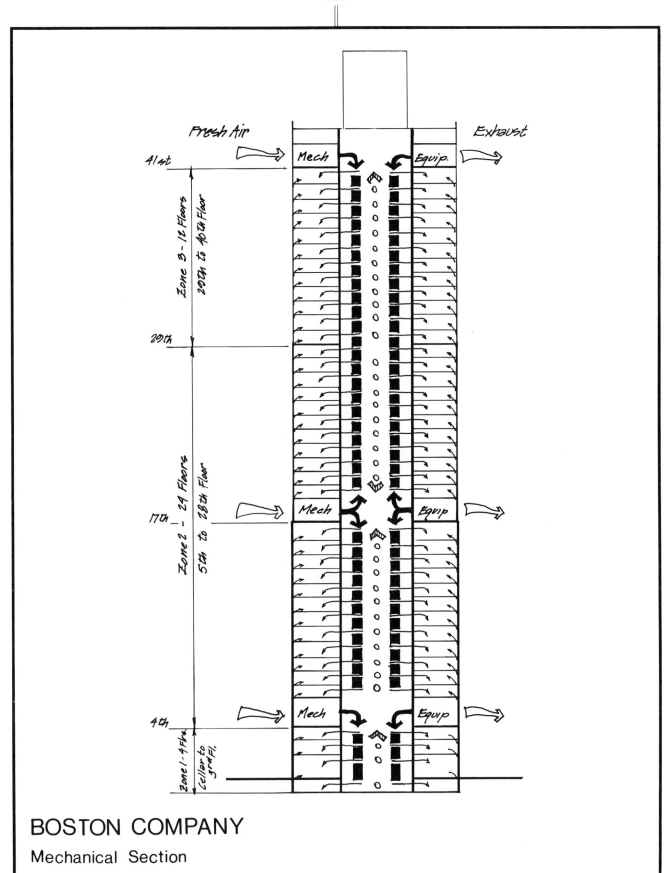

BOSTON COMPANY
Mechanical Section

WESTCOAST TRANSMISSION COMPANY BUILDING

ONE of the most critical areas of architectural expression is the manner in which a building meets its site. The Westcoast Transmission Company's headquarters in Vancouver, B.C., is an unusual building structurally in that its perimeter is supported from above rather than below. Cables are hung in pairs from outriggers that are attached near the top of the building's eighteen-story-high, concrete central core. These cables support the outer edges of this office tower. By suspending the perimeter in this manner, the architects emotionally and visually freed the ground space. The open plaza is handsomely sculptured with stairs and plantings that integrate well with the sloping hillside site, and the open plaza offers a magnificent view of the harbor. The 37-foot-square core occupies only a small part of the site area, and the office floors do not start until the third level above the ground.

Since the building core is the only part of the structure that touches the ground, it is called upon to contain all the wind bracing, mechanical shafts, and, ultimately, all vertical support, too.

The outer edge of the floor framing is clamped to the cables, which are suspended from the roof at twelve locations. The load placed on these cables must first rise up the cables to where they are attached to the core and then go back down through the core to the ground. In effect, this design adds 50 percent to the normal path length that the forces must travel. The cables support 50 percent of the floor load, while the core supports an additional 100 percent (50 percent at each floor, plus the 50 percent that the cables will transfer back to the core where they are attached at the top).

This longer and somewhat repetitive force path is not all negative. The loads received from the cable place additional compressive force on top of the core

walls, compressing the core more than a normal loading pattern, and thus making the building more earthquake resistant. But ultimately, the architectural ramification of having the building hover over the plaza is the real justification for this type of structural approach. The fact that the cable can be seen riding free between the top of the core and the facade wall renders the structural solution visually clear to anyone who approaches the building, and also allays feelings of insecurity that might be felt when walking under a huge floating mass. In fact, the statement could have been made even stronger if the core could have somehow occupied a smaller amount of the overhang dimension.

The visual weightlessness of the mirror-glass facade is subtly accented because its lower termination is free of any horizontal member to which the eye might attribute a load-carrying capacity. The vertical location of the support cables is articulated by covers that are considerably wider than the standard mullions. This latter statement, though intellectually understandable, is somewhat muddied by the fact that the cables are actually much smaller than their expressed visual bulk, which is almost column size. This increase in size is necessitated to a large degree by the fireproofing material that is used to protect the cables.

Mechanically, the building is low enough (12 office floors) to need only one vertical distribution zone. The fan rooms are contained within the core area in two levels located above the top office floor. The architects carefully kept the air-intake louvers low to the roof line so they could not be seen from the street—and mar the clean, visual lines of the extended core shaft. The heating plant and electrical generator are located in the garage area under the plaza. They have their own set of louvers and flue. These louvers are tucked out of sight, overlooking a small, rear alley. The flue is unfortunately visible from the plaza. The windows above the flue cannot be opened, so there is no problem for those inside the building, but one wonders how— or if—fumes affect the people using the plaza, especially since all equipment occasionally malfunctions.

The monolothic core provides all the necessary wind bracing. It is neatly and precisely laid out in plan so that there are only two penetrations into it at each level, which is the minimum amount possible to allow for the required two separate paths of egress. It is interesting to note that one must walk through the stair hall to reach the washrooms. This solution places two doors at each stair landing, one more than is currently permitted by most codes.

On balance, the architects have designed a handsome and neatly detailed building with clean crisp lines that strengthen its basic concept. Unfortunately, the

Cables suspended from two towers. Federal Reserve Bank of Minneapolis. Gunnar Birkerts, architect.

cables require fire protection, and thus their silhouette against the sky lacks a delicacy that could be briefly observed during construction. Once one is inside the building, the fact that the outer support is in tension rather than in compression is insignificant because the cover wrapping the pair of cables creates a bulk that closely resembles a load-bearing compression member. The magnificent, airy effect of the plaza level stays with one as the building is entered and is reinforced by the open plan of the executive floors, where a panoramic view strikes people from the moment they step off the elevator.

Other buildings have been constructed using cable systems to suspend floors from core-supported trusses, or even bridgelike from cables draped between two towers. The principal design advantage of these suspension approaches is that they free the ground level for architectural development. The Westcoast Transmission Company building is a modest, yet highly effective statement of a cable supported exterior.

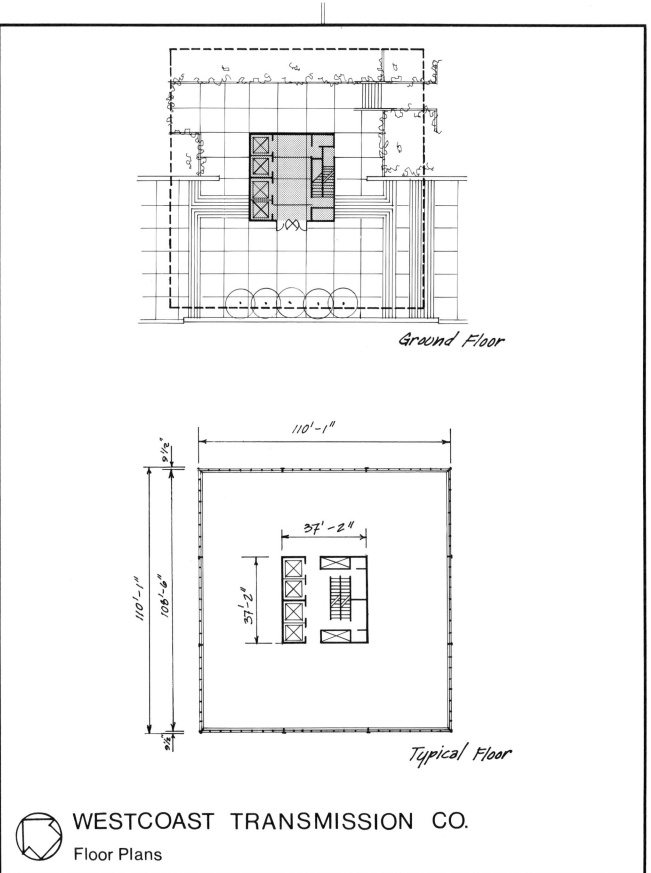

Ground Floor

110'-1"

37'-2"

37'-2"

108'-6"

110'-1"

9½"

9½"

Typical Floor

WESTCOAST TRANSMISSION CO.

Floor Plans

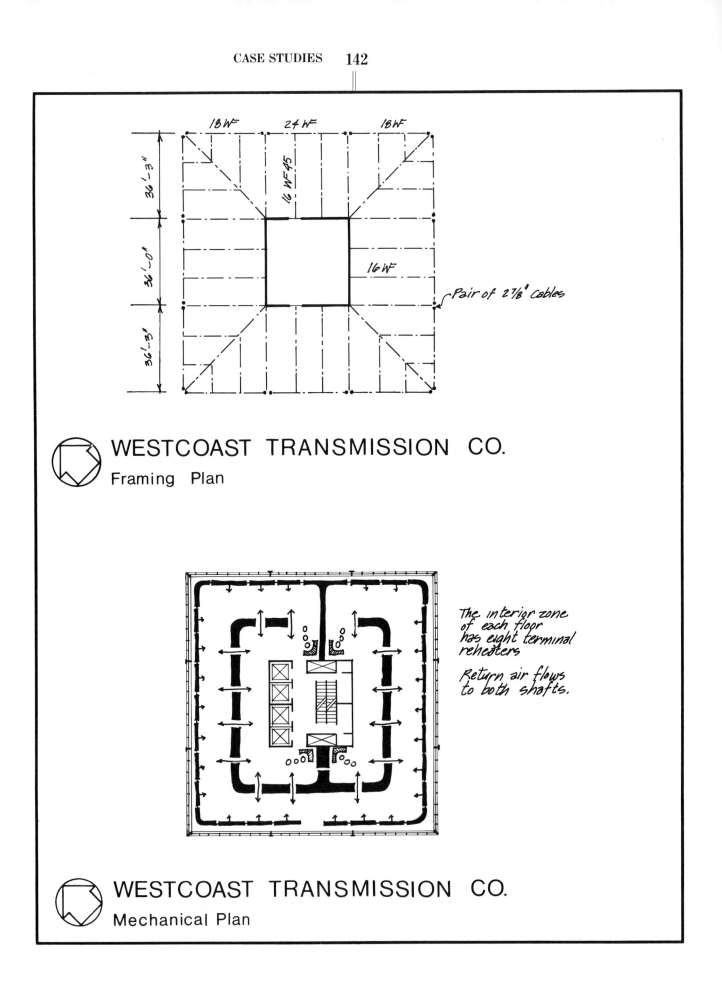

18 WF   24 WF   18 WF

16 WF 45

36'-3"

36'-0"

16 WF

36'-3"

Pair of 2⅞" Cables

WESTCOAST TRANSMISSION CO.
Framing Plan

WESTCOAST TRANSMISSION CO.
Mechanical Plan

The interior zone
of each floor
has eight terminal
reheaters

Return air flows
to both shafts.

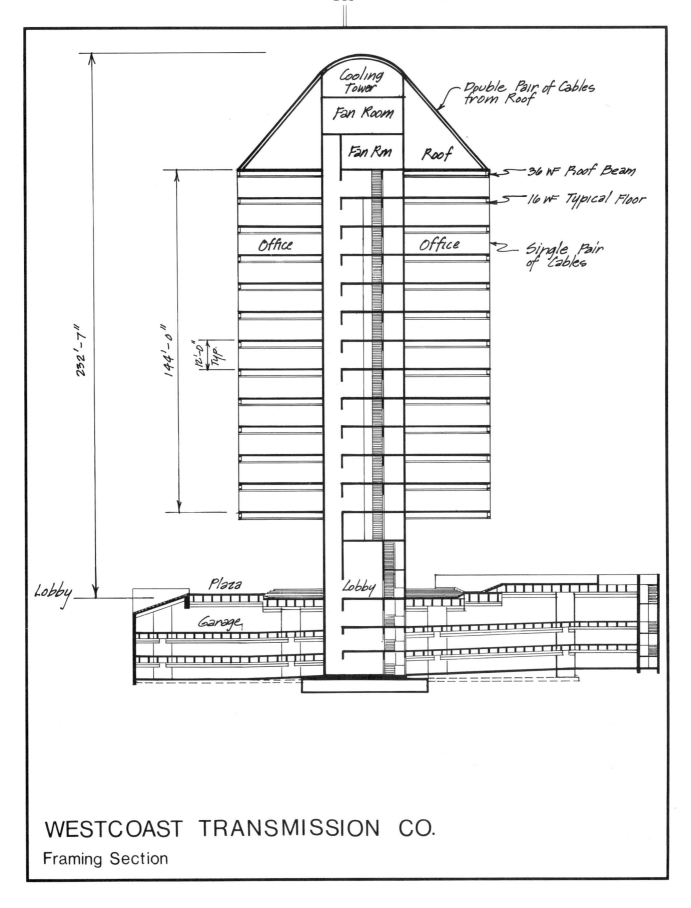

Cooling Tower

Fan Room

Fan Rm

Roof

Double Pair of Cables from Roof

36 WF Roof Beam

16 WF Typical Floor

Office

Office

Single Pair of Cables

252'-7"

144'-0"

12'-0" Typ.

Lobby

Plaza

Lobby

Garage

WESTCOAST TRANSMISSION CO.

Framing Section

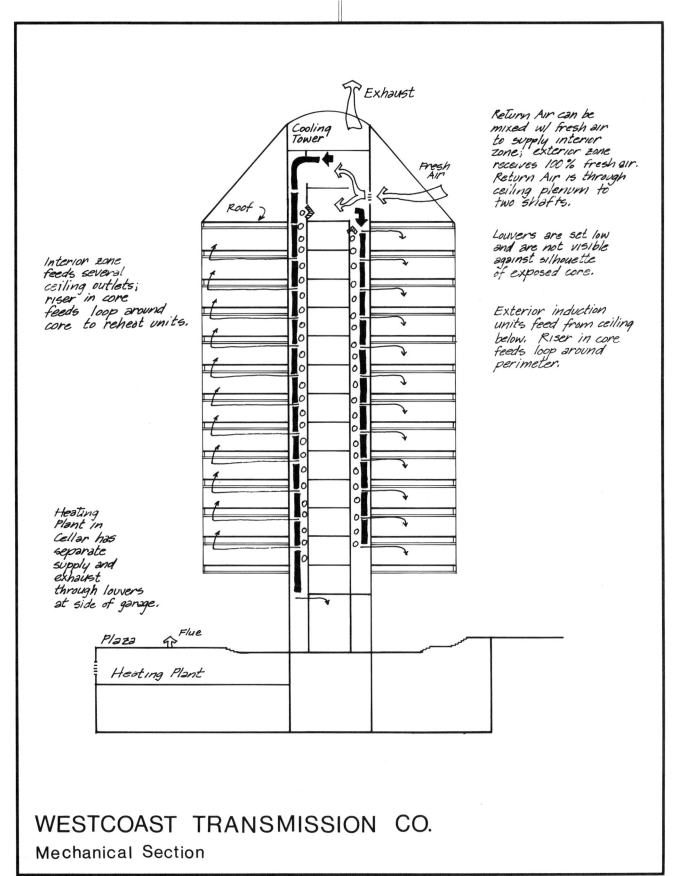

Exhaust

Cooling Tower

Fresh Air

Roof

Return Air can be mixed w/ fresh air to supply interior zone; exterior zone receives 100% fresh air. Return Air is through ceiling plenum to two shafts.

Louvers are set low and are not visible against silhouette of exposed core.

Exterior induction units feed from ceiling below. Riser in core feeds loop around perimeter.

Interior zone feeds several ceiling outlets; riser in core feeds loop around core to reheat units.

Heating Plant in Cellar has separate supply and exhaust through louvers at side of garage.

Plaza   Flue

Heating Plant

WESTCOAST TRANSMISSION CO.
Mechanical Section

U.S. STEEL BUILDING

THE main challenge that confronted the architects in designing U.S. Steel's headquarters tower in Pittsburgh was how to design the proposed megastructure as a symbol of the technical and aesthetic capacities of steel. One issue the designers definitely did not have to ponder was the choice of material for the framing system. In many ways, the building has been successful in achieving its goal of serving as an advertisement and showcase for innovations in the use of steel. Economics ultimately became a restraint however, even for this corporate giant.

Two powerful features of the building hit the viewer even from afar. The first is the use of what appears to be an exposed structural steel frame placed on the exterior side of the building's skin. Second is the frame itself, which produces a confusion of scale; the building is exceptionally tall, yet its texture, seen from afar, belies this. Closer inspection reveals that the articulated horizontal support beams occur at every third level rather than at each floor as your eye has been conditioned to expect.

A great many nontypical solutions were combined to create the total visual image of U.S. Steel's corporate symbol. The exterior structure is what first strikes the eye. The 18 massive, exterior columns of the structure are indeed exposed structural steel. They were fire-protected by filling their hollow rectangular shapes with water (carefully treated with antirust and antifreeze chemicals). The columns are all interconnected with piping, which permits the water to circulate. The water will begin to circulate automatically if a fire breaks out since the heat will cause the water that has been warmed by flames to rise, and this, in turn, will bring cool water into contact with the steel. The gigantic spandrel beams might also be assumed to contain water, but they do not, despite the fact that they are hollow box sections. Cost ultimately dictated that they would not, so the spandrel girders were sprayed with insulation and then covered with a sheet-steel wrapping to maintain a structural appearance. A close look at the exposed columns reveals that their decreasing need for load-carrying capacity as they rise from the lower floors has been expressed by reducing their depth at several intervals.

The building contains an unusual framing arrangement, which is responsible for the spandrel beams being expressed on only every third floor level. Behind the steel and glass skin of the building, two intermediate floors are supported on minicolumns rising from a major, or primary, floor. The primary floor spandrel beam is expressed on the exterior. This noncontinuous, two-story high support permits a certain flexibility in resisting horizontal wind forces. Another major wind-resisting system, in addition to the standard diagonal bracing in the core, is a deep truss located at the top of the building. This truss connects the exterior columns located on one side of the building with the columns on the opposite side, causing each pair of columns to act in unison, thus limiting the structure's sway. This cap truss, as it is called, has been used on other tall structures, and in some buildings, a second truss across the middle of the building has been added as an additional stiffening cross-tie. Usually, this middle level, or belt truss, as it is commonly called, is located at the same level as an intermediate mechanical-equipment room, where the diagonal members of the truss will not cause the interference problem they would on an occupied floor.

The building's height was divided into several zones to accommodate the vertical distribution of the heating and air-conditioning systems. The louvers for these zones have been strongly expressed on the exterior. The very large office area of each floor also meant that several climate control zones were needed on each floor. Fundamentally, there is a perimeter-induction system and an interior variable-volume, climate-control system. The huge floor area required an unusual number of vertical supply and return shafts. The owners are rather proud of the air-distribution system, which is a 30-foot-long linear slot that combines with a partition-attachment system. It is a neat, slick way of handling the ceiling texture, but the basics behind it are not unique.

What is special about this structure is the way its framing material, structural, and fire-protection systems combine to create a singular mood. The restrained color, scale, and texture of the building's rust-resistant steel make a statement that is unique to steel. The U.S. Steel Building is stately from a distance, perhaps a bit harsh up close, not always honest, but somehow regal and strong.

147

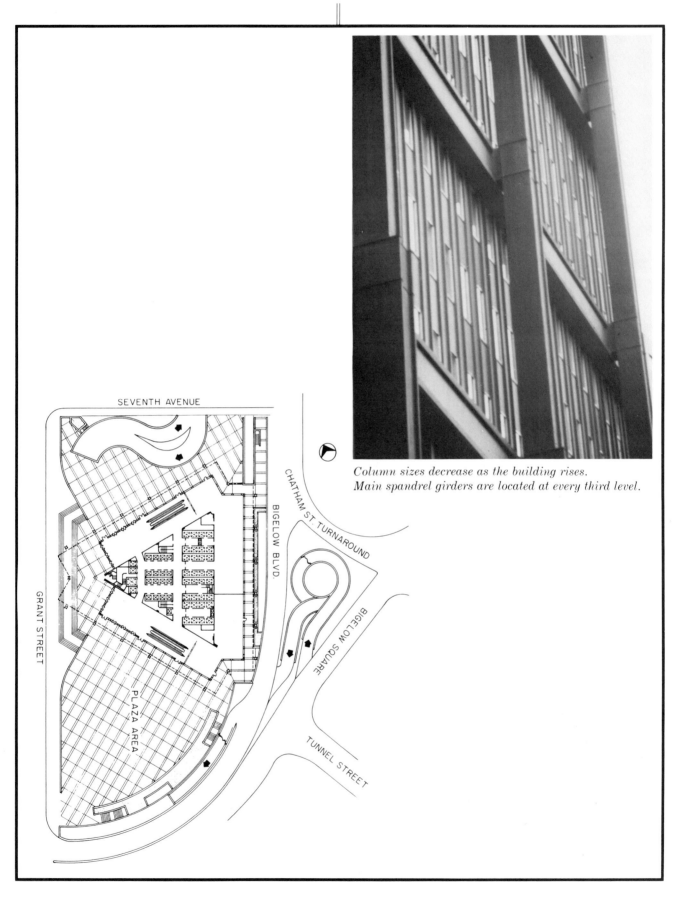

Column sizes decrease as the building rises.
Main spandrel girders are located at every third level.

SEVENTH AVENUE

CHATHAM ST. TURNAROUND

BIGELOW BLVD.

BIGELOW SQUARE

GRANT STREET

PLAZA AREA

TUNNEL STREET

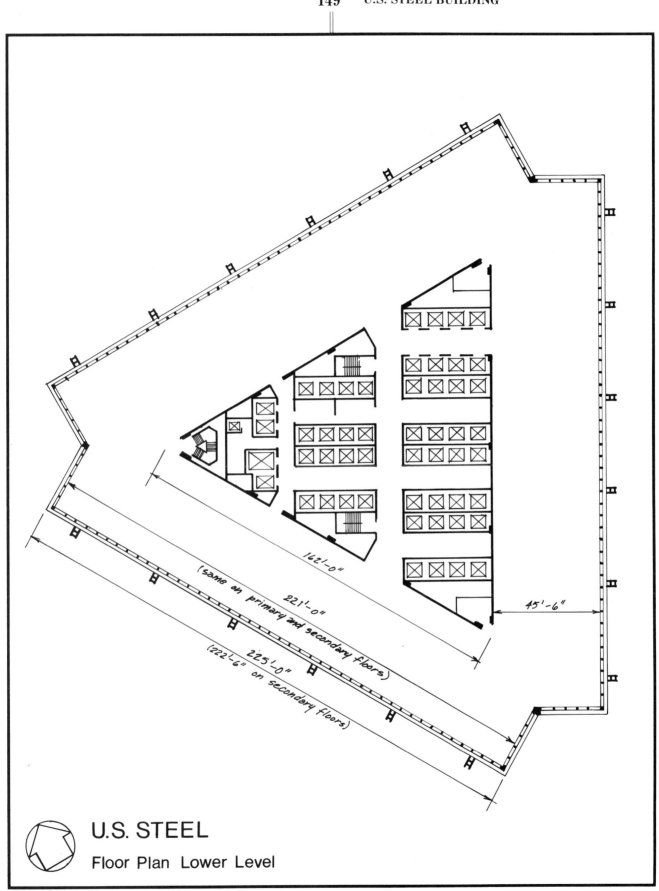

162'-0"

(same on primary and secondary floors)

221'-0"

225'-0"

(222'-6" on secondary floors)

45'-6"

U.S. STEEL
Floor Plan Lower Level

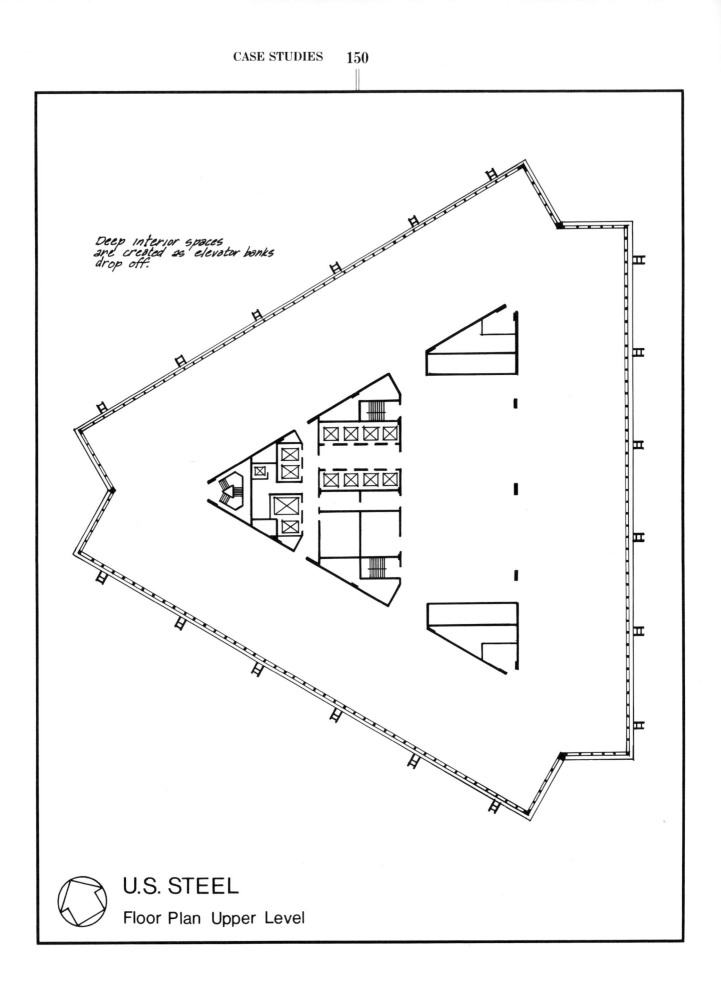

Deep interior spaces
are created as elevator banks
drop off.

U.S. STEEL

Floor Plan Upper Level

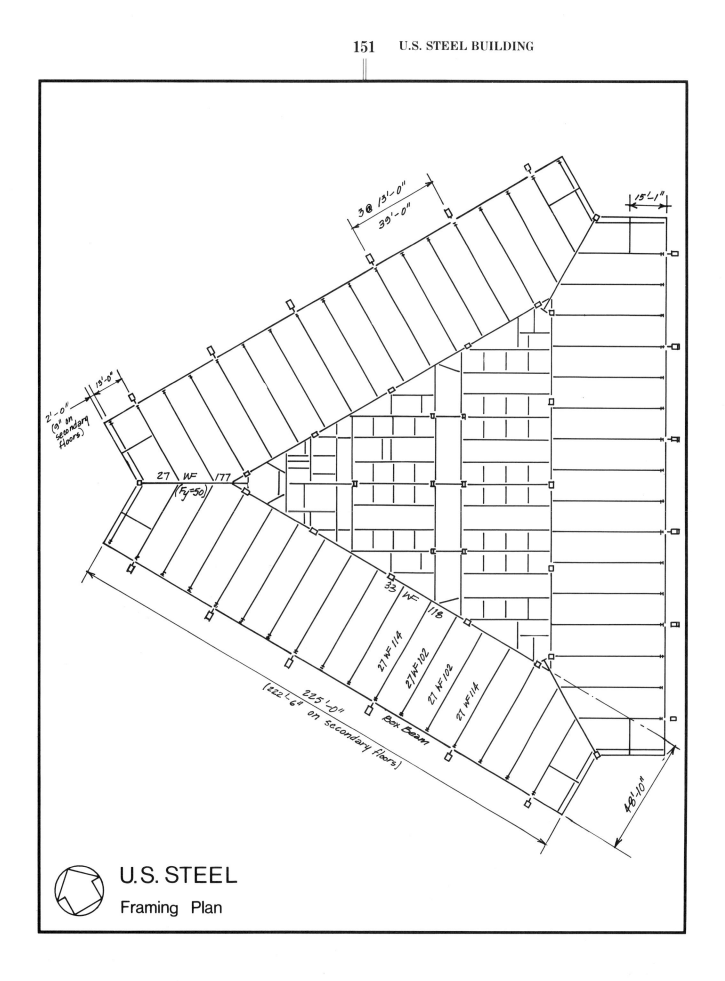

3 @ 13'-0"
39'-0"

15'-1"

2'-0"
(9" on secondary floors)

13'-0"

27 WF 177
(Fy=50)

33 WF 118

27 WF 114
27 WF 102
27 WF 102
27 WF 114

Box Beam

225'-0"
(222'-6" on secondary floors)

48'-10"

U.S. STEEL

Framing Plan

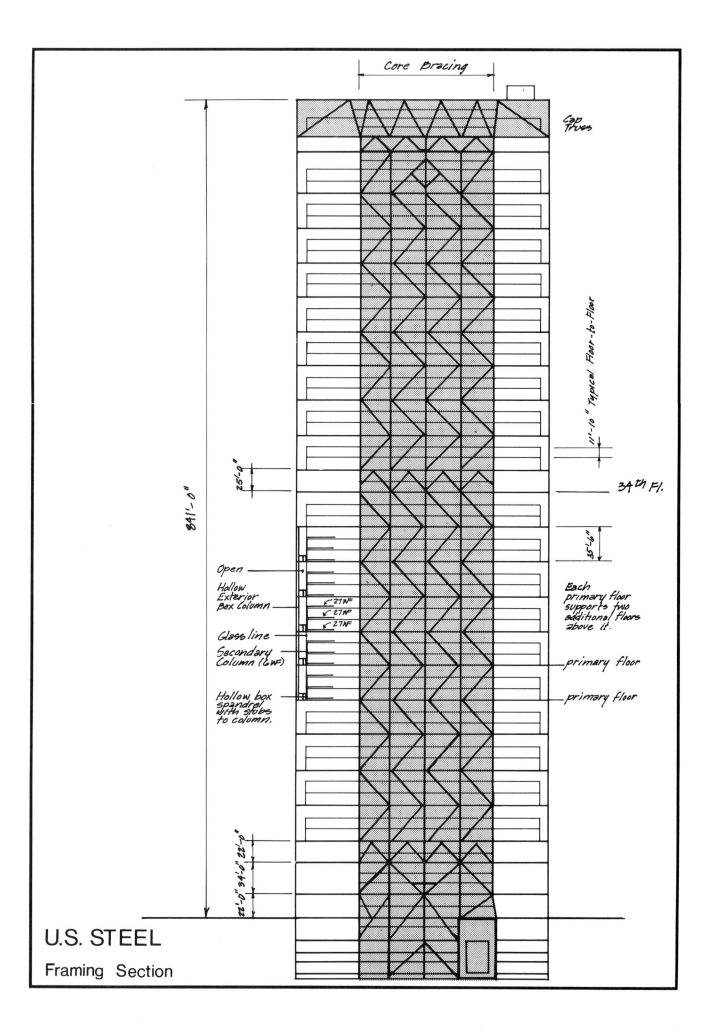

Core Bracing

Cap Truss

111'-10" Typical Floor-to-Floor

25'-0"

34th Fl.

35'-6"

Open

Hollow Exterior Box Column

27 W^F
27 W^F
27 W^F

Glass line

Secondary Column (6 W^F)

Hollow box spandrel with stubs to column.

Each primary floor supports two additional floors above it.

primary floor

primary floor

841'-0"

22'-0" 34'-0" 22'-0"

U.S. STEEL

Framing Section

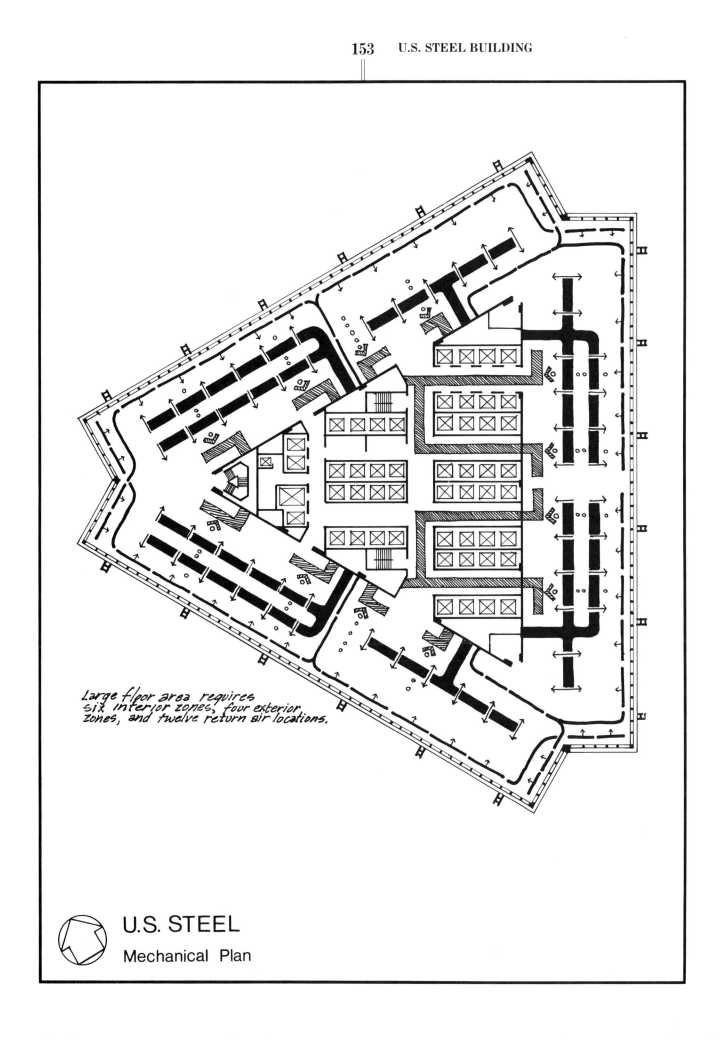

Large floor area requires six interior zones, four exterior zones, and twelve return air locations.

U.S. STEEL
Mechanical Plan

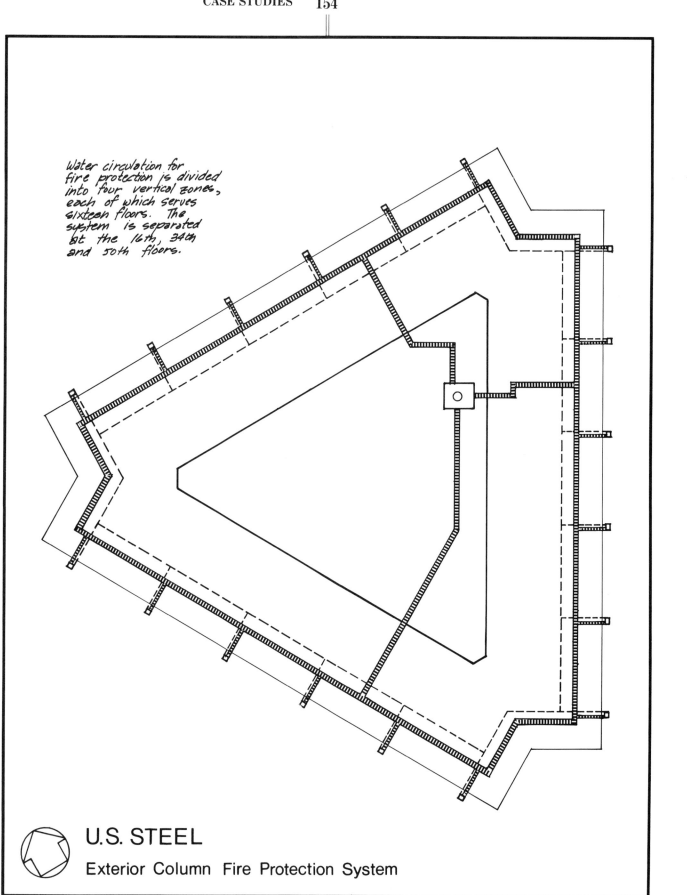

Water circulation for fire protection is divided into four vertical zones, each of which serves sixteen floors. The system is separated at the 16th, 34th and 50th floors.

U.S. STEEL

Exterior Column Fire Protection System

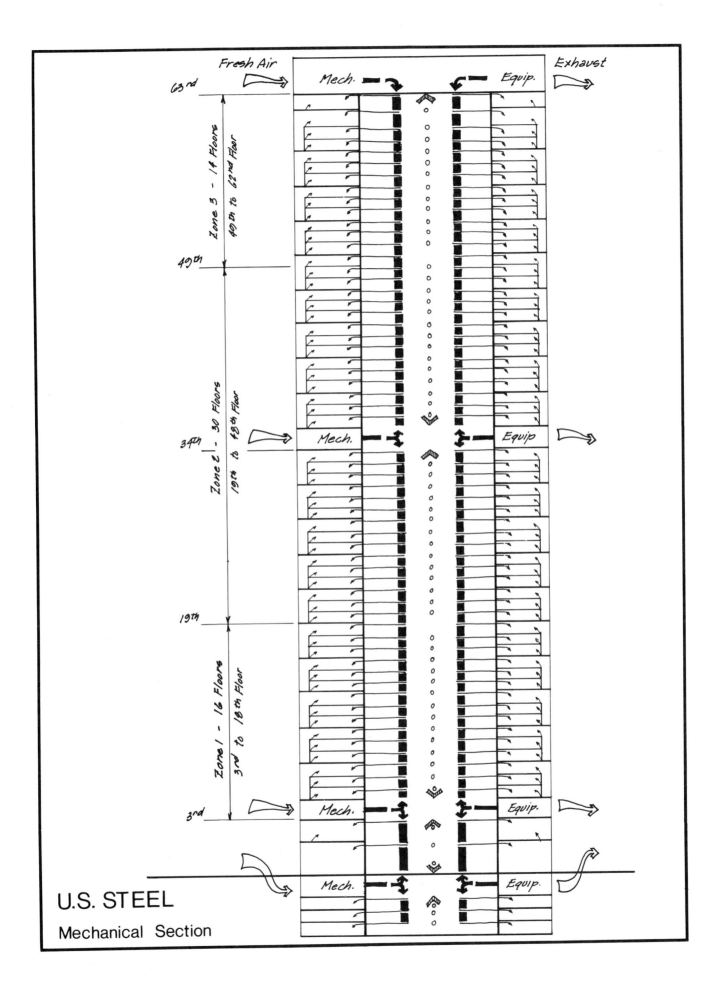

Fresh Air

Exhaust

63rd

Mech.

Equip.

Zone 3 - 14 Floors
49th to 62nd Floor

49th

Zone 2 - 30 Floors
19th to 48th Floor

34th

Mech.

Equip

19th

Zone 1 - 16 Floors
3rd to 18th Floor

3rd

Mech.

Equip.

Mech.

Equip.

U.S. STEEL

Mechanical Section

CITICORP TOWER

THE Citicorp Tower is a strikingly unusual building. Its massive feet, one in the middle of each of the building's four faces, support a tower that does not start until its legs have climbed nine floors above the street. A sloping shed roof stands out against the flat roofs and spires of its neighbors, its 70-plus stories soaring above most of the competition of New York City's skyline. Yet, despite all this, it is still in many ways a building that "might have been." Huge structural diagonals in the plane of the facade collect the vertical loads and bring them into a center column, and then, in turn, down to each of those four giant legs. However, this inherent inner potential is somehow never exploited. As the building's framing went up, it looked at times like a giant skeleton of a fish. One had only a short time to admire the eight-story-high chevron structural pattern with its fascinating, freestanding triangular bites where there is no corner column at the point where the chevron starts its path to the center mast. A mundane curtain wall was wrapped around this engineering tour de force, and the building's facade became another slick, tidily wrapped box.

The shed roof created to contain a solar collector was scrapped by the budget wielders, leaving a form without a purpose and creating an ice slide in the winter, which on occasion has caused the street below to be blocked off to protect passers-by.

One part of the wind-bracing system is particularly fascinating. It is based on the classic theory that "for every action, there is an equal and opposite reaction." In this case, the action is the horizontal displacement of the top of the building due to the wind (sway), and the balancing reaction is a huge four-hundred-ton concrete mass set on a bed of oil that permits it to slide in opposition to (and thus counteract) the building sway. There are bumpers to limit horizontal movement and all sorts of electronic controls, but the principle remains simplistic. Perhaps the most startling aspect of this system is the fact that less steel was required to support all this weight at the building's top than would have been needed to stiffen the building with traditional, structural wind-bracing members.

Mechanically, the building offers no surprises or unusual systems. The nine-story-high legs freed the underside of the office tower and permitted the architect to use the soffit to locate the louvers for the building's lower mechanical zone. The louvers for the upper mechanical zone are placed directly on the facade and are expressed in a simple, direct manner.

Another interesting device is the two-level or tandem elevators, which cut down on the core size by reducing the number of elevators and thus, in turn, the number of shafts. This solution carries a nuisance value, in that the elevators must be entered from two different lobby levels, depending on whether one is going to an even or an odd-numbered floor.

This tower, which was the world's seventh-tallest building at the time it was constructed, is a solid contribution to the city's texture, and contains a delightful multistory plaza under its main mass. It had the bones, guts, and majesty to be an even more exciting architectural statement than it is.

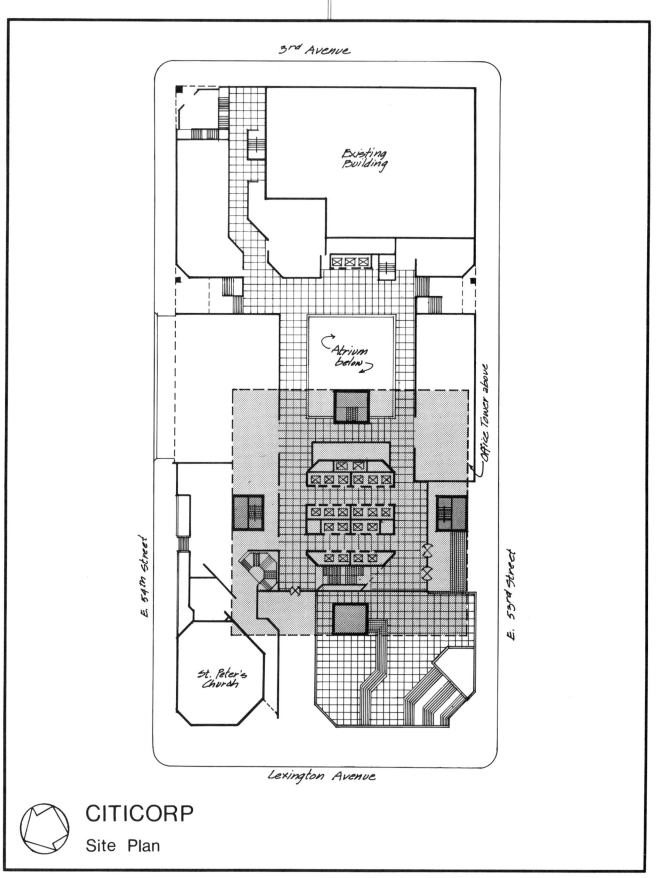

3rd Avenue

Existing
Building

Atrium
below

Office Tower above

E. 54th Street

E. 53rd Street

St. Peter's
Church

Lexington Avenue

CITICORP
Site Plan

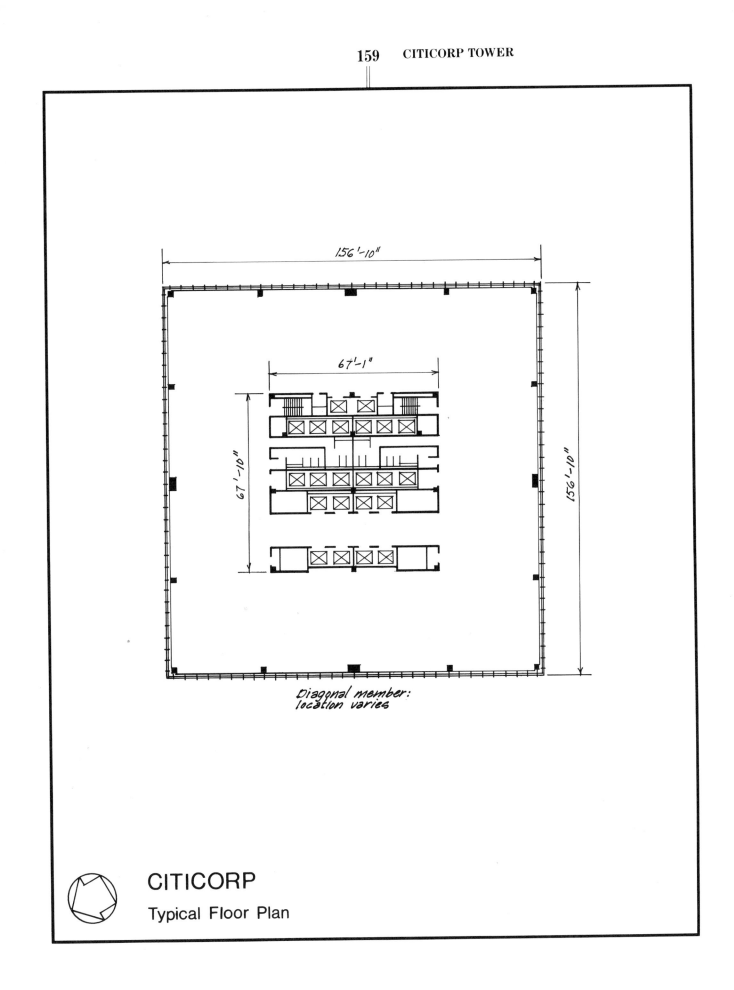

Diagonal member:
location varies

CITICORP

Typical Floor Plan

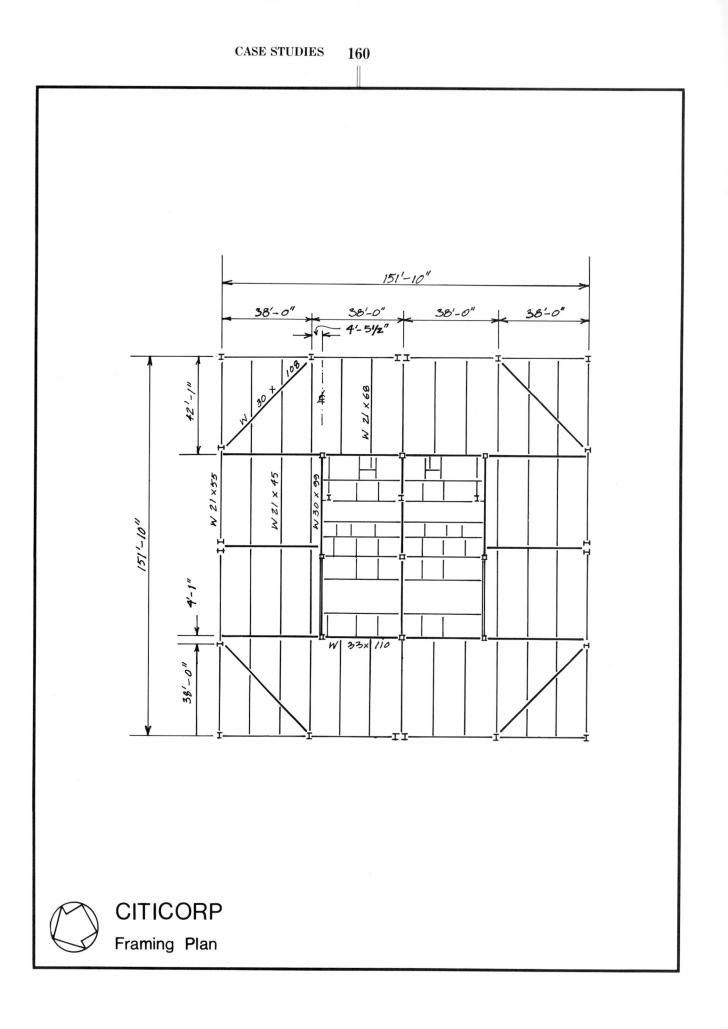

CITICORP

Framing Plan

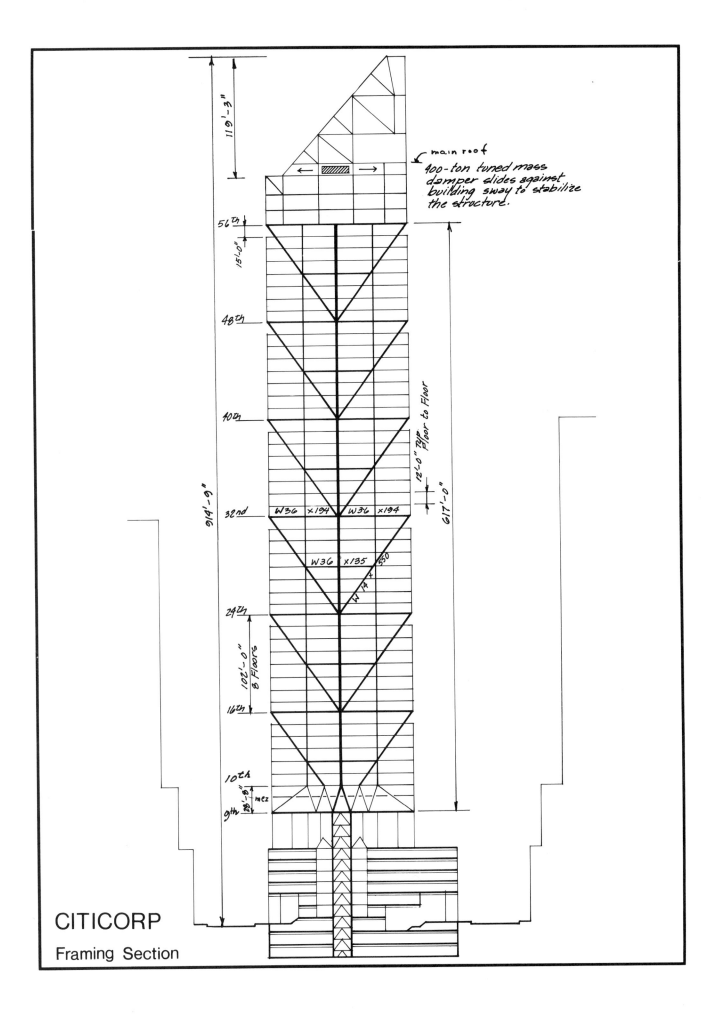

main roof

400-ton tuned mass damper slides against building sway to stabilize the structure.

119'-3"

56th

15'-0"

48th

40th

12'-0" Typ. Floor to Floor

617'-0"

32nd   W36 x194   W36 x194

W36 x135 50

914'-9"

W14 +

24th

102'-0"
8 Floors

16th

10th

mez

9th

20'-0"

CITICORP

Framing Section

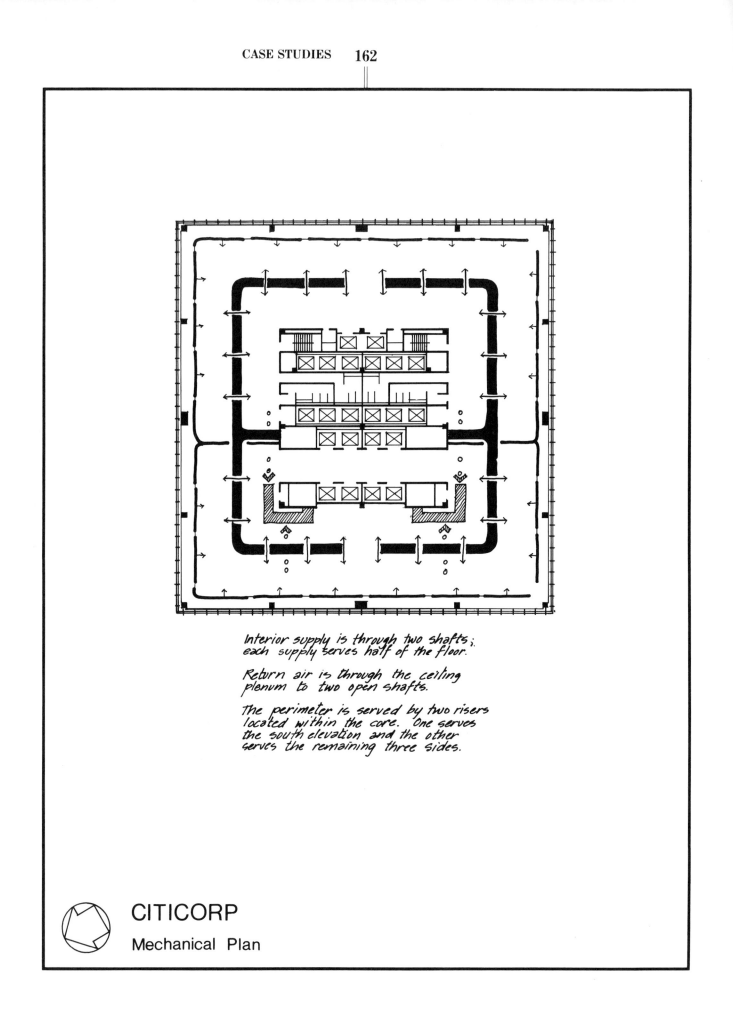

Interior supply is through two shafts;
each supply serves half of the floor.

Return air is through the ceiling
plenum to two open shafts.

The perimeter is served by two risers
located within the core. One serves
the south elevation and the other
serves the remaining three sides.

CITICORP

Mechanical Plan

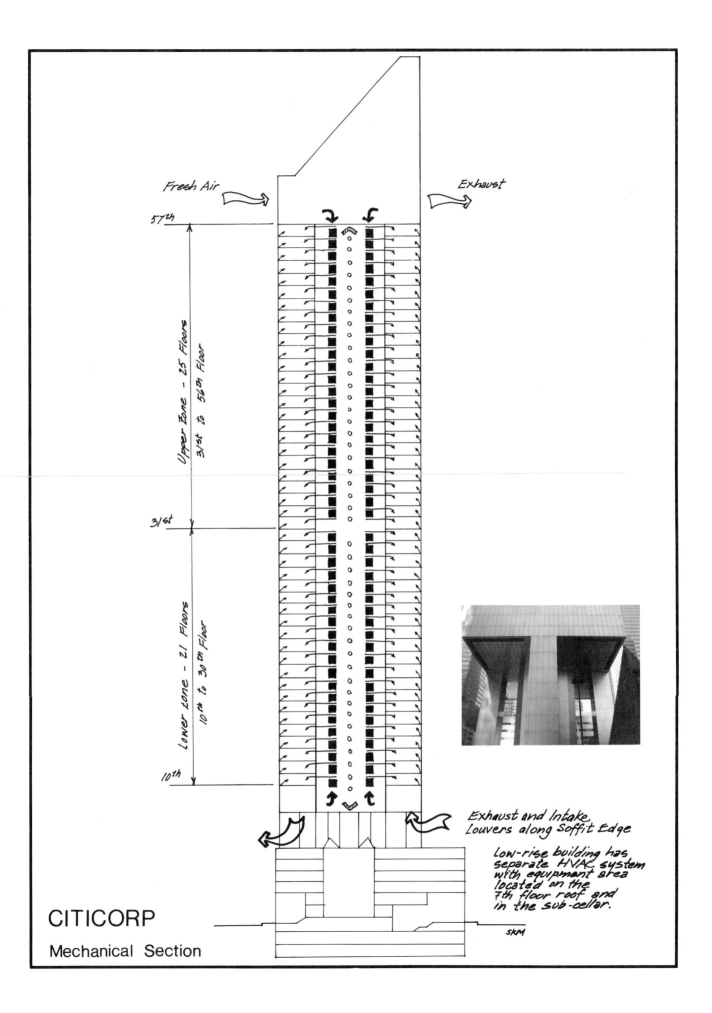

Fresh Air

Exhaust

57th

Upper Zone - 25 Floors
31st to 56th Floor

31st

Lower Zone - 21 Floors
10th to 30th Floor

10th

Exhaust and Intake
Louvers along Soffit Edge

Low-rise building has
separate HVAC system
with equipment area
located on the
7th floor roof and
in the sub-cellar.

SKM

CITICORP

Mechanical Section

BURLINGTON
INDUSTRIES

RUGGED, 75-foot-high, cross-braced exposed steel trusses march around the perimeter of Burlington Industries' solar-glass-clad office tower. This striking cubical building is part of a 400,000 square foot office complex that sits within a 34-acre suburban site. Manicured, tree-studded lawns surround the buildings, allowing them to create their own isolated image. The use of huge exposed steel-framing members, therefore, is not in as sharp a contrast with the residential neighborhood as one might suppose. The massive, meticulously detailed exterior trusses are simultaneously reflected and silhouetted by the mirror-like quality of the curtain wall located seven feet behind them. This unique combination of structure and cladding produces an eloquent statement which asks to be judged on its own merits.

The six-story tower is almost encircled by a 525-foot-long, two-story-high office structure, which also encloses a lush, gardened courtyard. Three bridges connect the second level of the low-rise structure to the off-centered tower, allowing it to remain as an isolated element, rising above its surrounding building and trees. One corner of the tower was left visually free and unencumbered by the low foreground building, permitting the total form of the tower to be sensed from the main highway and access road.

The perimeter edges of the upper four tower floors are suspended from a diagonal grid of roof beams, which are carried by the imposing three-bay-long trusses located along each exterior building face. The 7-foot separation between the trusses and building face isolates the structural steel from any flammable material within the building; and thus, in conjunction with a ring of sprinkler heads placed in the roof soffit between the truss and the curtain wall, serves as the fireproofing method for the trusses.

The suspended pristine glass "cube" is a four level 153' x 153' x 60'-high box which hovers over a two-story base that is supported by columns rising up from the cellar level.

The tension hangers carrying the upper floors, and the columns supporting the lower ones, are all concealed behind the opaque curtain wall, with the unfortunate result that the upper levels appear to be resting on the lower ones, despite the architect's use of a thin horizontal band of clear glass to separate them. Since none of the hangers or columns can be seen from the exterior, the actual structural discontinuity between the second and third floors simply cannot be properly perceived. The 8"-wide-flanged steel sections used as perimeter hangers are boxed out with gypsum boards for fireproofing, and thus when seen from the interior, they look exactly like any standard column.

The enormous cost of the exterior truss system might have been more justifiable if one could sense the actual suspension of the upper floors more clearly. Perhaps, the separation between the suspended levels and the lower floors could have been stronger, and there might have been a way to convey the fact that the roof is carrying the load of the floors below it rather than merely acting as a lid. In any event, the four, 75-foot-high by 170-foot-long trusses are "the" architectural statement that sets this building apart from the all too common stereotypes of mundane rectangular boxes, gift wrapped in curtain walls of varying quality. It is a shame that the purpose of such a strong design tool became less clear than it should or needed to become. However one might argue over the articulation, clarity, and expression of the cube, there is no question that this building draws its architectural statement and strength from a desire to express its structure. It is the vocabulary used to accomplish this end that one can quibble about.

As in the case of the Westcoast Transmission Company Building, when the perimeter of a structure is suspended, there is an unavoidable elongation of the path the vertical loads must travel. In this case, first up along the hangers to the roof, then over to the exterior truss, and then finally down through the truss to the ground. When one is inside the tower office space, there is little sense of being within a suspended structure, because the visual bulk of the 8"-wide steel sections being used as hangers becomes large enough to appear capable of supporting the floors as normal standard compression columns. Of course, had the exterior hangers actually been used as columns, it would have eliminated the need for the massive wall trusses and costly roof framing. The central core of the tower is framed with a conventional steel skeleton system of beams, columns, and girders; which support the interior ends of the main floor girders that span 45 feet to the hanger supports located just inside the curtain wall.

The fan-room that services the tower structure's HVAC system is located on the top, or sixth, floor, adjacent to the building's core. A 60-foot square, by 7-foot high penthouse volume punches up through the main roof level, providing headroom for the bulky fan-room equipment. The penthouse's perimeter walls provide a vertical surface for the fresh air intake louvers, and its flush unpierced roof doubles as a helicopter landing pad. The 22-foot high space between the penthouse roof and the sixth floor is also tall enough to contain the elevator-run-by space.

The chillers for the air-conditioning systems of both the tower and the rambling low-rise building are located in the tower cellar. The fan-room for the low-rise structure is situated partially under the tower and partially under the upper level of the terraced courtyard located between the high- and low-rise buildings. The requisite fresh air intake louvers are quietly concealed behind evergreen plants.

Each tower floor is serviced by two separate environmental air-supply systems. The interior spaces are supplied by a variable-air-volume system, with its supply ducts running above a hung acoustical-tile ceiling. The perimeter of the building is serviced by a dual-duct air system. A loop of warm and cool air ducts run under the floors of the level they will supply. A series of small branch ducts tap into the main ducts, and these branches lead to a mixing box located near the exterior wall. From there the mixed air is conveyed up and over the spandrel beam to a windowsill supply slot. A pattern of grilles in the hung ceiling permit the return air from both the interior and perimeter systems to flow into the open plenum created between the hung ceiling and the underside of the floor above, and then through this plenum back to the return air shaft.

The dual-duct perimeter supply system has fourteen separate thermostatically controlled mixing boxes, which permits the HVAC system to compensate for the wide variations in solar loads nature often places simultaneously on the different sides of the building. Certain not uncommon circumstances (such as a sunny 45-degree day) will require cooling for the rooms located along the sun-warmed southern elevation at the same time as the Chilled north facing rooms need heating.

Because a dual-duct system requires the simultaneous operation of both a heating and cooling plant, it is not nearly as energy efficient as a variable-volume air system which simply modulates the amount of whatever temperature air is generated. Additionally, the installation of two separate parallel duct systems and mixing boxes adds considerably to construction costs.

As a result of their high construction and operating costs, dual-duct systems tended to be limited to prestige high-quality buildings, such as this and the Seagram Building. Exacerbated by recent skyrocketing fuel costs, the use of dual-duct systems in new construction has greatly diminished. In fact, many luxury buildings (including the Seagram Building) are changing their original dual-duct systems to variable-volume systems, in order to constrain rapidly rising operating expenses. However, it must be pointed out that a dual-duct system can provide a higher level of environmental comfort control than a variable-volume system can.

The major drawback of a variable-volume system is, despite recent advancements in thermostatically activated motorized controlled dampers, that they often provide an inadequate amount of air changes. The reason this happens is that if the room thermostat indicates that the current temperature doesn't require any modulation, then it will throttle down the damper located in the air-supply duct because no additional tempered air is needed in order to change the current temperature within the particular room or space monitored by the thermostat. What is really needed under these circumstances is some fresh air to replace the stale air; but since the temperature in the space doesn't require any modulation, only a preprogrammed minimum amount of air will be supplied past the almost closed damper, and this amount is often inadequate. When larger volumes of air are provided (to raise the temperature in winter or, lower it in summer), then the air-change problem automatically solves itself.

A dual-duct system always delivers a constant total volume of the proper amount of air. Depending on the requirements of the moment, the system will furnish the correct proportions of warm to cool air. The dual-duct system works on a similar principle to that of a kitchen faucet supplied by a hot and cold water pipes.

In general, the architects for Burlington Industries chose to tuck a rather expensive mechanical system into their building in an unobtrusive way. The principle heat source for the structure is the reclaimed heat picked up, from the light fixtures and computers, by the return air. Additional heat is obtained from the water used to cool the compressors and from a relatively small electric furnace. The issue of where to place the chimney never needed solving, since one was never needed. Spill, or exhaust, air leaves the building through washroom and kitchen exhaust ducts, as well as by door openings and leakage.

It is interesting to realize that by minimizing the visual impact of the mechanical features, it became easier to maximize the impact of the structural characteristics. The bulk and symmetry of the massive omnipresent trusses are so dominating, that even the eccentric placement of the lower two column-supported floors in relation to the upper four suspended-tower levels, is not readily noticeable.

The architects surrounded their building with imposing exposed trusses, and then dropped the actual building inside this frame, securing it by its ears, so to speak, to a structural roof grid which is carried by the perimeter truss frame and central core. One can not help wondering if the effect would have been even stronger had the diagonal roof framing been left exposed in a similar manner to the exterior trusses, and if the upper four suspended floors were more clearly separated from the lower levels which are directly supported by the ground below them.

Much of the building's overall aura of controlled power comes from a sense of scale, and meticulous attention to detail. The precise uncluttered connections, rich but unadorned background texture of the curtain wall, all contribute to the majesty of the complex which has become part of Burlington Industries' corporate image. There has been a sufficient test of time for us to ascertain that both the people who work here, as well as those who live nearby, have accepted a building that is radically different architecturally from the mundane-new and pseudocolonial structures that are so prevalent in the vicinity. Burlington Industries' headquarters is a building where the relationship between technology and aesthetics, while possibly slightly contrived, is successfully bold and inseparable.

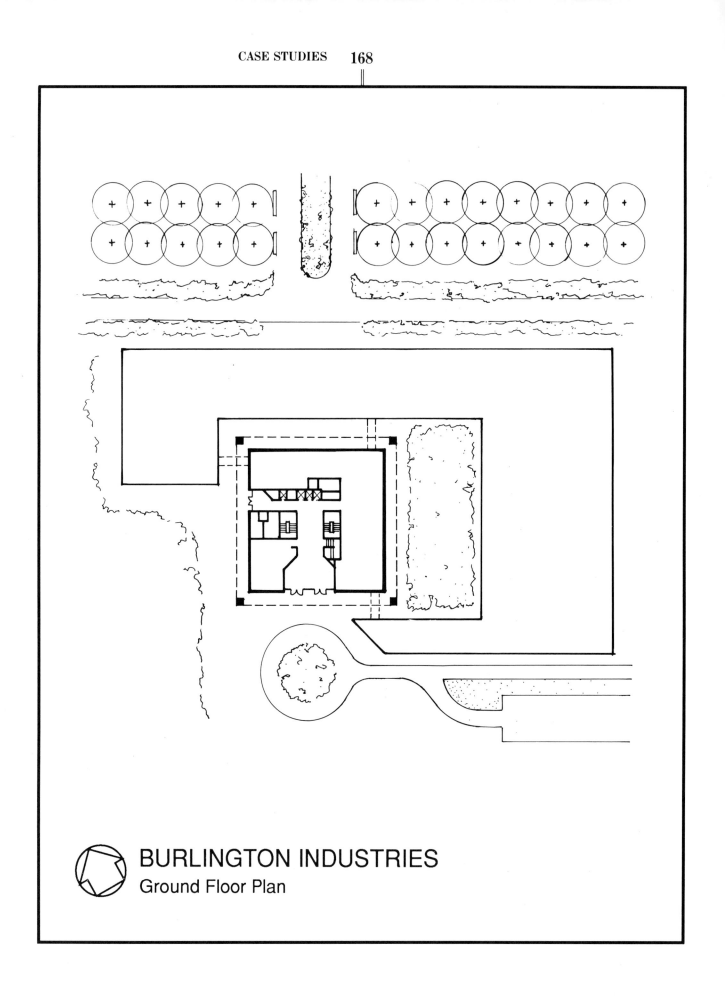

BURLINGTON INDUSTRIES
Ground Floor Plan

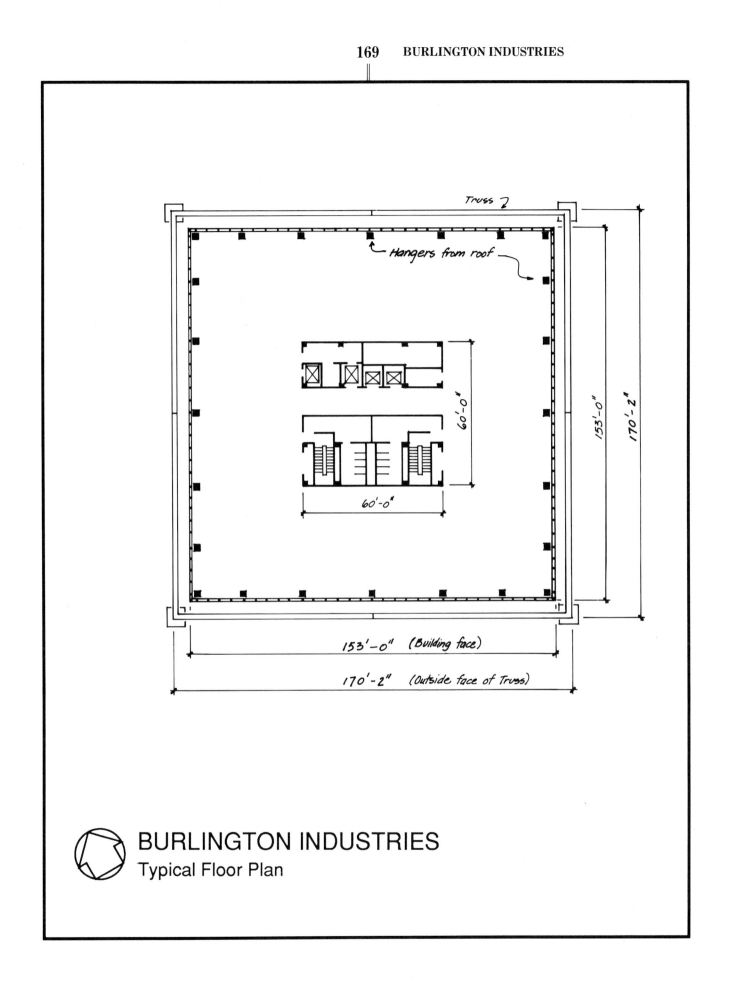

BURLINGTON INDUSTRIES
Typical Floor Plan

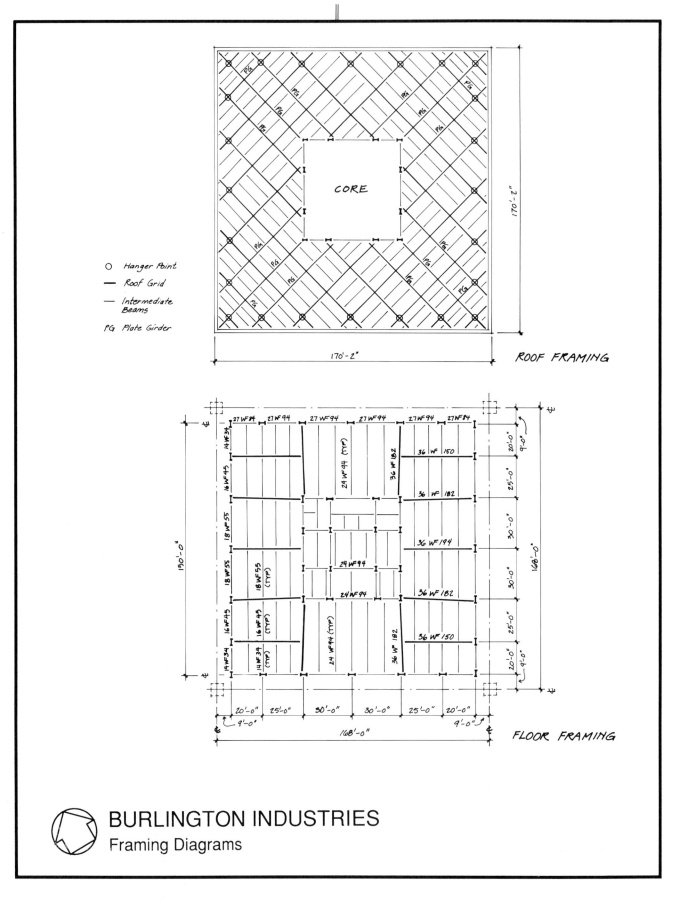

O   Hanger Point
—   Roof Grid
—   Intermediate Beams
PG   Plate Girder

CORE

170'-2"

170'-2"

ROOF FRAMING

150'-0"

168'-0"

FLOOR FRAMING

BURLINGTON INDUSTRIES
Framing Diagrams

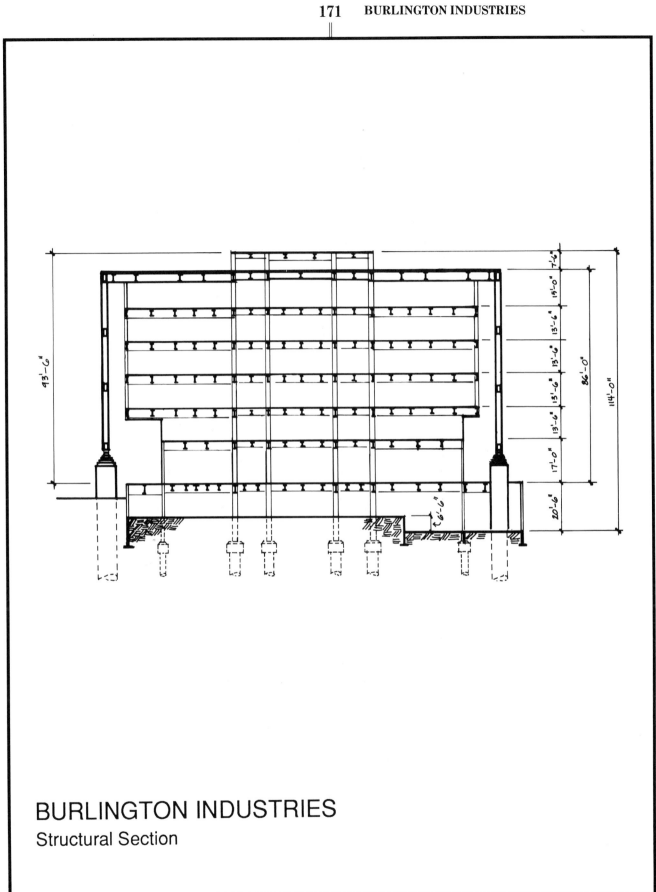

BURLINGTON INDUSTRIES
Structural Section

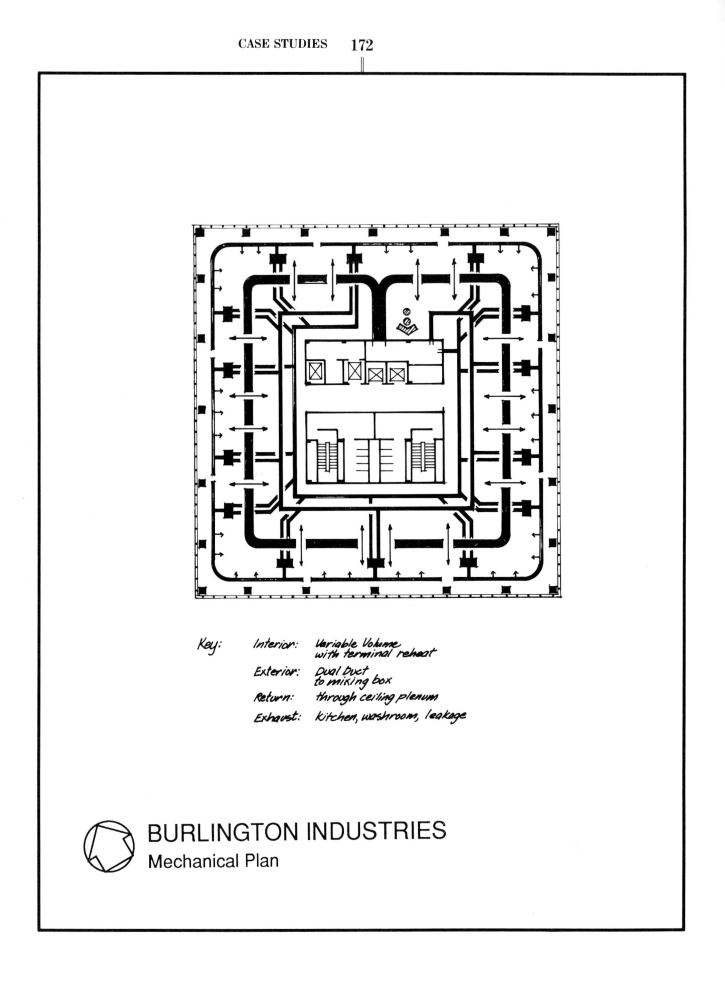

Key: Interior: Variable Volume
                     with terminal reheat
        Exterior: Dual Duct
                     to mixing box
        Return: through ceiling plenum
        Exhaust: kitchen, washroom, leakage

BURLINGTON INDUSTRIES
Mechanical Plan

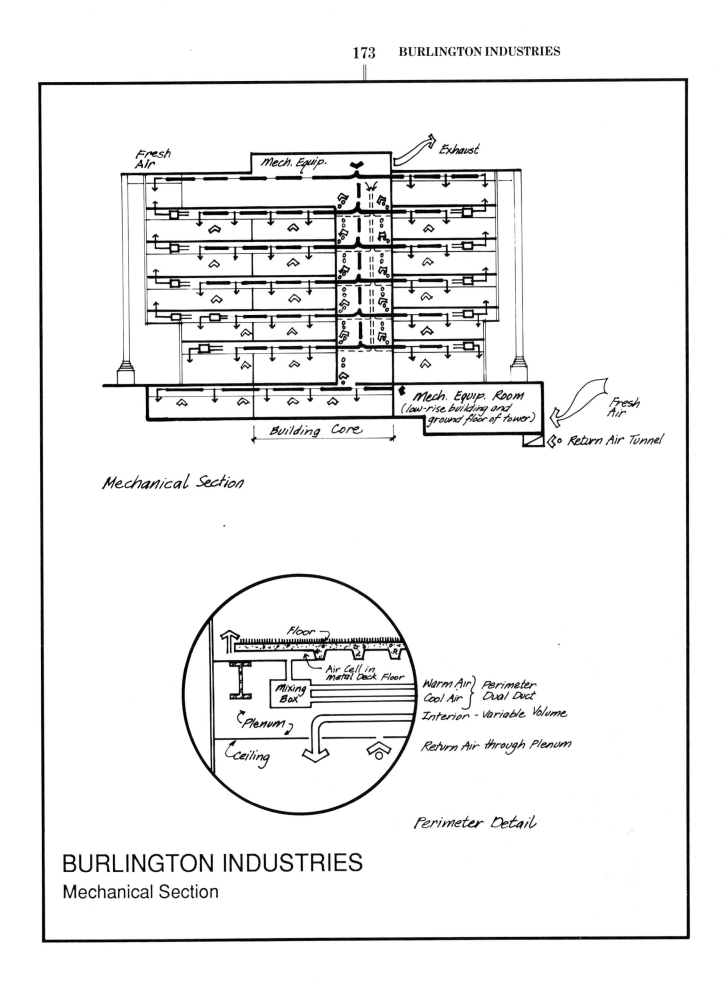

Fresh Air

Mech. Equip.

Exhaust

Mech. Equip. Room
(low-rise building and
ground floor of tower)

Fresh Air

Return Air Tunnel

Building Core

Mechanical Section

Floor

Air Cell in metal deck Floor

Mixing Box

Plenum

Ceiling

Warm Air
Cool Air } Perimeter
Dual Duct

Interior - Variable Volume

Return Air through Plenum

Perimeter Detail

BURLINGTON INDUSTRIES
Mechanical Section

CBS TOWER

CLOTHED in a somber mantle of black granite, the CBS tower stands as a sophisticated symbol of corporate propriety. With their 500-foot height, the stern row of 5-foot wide columns spaced 5 feet apart create a staid rhythm when viewed head-on, and create the illusion of a solid texture when viewed obliquely. Everything is subordinated to this 5-foot rhythm. Entrance doors, windows, and air-conditioning louvers all march to the five-foot module. The entire building sits in a dry moat that sets it apart from its neighbors. A tiny separate building off to one side contains the service entrance and permits truck ramps to enter the main building's cellar without violating the pristine rhythm of the main structure's columns.

The CBS tower in New York City and the One Shell Plaza tower in Houston (see the next case study) constitute an interesting pair of buildings. At first glance, both appear to accomplish the same ends via the same means. More careful inspection reveals a vast difference in their underlying philosophical statements and in the visual expression of the structural rationalization of their designs. Both buildings are high-rise office towers, built of poured-in-place concrete. Both buildings are squarish rectangles. Both are designed with a central core surrounded by an outer ring of closely spaced columns, each separated from its neighbor by only a single window. In one leap, the structural floor of both buildings spans the distance between the central core and the band of outer columns, creating a large, open space that can easily be subdivided by partitions.

The most important physical difference between these two structures lies in how each handles the exterior expression of its columns, especially those located at the four corners. In both buildings, poured-in-place concrete ribs extend from the bearing wall surrounding the core to the closely spaced columns forming the exterior wall. In the CBS building, the issue of how to frame the corner was resolved by making the closely spaced beams or ribs go in both a north-south and an east-west direction. This solution creates an additional load in the rib b–B (see illustration), caused by the loads produced by ribs e–E and d–D, which terminate on rib b–B. Architect Eero Saarinen solved this problem by increasing the load-carrying capacity of rib b–B, and in turn, of column B, while keeping column B's visual appearance consistent with the typical column A. The schematic sketch shows that columns D and E support lighter loads than does the typical column A and that the corner column C supports a very light load. Therefore, it is interesting to observe that just as column B was not made visually larger, columns E, D, and C were not made visually smaller. In fact, in order to maintain an even appearance among the columns on all four facades, the corner column C which supports the least load of all was made exactly double the size of all the other columns. A preconceived symmetry was imposed upon the building with total disregard for the loads. An intriguing photograph taken during construction shows the corner column construction completed from the third floor up—but with the second floor section still unbuilt. This was done to facilitate the installation of large pieces of equipment into the second floor mechanical-equipment room by unloading them directly from delivery trucks parked in the street.

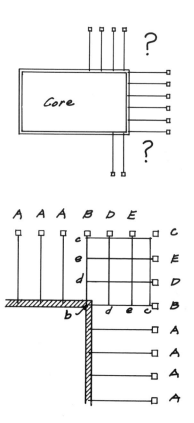

When walking past the building, one senses that it is supported on diamond-shaped columns. This is a logical assumption, since on the ground-floor level, one can look through the windows into the bank area and the public spaces and see all sides of the free-standing columns, which are indeed diamond or double triangles in cross-section. These columns are double their necessary size. On the floors above the ground, where one can see only the exterior portions of the columns from the street, they are actually triangular, or half of their ground-floor statement.

The inside of the columns is intriguing because they contain a void and are not solid concrete triangles. The area of this void increases in the columns on the upper floors as the need for structural support decreases. The majority of the tenant floors are furnished with perimeter heating and cooling from a mechanical floor located at the top of the building. Therefore, as the ducts and pipes descend, their cross-sectional size decreases, which dovetails nicely with the increase in the required area of the columns as they descend and accumulate loads. This compatability would seem to be a purist's delight. Unfortunately, every column does not contain a high-speed duct. The dovetail fit concept does not apply to the lower-level floors supplied by ducts rising from the second-floor fan room. Furthermore, and more important architecturally, the wide columns limit the amount of prestige window space available to tenants.

Despite the inconsistencies between what is actually taking place structurally and mechanically and what is visually apparent, Saarinen has produced a subdued building with a strong corporate image. His client and the average passer-by do not sense the incongruities. They see the strength of the massive supports and assume they are necessary, and most people appreciate the structure's dignity set amidst the glitter of its neighbors.

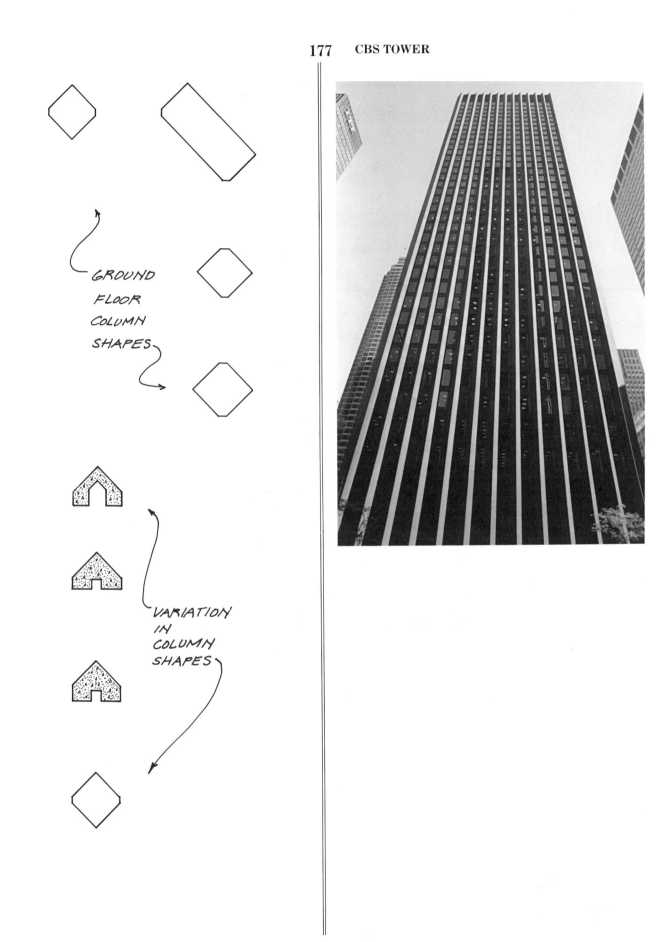

GROUND
FLOOR
COLUMN
SHAPES

VARIATION
IN
COLUMN
SHAPES

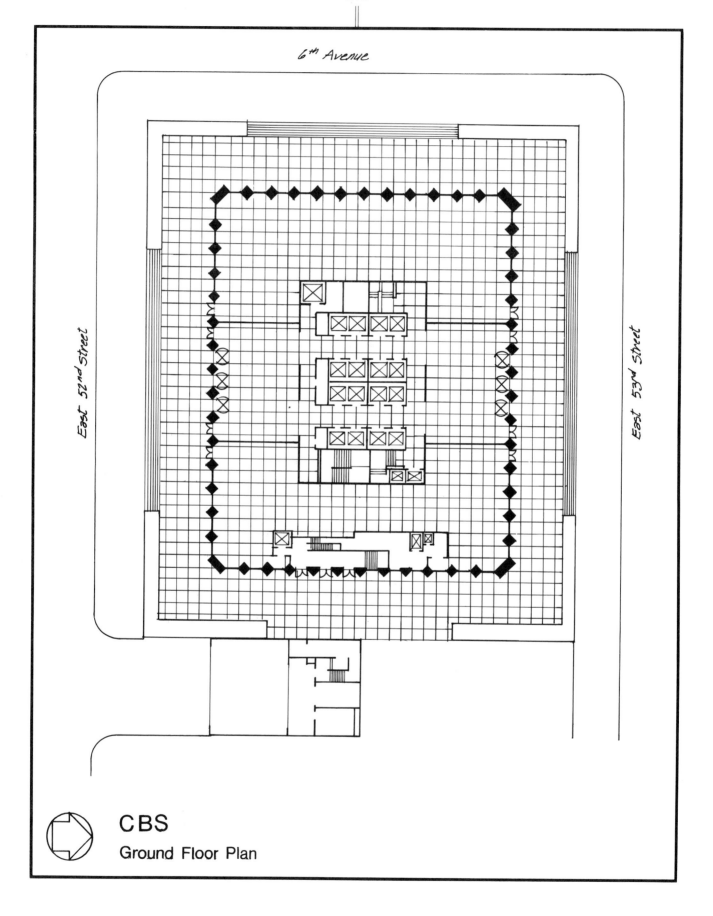

CBS
Ground Floor Plan

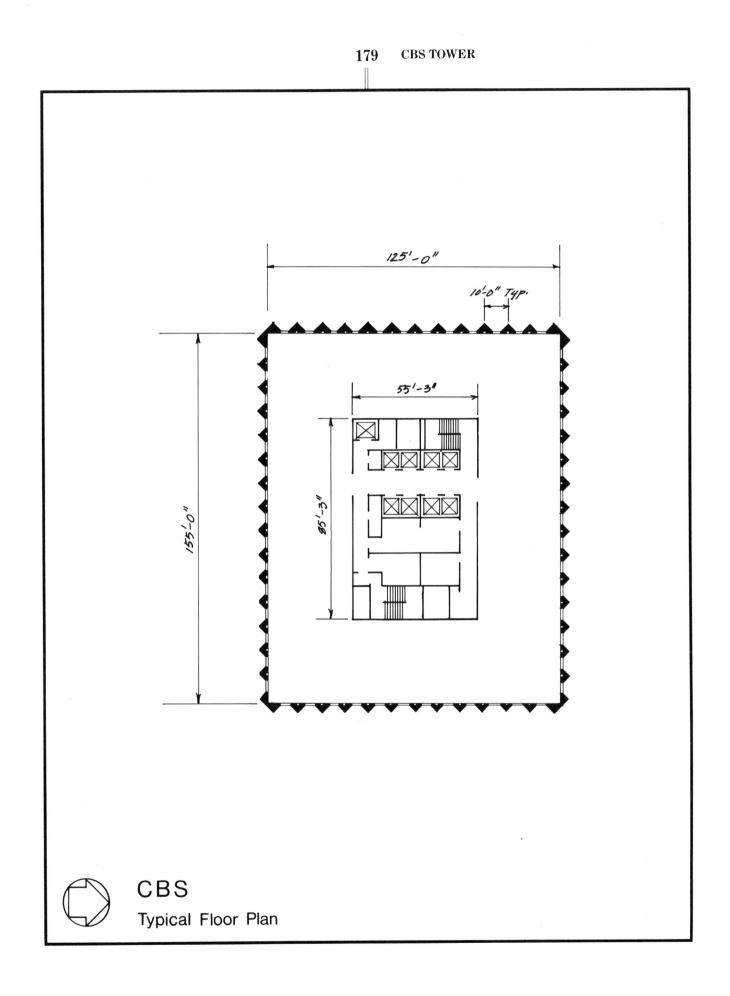

CBS
Typical Floor Plan

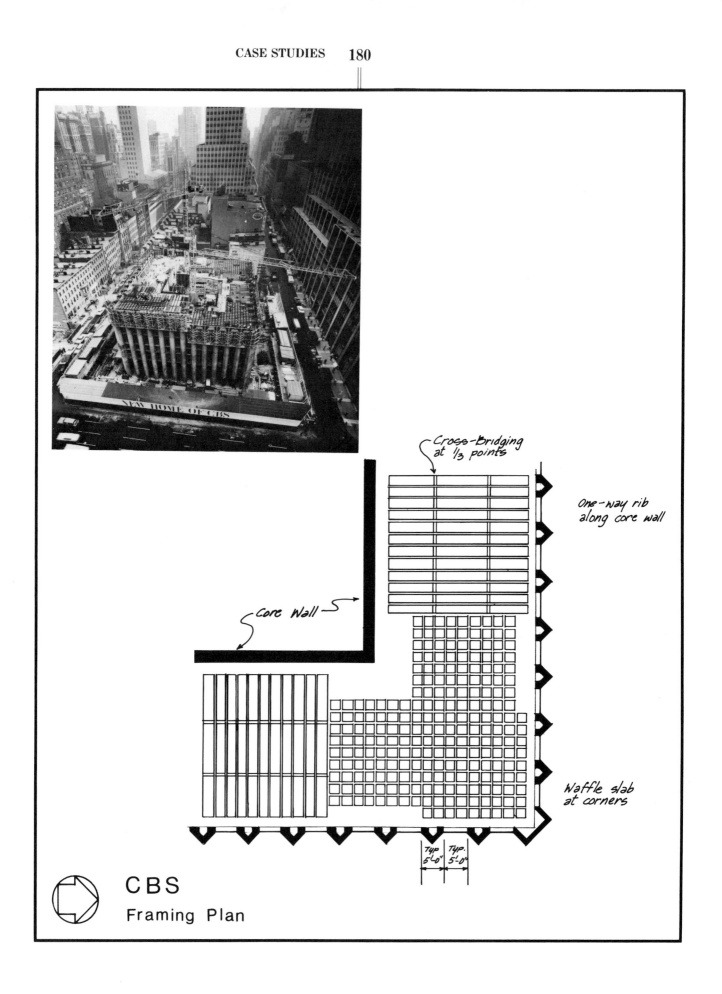

Cross-Bridging
at ⅓ points

One-way rib
along core wall

Core Wall

Waffle slab
at corners

Typ
5'-0"   Typ.
5'-0"

CBS
Framing Plan

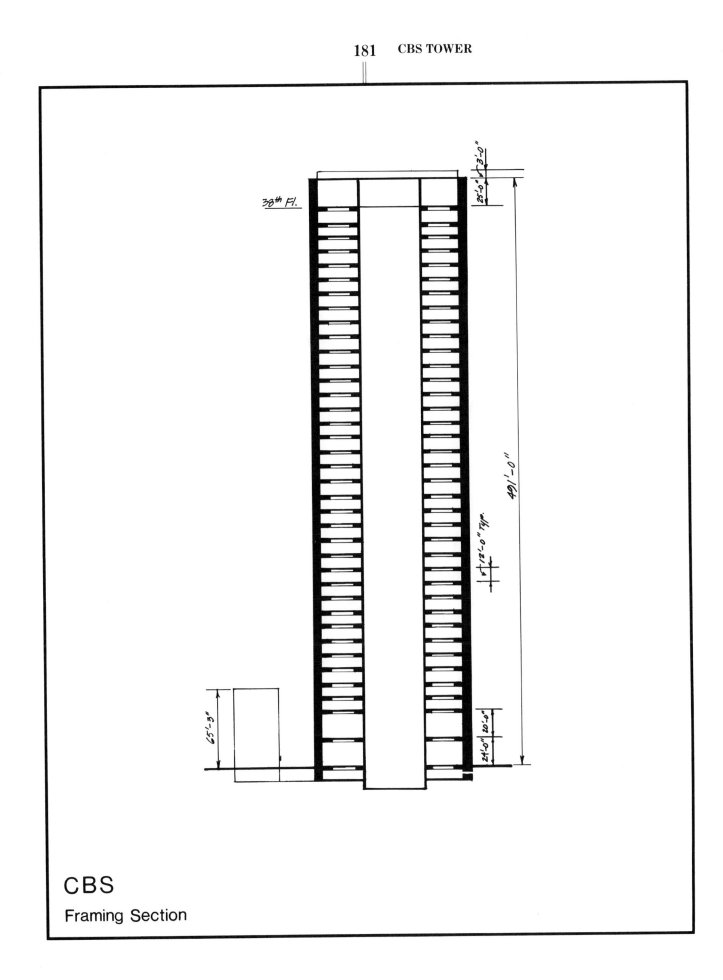

38th Fl.

3'-0"
25'-0"

491'-0"

12'-0" Typ.

65'-3"

10'-0"
24'-0"

CBS
Framing Section

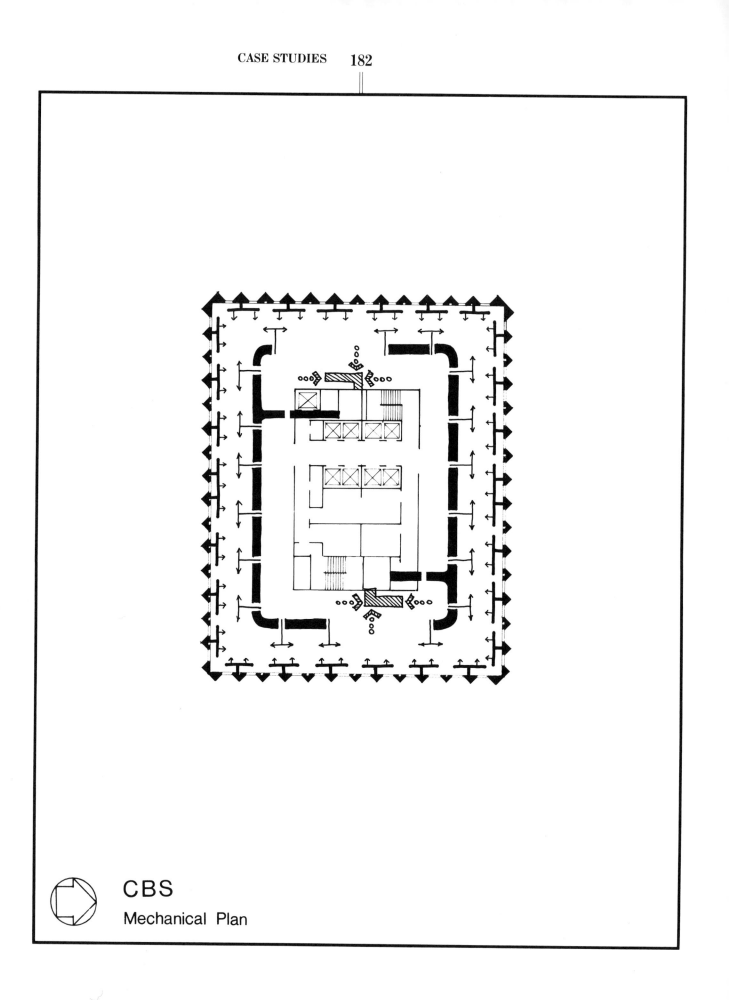

CBS

Mechanical Plan

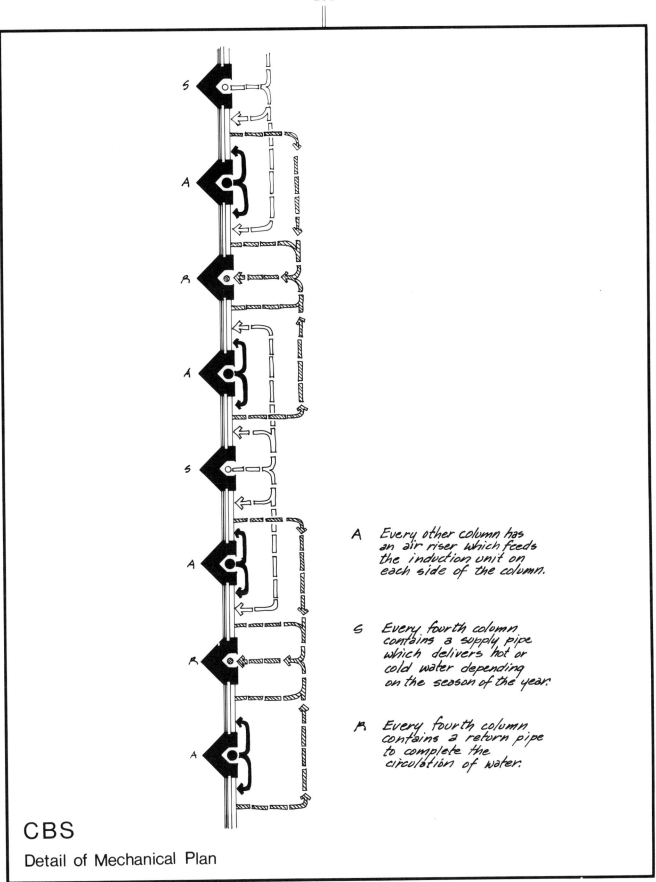

A   Every other column has an air riser which feeds the induction unit on each side of the column.

S   Every fourth column contains a supply pipe which delivers hot or cold water depending on the season of the year.

R   Every fourth column contains a return pipe to complete the circulation of water.

CBS
Detail of Mechanical Plan

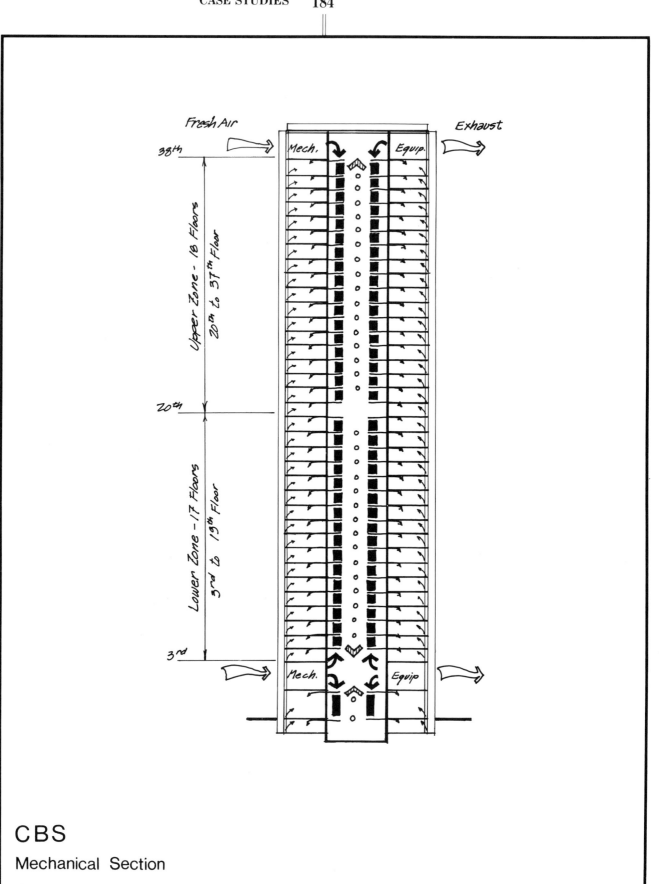

Fresh Air

Exhaust

38th

Mech.   Equip.

Upper Zone - 18 Floors
20th to 37th Floor

20th

Lower Zone - 17 Floors
3rd to 19th Floor

3rd

Mech.   Equip

CBS
Mechanical Section

ONE SHELL PLAZA

ONE Shell Plaza's structure undulates across its facade, revealing its structural anatomy with a sophisticated subtlety that makes a clear and eloquent statement about high-rise concrete technology as a determiner of form.

Where the columns in the CBS building conform to an absolutely rigid, unvarying module, consistent in appearance irrespective of the variation in the loads they carry, the columns at One Shell Plaza vary in size depending on the loads they are required to support.

The basic structural framing is the same as that of the CBS tower. The floor framing spans between a load-bearing core and closely spaced exterior columns.

The designers employed two basic engineering truths in shaping the facade columns that surround the building as the form-givers for their architectural statement. Due to their specific location in a building, certain columns are required to carry either a greater or lesser load than other columns. For example, the columns opposite the core corners are called upon to carry more of a load than those parallel to the core walls, and those columns between the core corners and the facade corners carry progressively lesser loads. These different load-carrying requirements are expressed in One Shell Plaza by adjusting the cross-sectional size of the affected columns to reflect their specific difference in support capacity. It is this change in the size of the regularly spaced columns that gives the building its undulating shape. All the columns are spaced four feet apart, and all the columns are two feet wide; the change in size is effected by changing the column's depth, or dimension perpendicular to the facade. The columns also taper as they rise up from the ground, in response to the decrease in their required load-carrying capacity as the number of floors they support decreases.

In only two minor ways does the building violate the clarity of its basic statement: first, by collecting several columns in order to provide a monumental en-tranceway at the base of the building and second, by exceeding the structurally required size of the corner columns in order to turn the corner symmetrically. As a result of the latter, when One Shell Plaza is viewed on its diagonal, the corner column presents a larger impact than the adjacent columns.

Mechanically, the building deviates from the stereotypic solution of having several major mechanical levels interspersed throughout the building (each such separate mechanical level providing the heating and cooling needs for a group of floors located above and below it). In the case of One Shell Plaza, each floor is provided with two small mechanical-equipment rooms. Each of these rooms serves one-half of the floor on which it is located. The fresh air for these mini-mechanical rooms is introduced through louvers that are recessed at the head of individual windows. Only two mechanical spaces are common to the structure as a whole; one, containing boilers and chillers is located on part of the fiftieth floor, and another, containing cooling towers, is located on the roof.

By placing the structure on the exterior and then using the variation in the load-carrying needs of each individual column, the architects developed a shape that is as inherently true to the building's needs as the flying buttress was to the Gothic cathedral. This type of truthful expression bears up well to the test of time. The preeminence of this structure should grow while other arbitrarily stylistic designs fade into the obscurity reserved for fads.

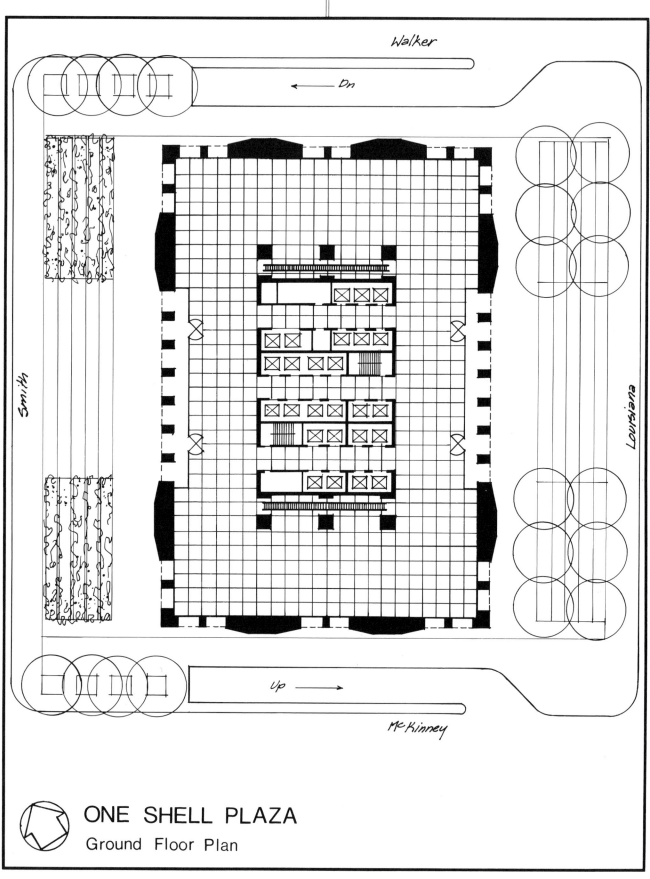

ONE SHELL PLAZA
Ground Floor Plan

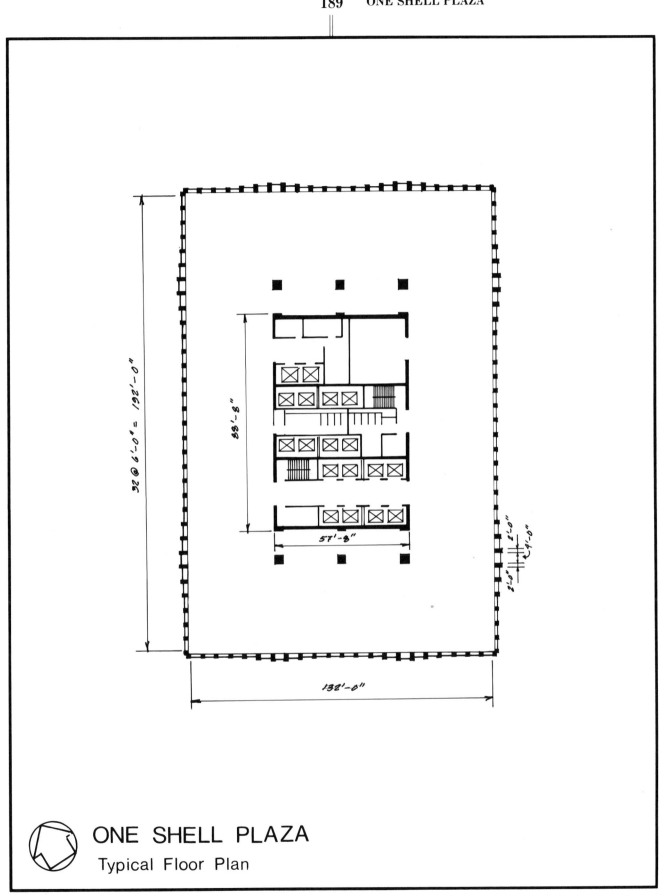

ONE SHELL PLAZA
Typical Floor Plan

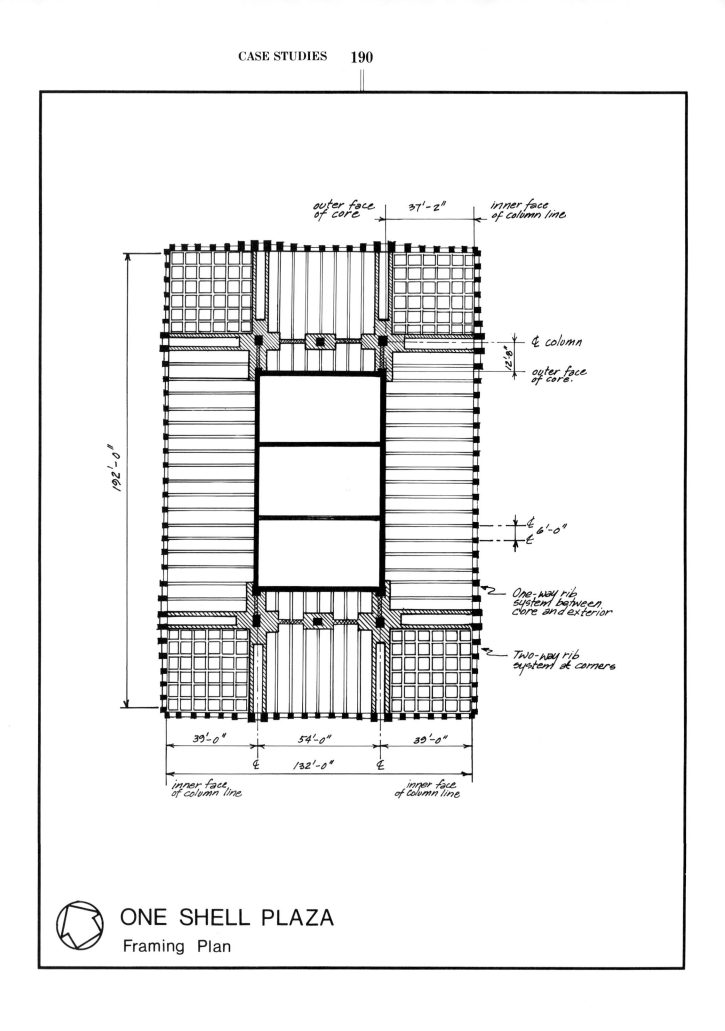

outer face
of core

37'-2"

inner face
of column line

₵ colomn

12'-8"

outer face
of core.

192'-0"

₵ 6'-0"
₵

One-way rib
system between
core and exterior

Two-way rib
system at corners

39'-0"   54'-0"   39'-0"

₵   132'-0"   ₵

inner face
of column line.

inner face
of column line

ONE SHELL PLAZA
Framing Plan

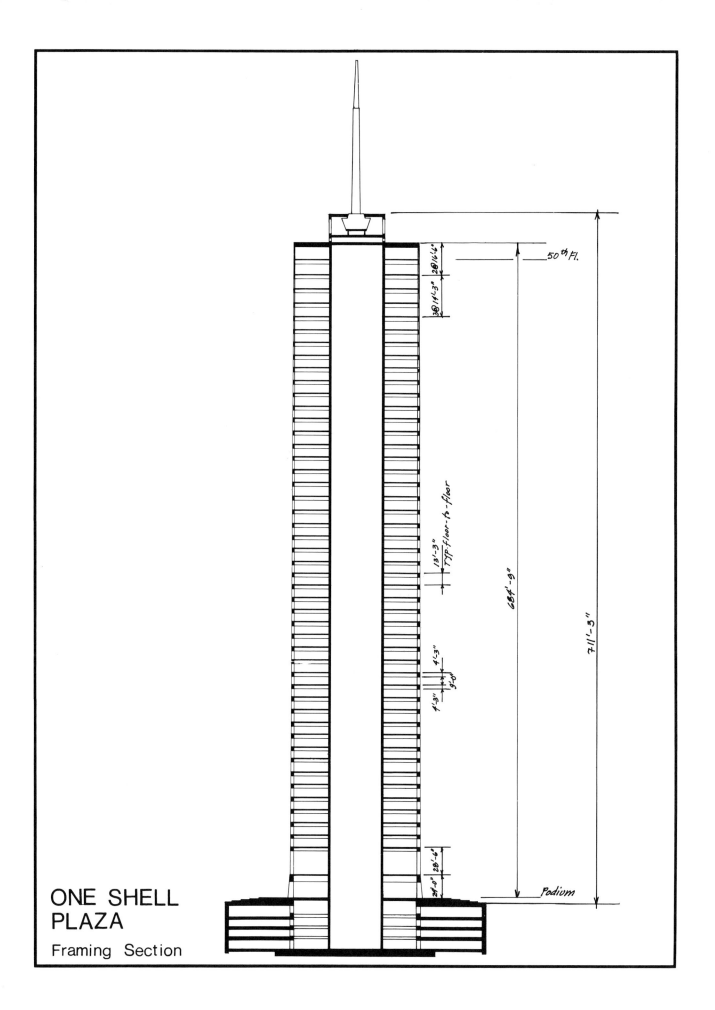

50th Fl.

28'-6"

38'-11'-3"

13'-3"
TYP-floor-to-floor

684'-9"

711'-3"

4'-3"

9'-0"

1'-3"

28'-6"

24'-0"

Podium

ONE SHELL
PLAZA

Framing Section

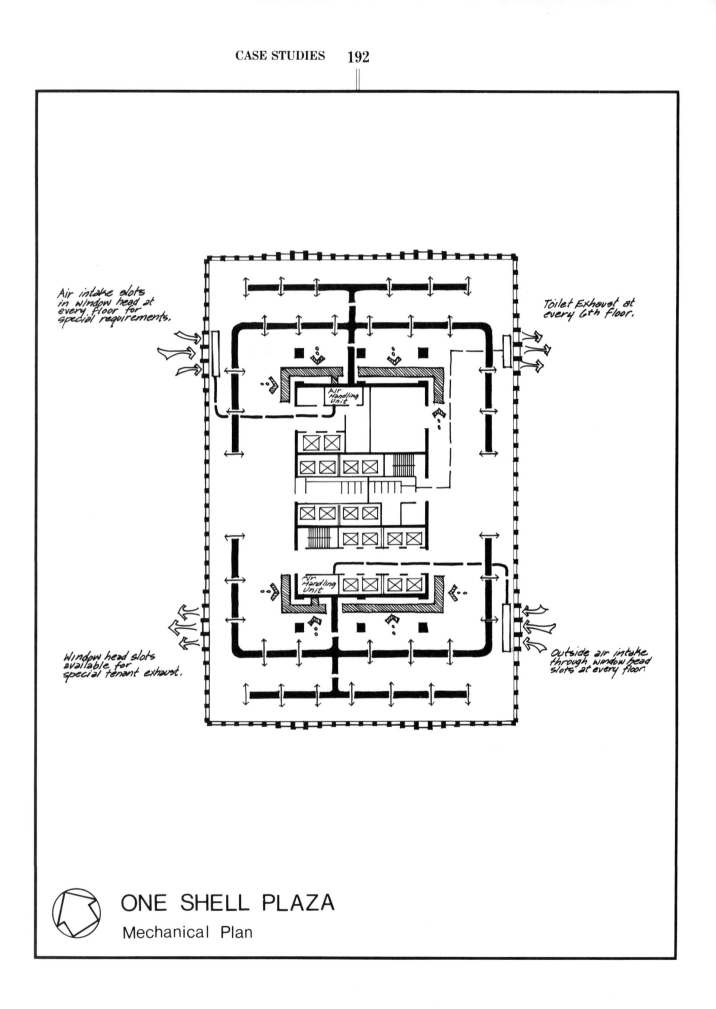

Air intake slots in window head at every floor for special requirements.

Toilet Exhaust at every 6th floor.

Window head slots available for special tenant exhaust.

Outside air intake through window head slots at every floor.

Air Handling Unit

Air Handling Unit

ONE SHELL PLAZA

Mechanical Plan

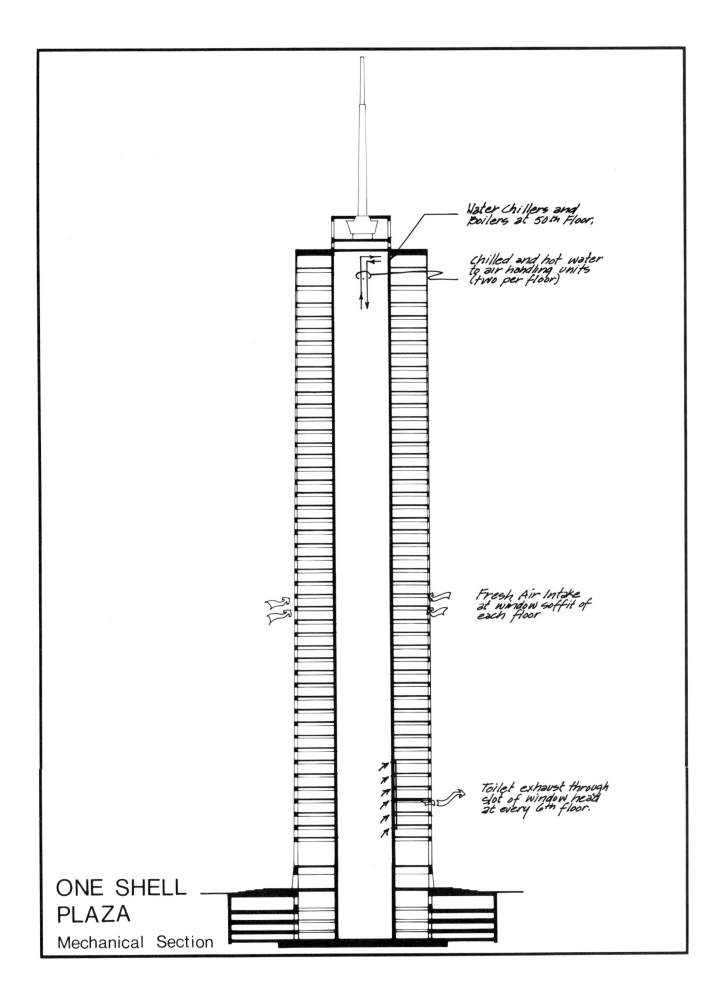

Water Chillers and Boilers at 50th Floor.

Chilled and hot water to air handling units (two per floor)

Fresh Air Intake at window soffit of each floor

Toilet exhaust through slot of window head at every 6th floor.

ONE SHELL PLAZA
Mechanical Section

RICHARDS MEDICAL LABORATORY

THE Richards Medical Laboratory complex at the University of Pennsylvania is one of the more influential structures erected in the United States since World War II. The building's significance is derived from the architect's sophisticated use of an exposed, precast concrete framing system, the articulation of mechanical equipment, and the use of shafts as major form generators.

This structure received worldwide publicity when it was completed and established Louis Kahn as an international force in the architectural world. The three-dimensional expression of what he referred to as "served" (areas used by people) and "servant" (areas needed for equipment and/or circulation) spaces became a new and powerful means of creating structural rhythms and forms. This type of architectural clarity has been adopted by an entire generation of architects.

Imposing brick clad shafts, which are used to bring the air supply to the occupants, to remove exhaust air from the laboratories, and to enclose the stairs, are the dominating form-givers in this cluster of eight-story-high research buildings. From certain perspectives, these towers almost overpower the spaces they serve.

In this type of laboratory building, all the used air must be exhausted directly to the outside because of the dangers of toxicity and cross-contamination. This means that the air circulated throughout the building must all be fresh, rather than being the usual combination of approximately 15 to 25 percent fresh air mixed with recirculated air. The ramification of this is that the shaft sizes for this building's exhaust and fresh air supply must be considerably larger than those of other buildings that can use recirculated air. In designing this laboratory building, Kahn had available in this mechanical system a form-generating source that possessed a significant-enough scale to allow him to create a bold statement by expressing certain truths about how the building functioned. By placing the shafts on the building's exterior rather than concealing them within a central core, and by totally exposing the precast, structural support system, the architect revealed a palette that had no precedent.

While this building has earned a place in history for its innovations, the results seem to have pleased the architectural world far more than the scientists who are forced to live with what is, at best, a very awkward building for their needs. The buildings, however, have received some criticism by other architects as well as by those who use the laboratories. The proper orientation of glass areas in relation to the sun was ignored in favor of compositional organization. One of the four laboratory structures has an extra exhaust flume for reasons of symmetry and balance rather than need. The exposed chords of the precast truss system delight most architects while they frustrate the scientists who must work under them; the scientists are concerned that dust from these trusses may contaminate their experiments. By subdividing the laboratory space into separate building forms, the needed flexibility to rearrange interior work spaces was sacrificed, and a severe limit was placed on the maximum area of contiguous space.

Despite these drawbacks, the Richards Medical Laboratory served as a philosophical and stylistic breakthrough, and it has become the cornerstone of what is known as the "Philadelphia School," which is composed mostly of architects who taught with Kahn at the University of Pennsylvania.

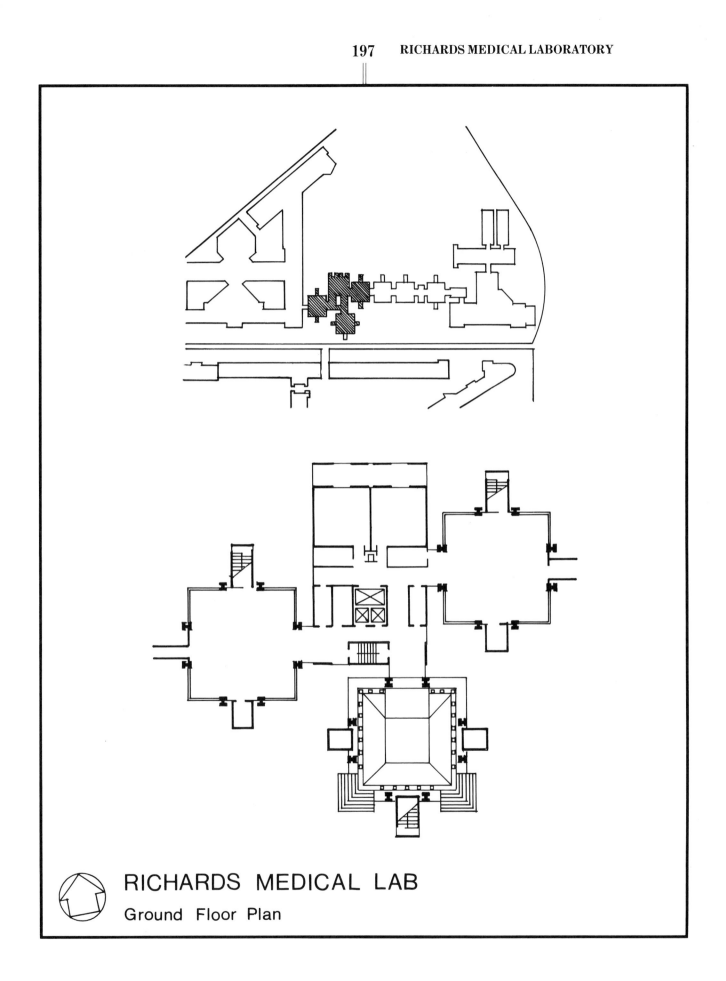

RICHARDS MEDICAL LAB
Ground Floor Plan

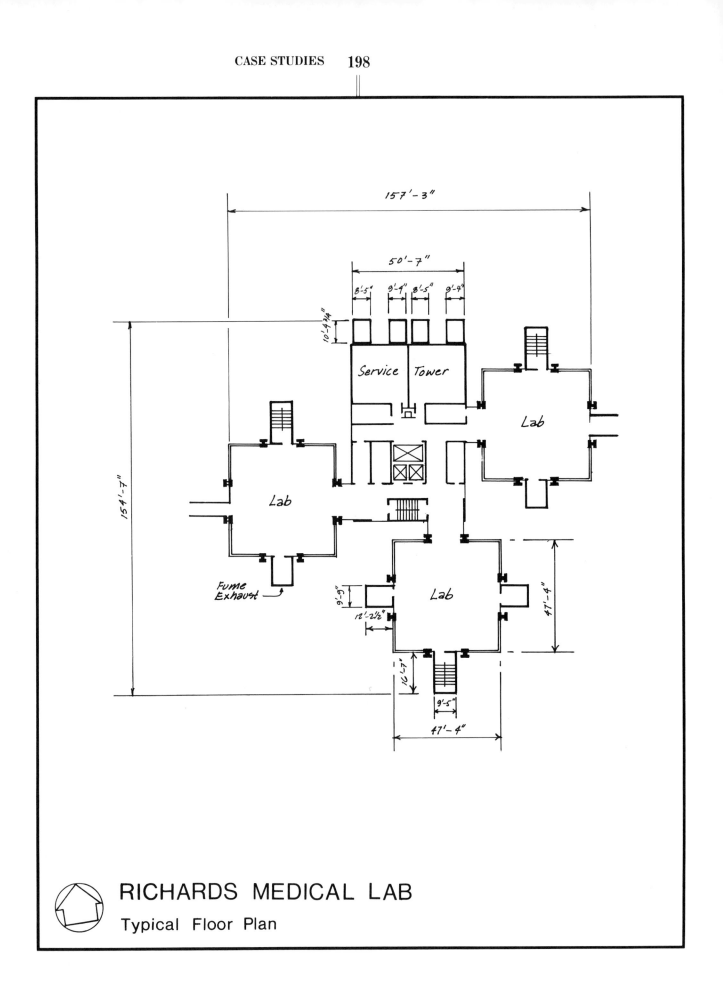

RICHARDS MEDICAL LAB

Typical Floor Plan

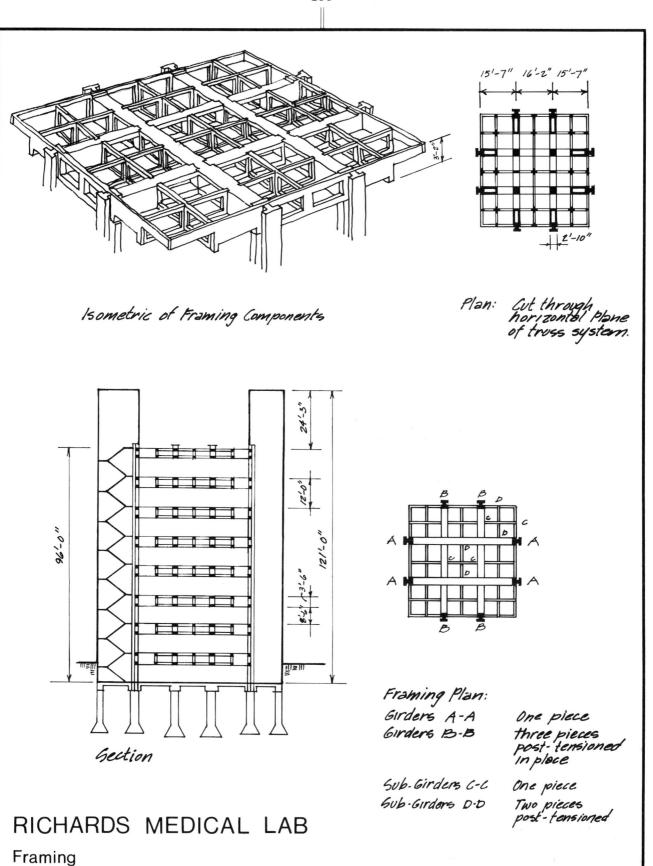

15'-7" 16'-2" 15'-7"

2'-10"

Isometric of Framing Components

Plan: Cut through horizontal Plane of truss system.

24'-3"

12'-0"

121'-0"

8'-4" 3'-6"

96'-0"

Section

B   B   D
         c   C
A   b   A
    D
A   c c   A
    D
B   B

Framing Plan:
Girders A-A   One piece
Girders B-B   three pieces
                   post-tensioned
                   in place

Sub-Girders C-C   One piece
Sub-Girders D-D   Two pieces
                   post-tensioned

RICHARDS MEDICAL LAB

Framing

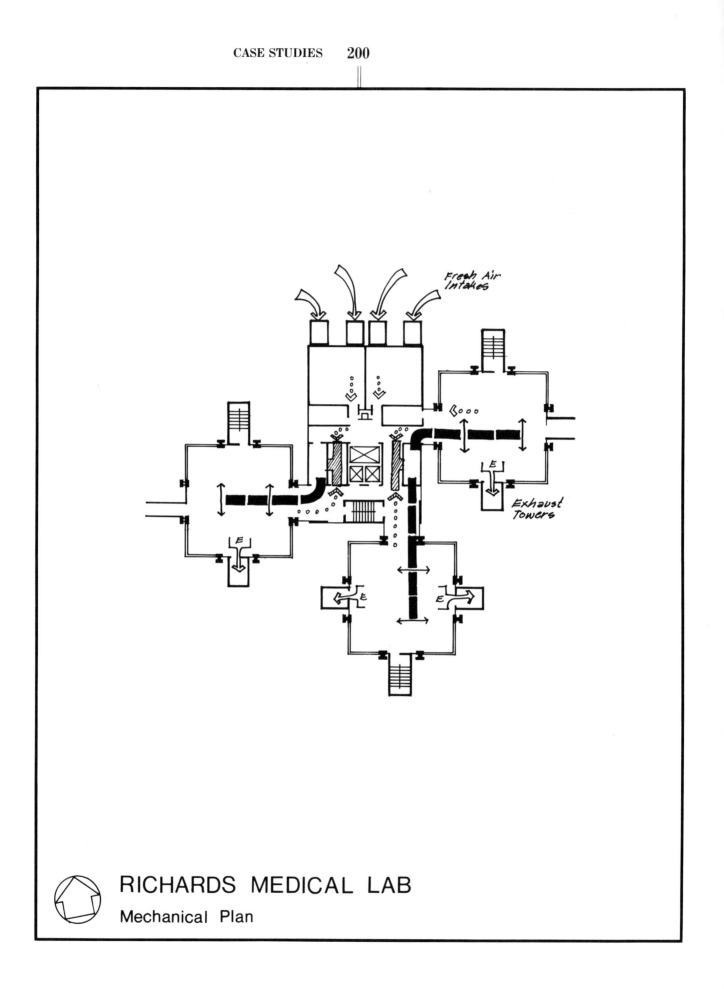

Fresh Air Intakes

Exhaust Towers

RICHARDS MEDICAL LAB
Mechanical Plan

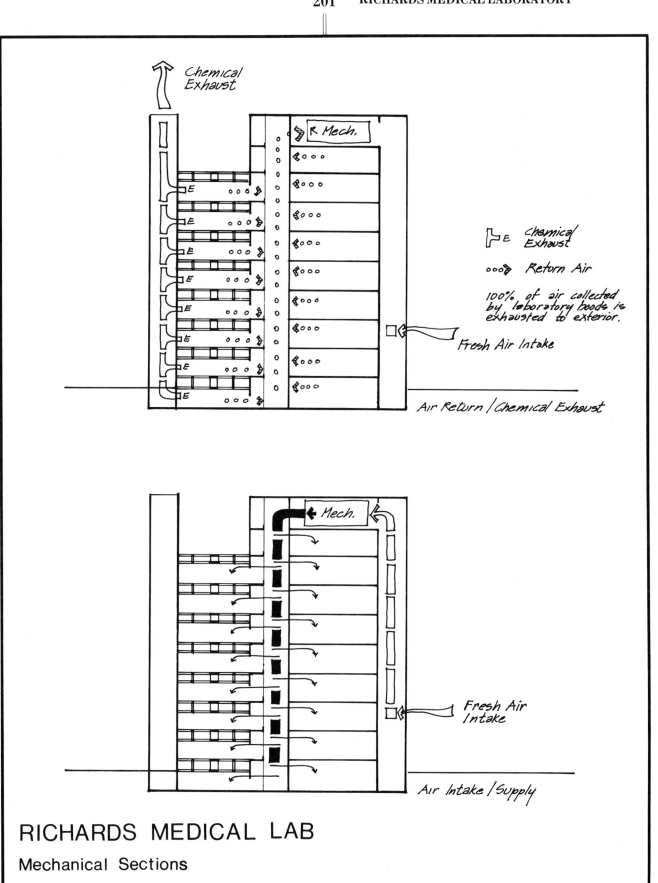

Chemical Exhaust

R Mech.

⌐E Chemical Exhaust

ₒₒₒ↗ Return Air

100% of air collected by laboratory hoods is exhausted to exterior.

Fresh Air Intake

Air Return / Chemical Exhaust

Mech.

Fresh Air Intake

Air Intake / Supply

RICHARDS MEDICAL LAB

Mechanical Sections

HOFFMANN
LaROCHE
BUILDING

THE Hoffmann LaRoche office is an elegant and deceptively simple architectural statement. The building's almost cubic mass is accumulated from an unyielding checkerboard module created by the vertical lines of exterior columns marching around the perimeter at 7½-foot intervals and the horizontal banding of the floor system. The poured-in-place, waffle-concrete floor framing is expressed as the exposed ceiling of every floor. All the air ducts, as well as the spaghetti of wire and telephone lines that are normally stuffed between a structural floor and a hung ceiling of acoustical tile below, are organized and placed above rather than under the structural floor slab. Everything is regulated by and subordinated to the exposed two-way grid of the concrete ribs. Each and every lighting fixture, supply or return air grille is neatly fitted into the recessed 2-foot-by-2-foot-by-18-inch-deep coffered space created between the exposed structural ribs.

Exterior columns, located modularly at the end of every third rib, carry a continuous spandrel beam, which, in turn, supports the ribs. The spandrel beam has been held to the same depth as the waffle slab in order to keep a flush ceiling plane. The spandrel also serves as a sun shield for the recessed glass panels of the facade. Unfortunately, all four building faces are the same, which ignores the effect of the moving sun. A curved, freeform shape containing one of the two required exit stairways is offset slightly beyond the building's otherwise uniformly symmetrical elevations. This oval tower serves as an interesting relief and welcome counterpoint to the building's uncompromising severity.

The horizontal distribution of all the mechanical trades takes place above the structural floor. Above all these ducts and conduits is a walking surface that completes the top layer of the floor sandwich. This floor surface is 4-inch-thick concrete poured over a metal deck. Its span is trivial since it is supported by rows of blocking, which rest on the structural ribs below. In fact, structurally, it could have been thinner, but a minimum of 4 inches is required as a fire separation between floors.

The building can be perceived as a grid of nine equal bays (see structural plans), each one a 40-foot square, with the center one being the core, and the surrounding ones the exposed two-way waffle slabs of the office space. The ribs running parallel to the facade extend for three of these bays, or 120 feet, and are thus three times as long as the ribs merely going from the inner core to the outer wall. These longer ribs must logically be either much larger in cross-section than the shorter ribs or somehow must be supported intermediately. What takes place is that the ribs, which start at the corners of the central core and span over to the exterior spandrel beam, contain more steel reinforcement than the other ribs. This additional reinforcement makes those ribs strong enough to allow them to function as a beam that supports the long ribs at their ⅓ points. The result is that each side of the building is divided into three major structural bays, and the entire building is divided into eight equal major framing bays surrounding the core. All the ribs, however, appear to be uniform, and the visual effect is that of a uniform checkerboard ceiling pattern surrounding the core.

Those columns opposite the core corners support the extra load-carrying ribs, and so they, in turn, must support a greater load than the other columns. The close spacing of the columns around the perimeter, along with help from the continuous spandrel beam, distributes this extra load fairly efficiently to adjacent columns, and thus somewhat equalizes the stress differences. All the columns were constructed with the same outside dimensions, regardless of the amount of load they carry.

By suppressing a precise visual expression of how the stresses are distributed in the floor system, the architects were able to make all the exposed ribs of the floor system constant in size, depth, and spacing. The resulting ease of subdividing the space with partitions placed beneath the uniform pattern provided by the rib bottoms located every 2½ feet in both directions makes the basic decision understandable and perhaps even forgivable.

The coffered ceiling texture has excellent acoustical features. The mess of mechanical equipment remains concealed, with access from removable panels. In addition, the total depth of structural and mechan-

ical space is less than the amount that a standard hung ceiling system normally requires.

This tidy logical integration of systems, which lets one see and thus sense the total framing structure from within every office, is clearly visual from the exterior. At night when the lights are on, the layers of the waffle system glow and hover in place.

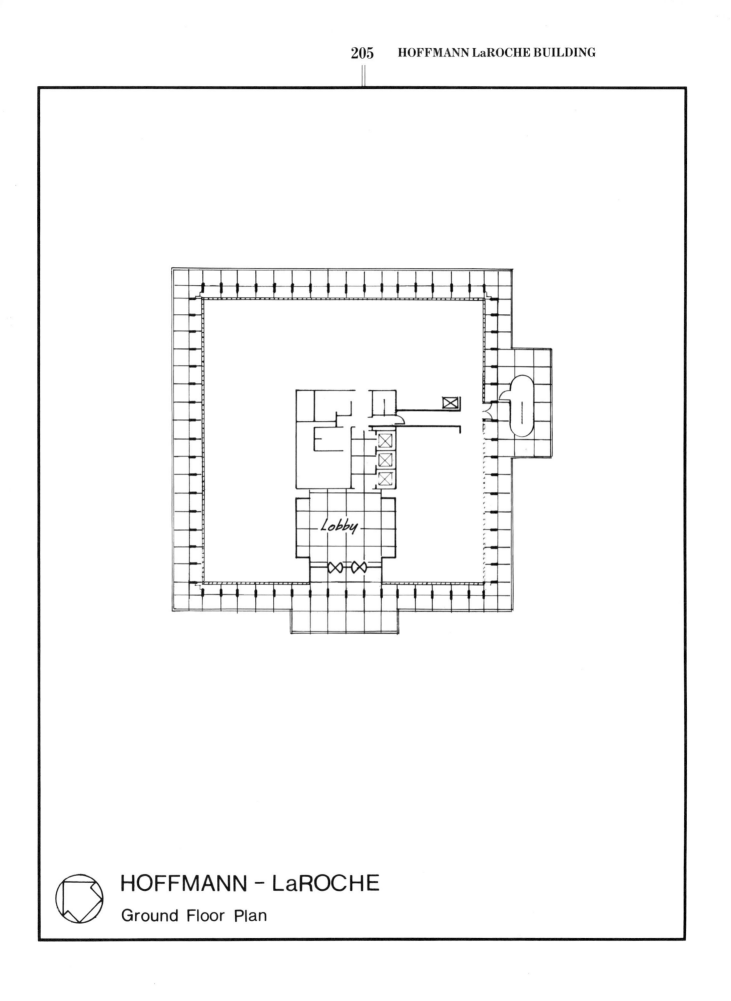

Lobby

HOFFMANN - LaROCHE

Ground Floor Plan

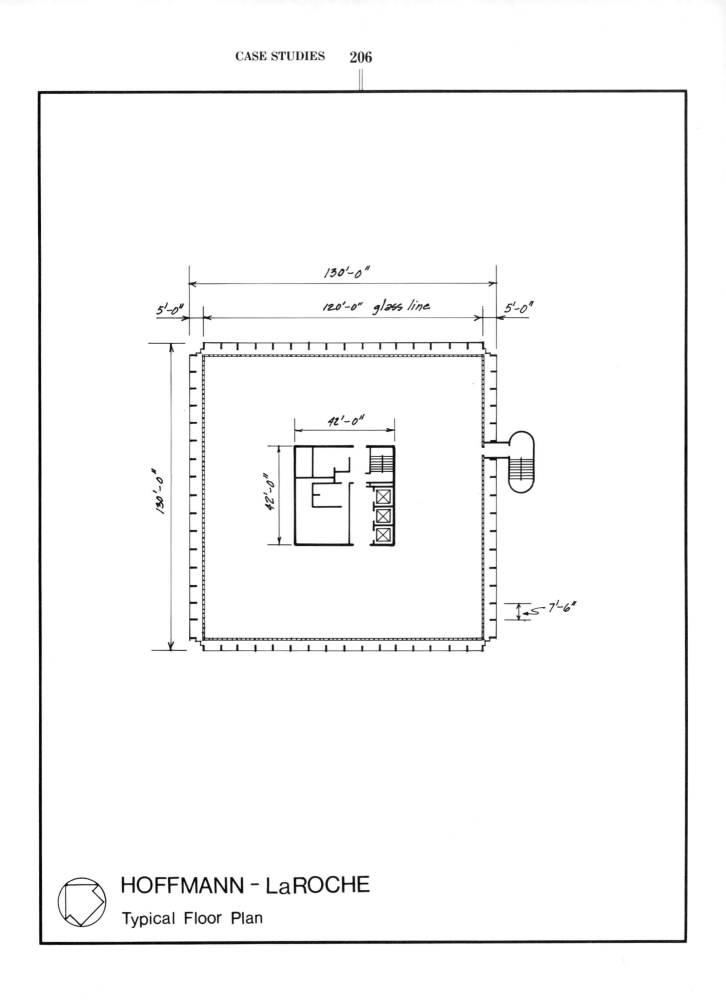

130'-0"

5'-0"   120'-0" glass line   5'-0"

130'-0"

42'-0"

42'-0"

7'-6"

HOFFMANN - LaROCHE

Typical Floor Plan

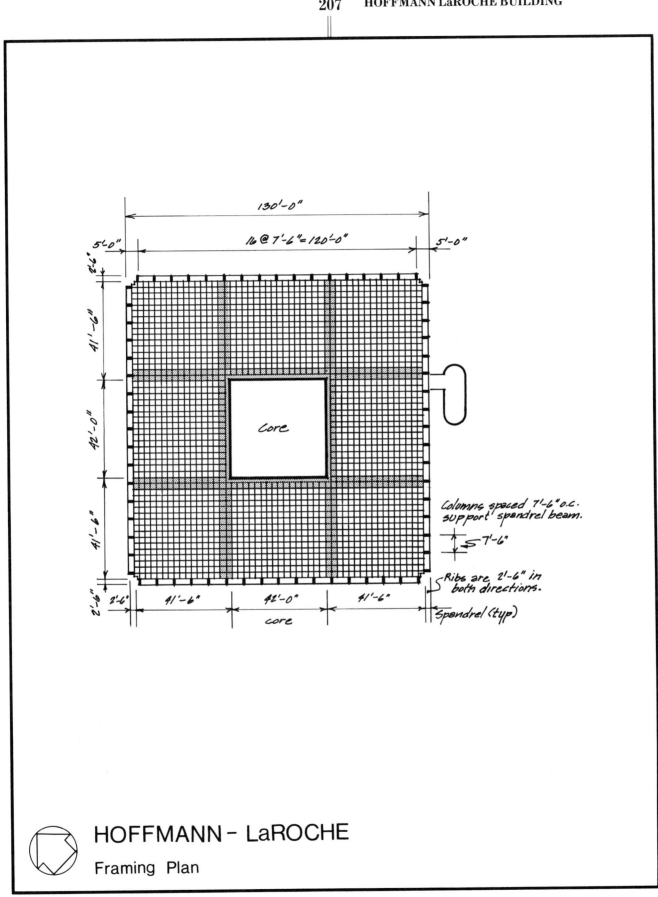

HOFFMANN - LaROCHE

Framing Plan

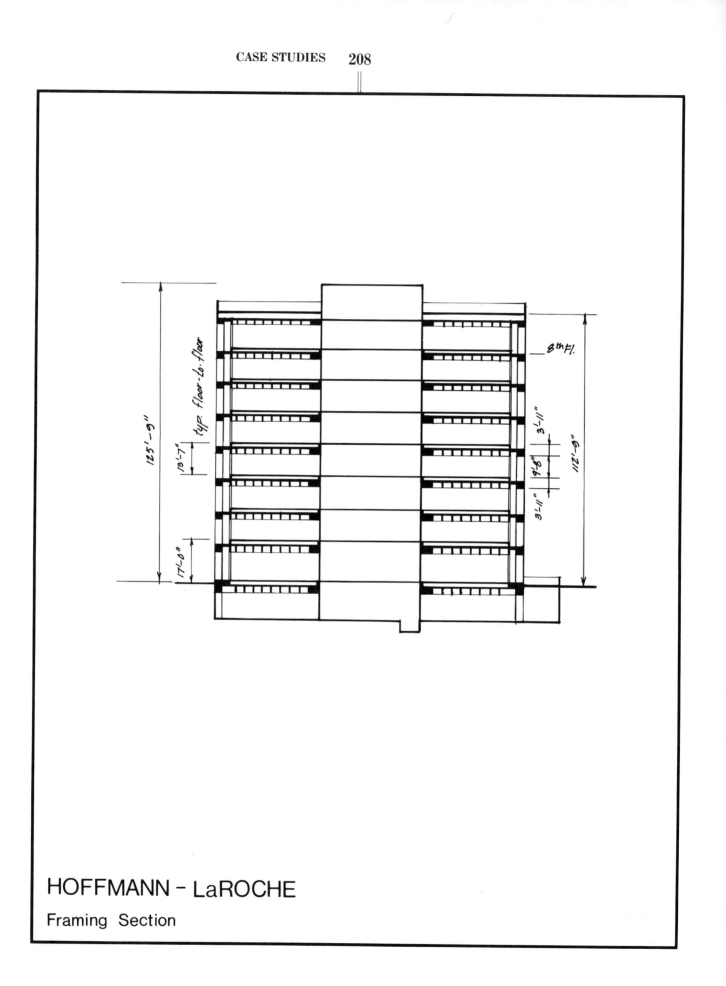

HOFFMANN - LaROCHE

Framing Section

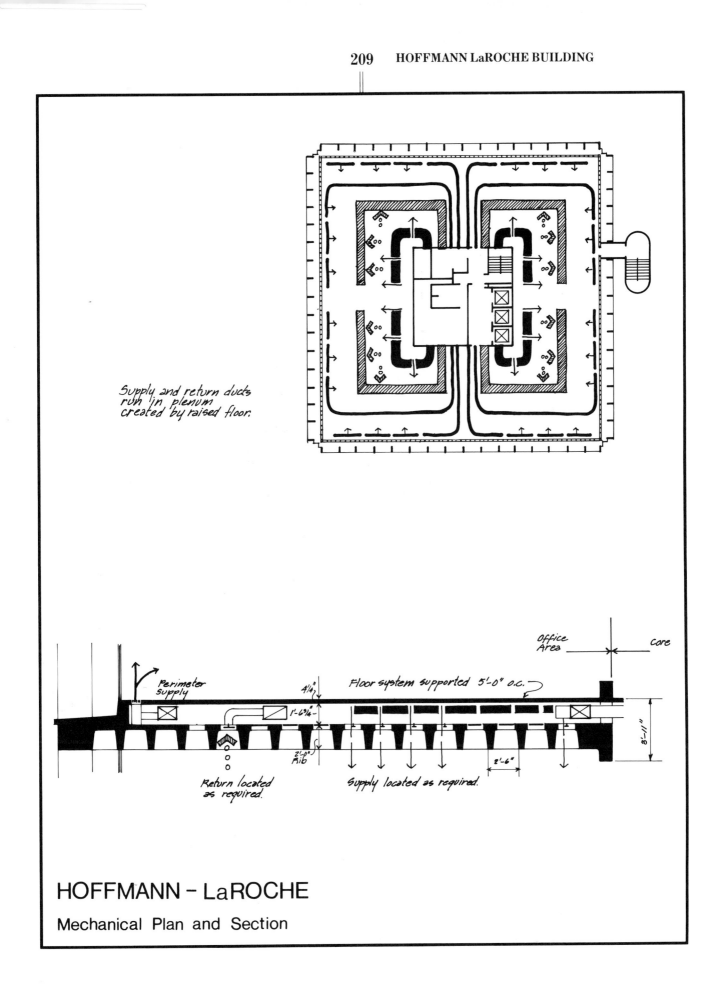

Supply and return ducts run in plenum created by raised floor.

Office Area   Core

Perimeter supply

Floor system supported 5'-0" o.c.

4¼"

1'-6¾"

2'-0" Rib

8'-11"

2'-6"

Return located as required.

Supply located as required.

HOFFMANN – LaROCHE

Mechanical Plan and Section

YALE ART GALLERY

THE Yale University Art Gallery, or Design Laboratory, as it was originally called, was Louis Kahn's first major work. Although the stylistic influences of Corbusier and Mies are apparent, Kahn's unique organization of spaces and services emerges clearly. Once inside the building, the most distinguishing and notable architectural feature is the mood created by the stark, rhythmic texture of the triangular ceiling grid, which consists of exposed concrete ribs spaced 2½ feet apart in all three directions.

Essentially, the basic floor plan consists of three segments. There are two 40-foot-wide exhibit spaces separated by a 27-foot-wide central core. This central module contains the vertical movement through the building in the form of two stairhalls and a service elevator, as well as mechanical-equipment shafts. The ceiling of the core is wire mesh, which has an interesting texture and also functions as the central, return-air grille for the entire floor.

The ceiling in the approximately 40-by-80-foot exhibit spaces incorporates the structural load-carrying members; ducts for the supply air; recesses for the lighting and, as an extra bonus, provides good acoustical baffling. An inspection of the omnidirectional texture of equilaterial triangles on the ceiling surface reveals the grid to be the underside of 2-foot-deep triangular pyramids or tetrahedrons. Further analysis reveals that one direction of the triangular pattern is actually a continuous sloping rib that spans across the exhibit space to girders at each edge. These girders were made very wide in proportion to their depth so their depth would exactly match that of the ribs. The result is that the underside of the ribbing and girders creates an absolutely flat, horizontal ceiling plane throughout the entire building. The other two ribs of the three-way rib pattern turn out to be little more than decorative structurally, but they do provide contiguous voids for the small, round air-supply ducts and electric raceways for the lighting, both of which are placed between the structural ribs. An intriguing aspect of all this is that while the ducts and raceways are actually exposed, they are recessed and shielded by the three-dimensional aspects of the tetrahedron so that they blend unobtrusively into the ceiling texture.

It is interesting to note that Kahn's original concept was to make all three sides of the tetrahedron load-carrying, but a combination of building-code restraints and unresolvable construction problems prevented this. The actual structure has much of the originally intended appearance, even though Kahn did have to make compromises. Careful visual inspection reveals that the load-carrying rib is actually slightly thicker than the texture ribs, thus subtly expressing its different responsibility.

Few ceilings dominate a space to the degree that this one does. The Yale art gallery possesses an interior as striking and as successful today as when it was built. Perhaps the richness of the building's interior in contrast to its exterior, unconsciously borrows from Kahn's heritage, where the tsar and the very rich wore their mink coats with the fur side in.

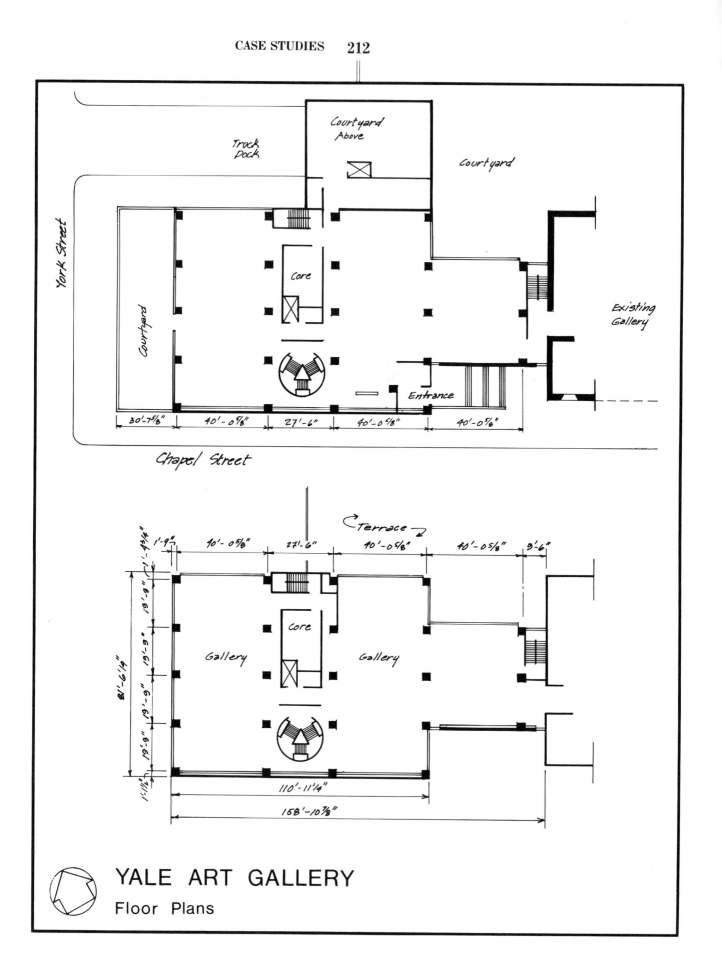

YALE ART GALLERY
Floor Plans

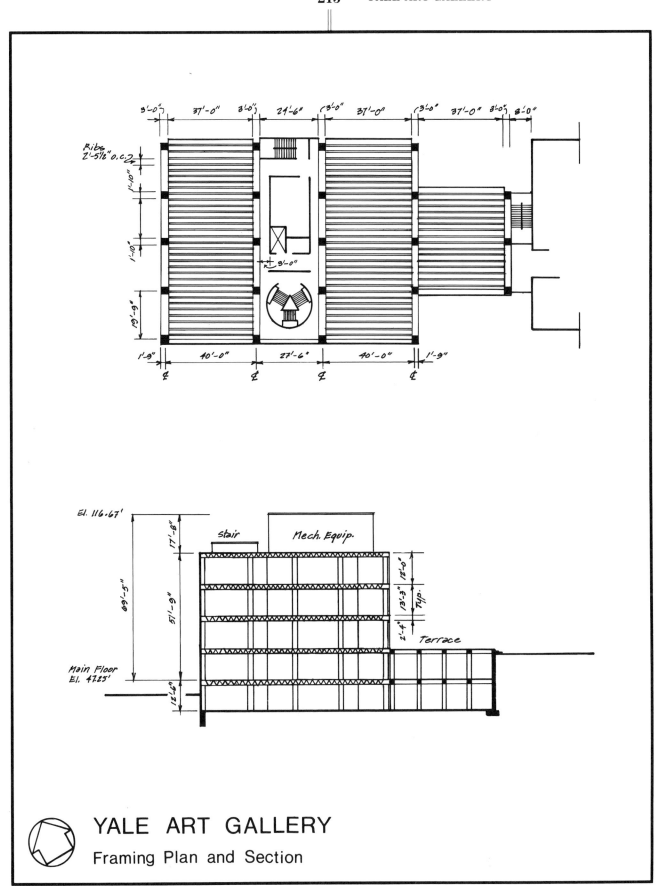

YALE ART GALLERY
Framing Plan and Section

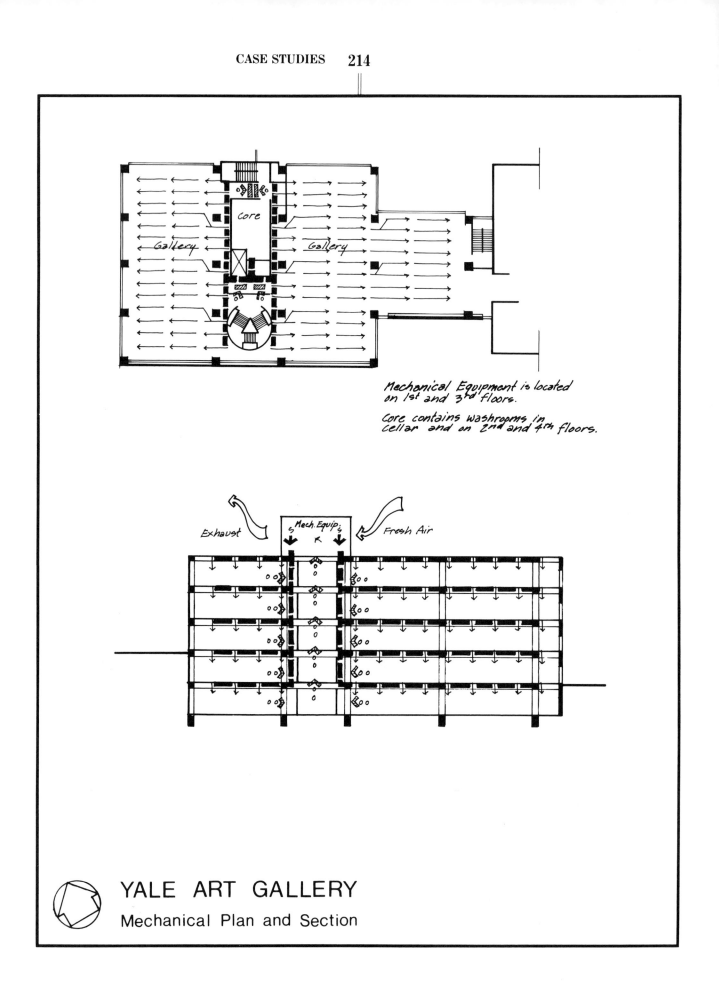

Mechanical Equipment is located
on 1st and 3rd floors.

Core contains washrooms in
cellar and on 2nd and 4th floors.

Exhaust   Mech. Equip.   Fresh Air

YALE ART GALLERY

Mechanical Plan and Section

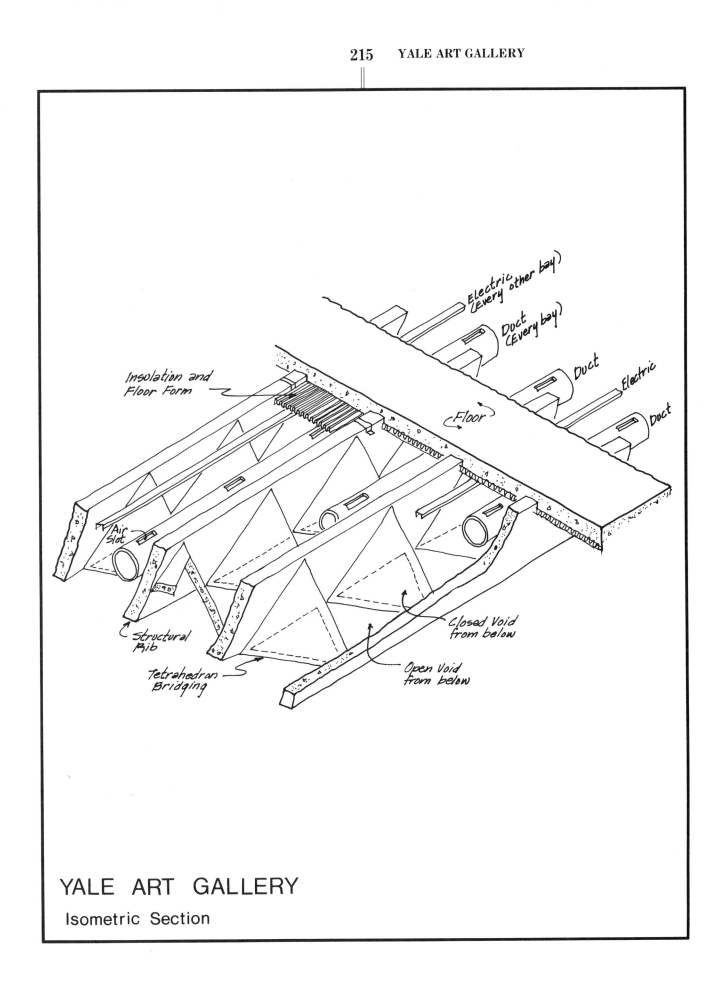

Electric
(Every other bay)

Duct
(Every bay)

Duct

Electric

Duct

Floor

Insulation and
Floor Form

Air
Slot

Structural
Rib

Tetrahedron
Bridging

Open Void
from below

Closed Void
from below

YALE ART GALLERY

Isometric Section

M.I.T.
EARTH
SCIENCE
LABORATORY

IN the Earth Science laboratory at MIT, the architects attempted to do several interesting things. Most significantly, they took the standard core functions, divided them into two parts, and placed each of these half cores at longitudinally opposite ends of the building. The immediate advantage is that this leaves the usable part of every floor undivided.

The framing system consists of 3′-6″ deep concrete I-beams, which span parallel to the end cores across the short dimension of the building. The vertical support system is a row of columns individually placed under each end of every floor beam. The relatively close, 9-foot, center-to-center spacing of these 2′-6″ wide columns led to a determination to collect them before they reached the ground with a 13½-foot-deep post-tensioned girder, in order to provide a more open entrance area. This strong, visible horizontal band is matched with a similar one at the building's top. The upper band serves as a nonstructural mask for the mechanical equipment located behind it. The air intake at this top level is disguised by using cleverly concealed scoops that are similar in appearance to the concrete member used to house the peripheral induction units at each floor. The building's overall form evolves from the crisp clean articulation of the end cores, which are in consort with the rhythm of closely spaced columns perched securely on their oversized pedestal-like girders.

Locating the cores at the ends of the building, rather than at the more traditional center, created a number of advantages in addition to providing the uninterrupted, open floor space. Each of the two required stairs is located in an opposite core. This solution provides maximum exiting safety because it eliminates all dead-end spaces. All the elevators are placed in one core, and the washrooms in the other, providing a clarity of circulation. Unfortunately, the amount of vertical shaft space provided within the cores turned out to be woefully inadequate for the high demands and constant layout changes that user needs impose upon a university research laboratory.

Since it was decided not to install a hung ceiling because it would impede access to the mechanical equipment above it, Pei was faced with a problem of how to integrate the horizontal ducts which would have to emerge from the end cores and then run across the directional grain of the floor beams. This problem was solved by casting a series of chamfered, rectangular openings into the beams to permit the ducts to penetrate them. The exposure of beams, ducts, and lights create interesting statements of what is taking place.

Return air is transferred through sound-buffered ducts into the open, central corridor. The air then flows down the corridor to a vertical return shaft. This method of using an exit corridor as an open return-air space is not acceptable as a fire hazard under most of today's building codes. Exhaust air from the laboratories is handled by a separate system. One interesting aspect of this system is that return air collected from nonlaboratory areas is used as a separate supply-air source which is provided for each toxic laboratory exhaust hood. The air for the building's occupants contains the usual mix of fresh air and recirculated air. In keeping with the theme of expressing most elements, the rooms, laboratories, and corridor do not have a hung ceiling to conceal the structure or mechanical systems.

Despite the problem the university has had with the lack of adequate mechanical shaft space, as well as some terrible wind-tunnel effects in the portico entrance area, which eventually led to a redesign of the entrance, the building makes a handsome contribution to the campus. One could wish for more honesty in the handling of the two similarly scaled, horizontal bands at the top and bottom, but must admire the handsome use of texture and subtle reveal to create a structure that will probably age more gracefully than most other poured concrete edifices.

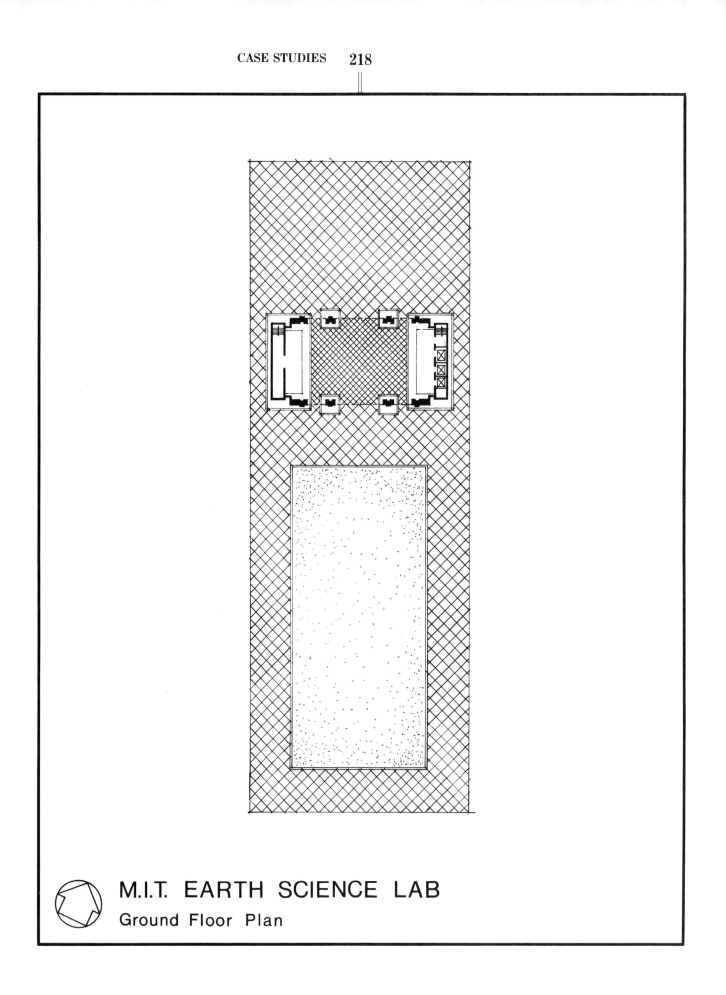

M.I.T. EARTH SCIENCE LAB
Ground Floor Plan

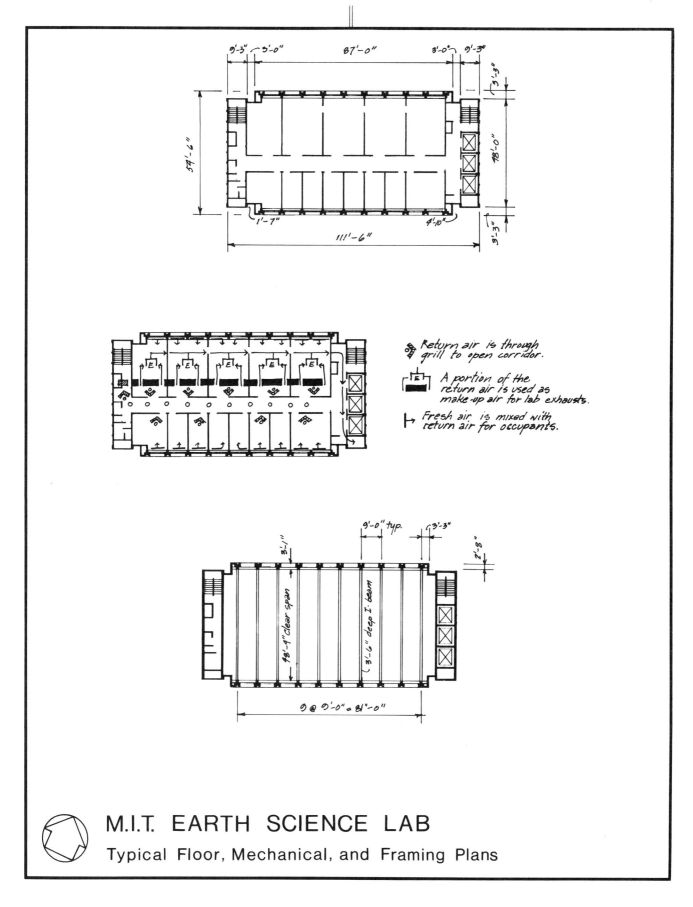

Return air is through grill to open corridor.

A portion of the return air is used as make-up air for lab exhausts.

Fresh air is mixed with return air for occupants.

M.I.T. EARTH SCIENCE LAB
Typical Floor, Mechanical, and Framing Plans

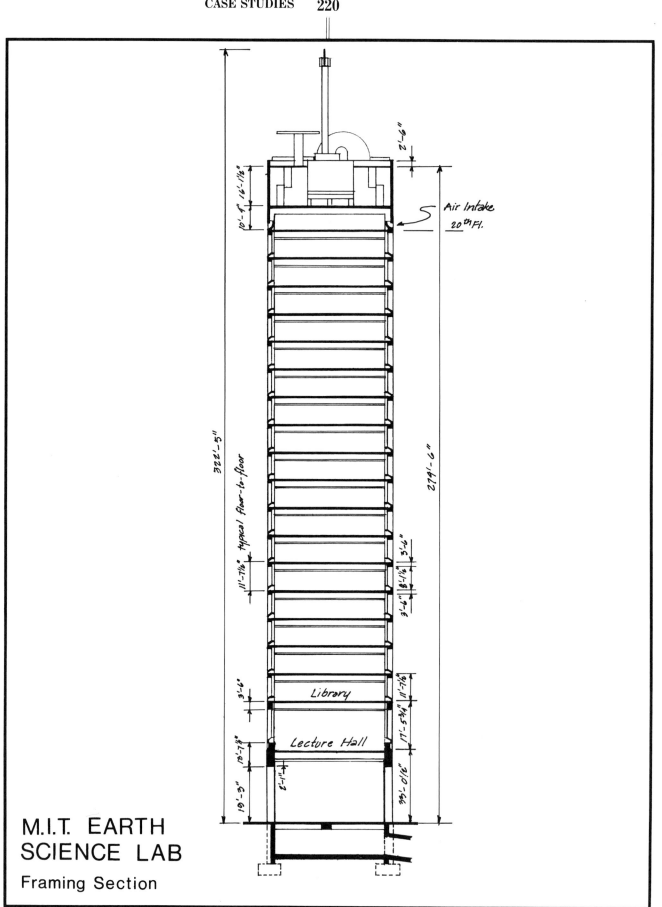

Air Intake
20th Fl.

Library

Lecture Hall

M.I.T. EARTH
SCIENCE LAB

Framing Section

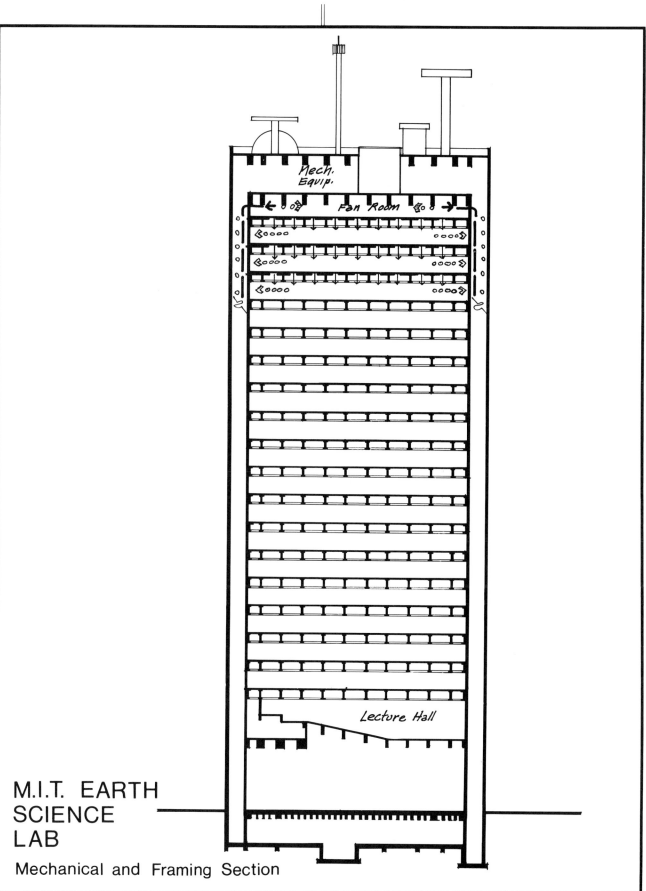

Mech.
Equip.

Fan Room

Lecture Hall

M.I.T. EARTH
SCIENCE
LAB

Mechanical and Framing Section

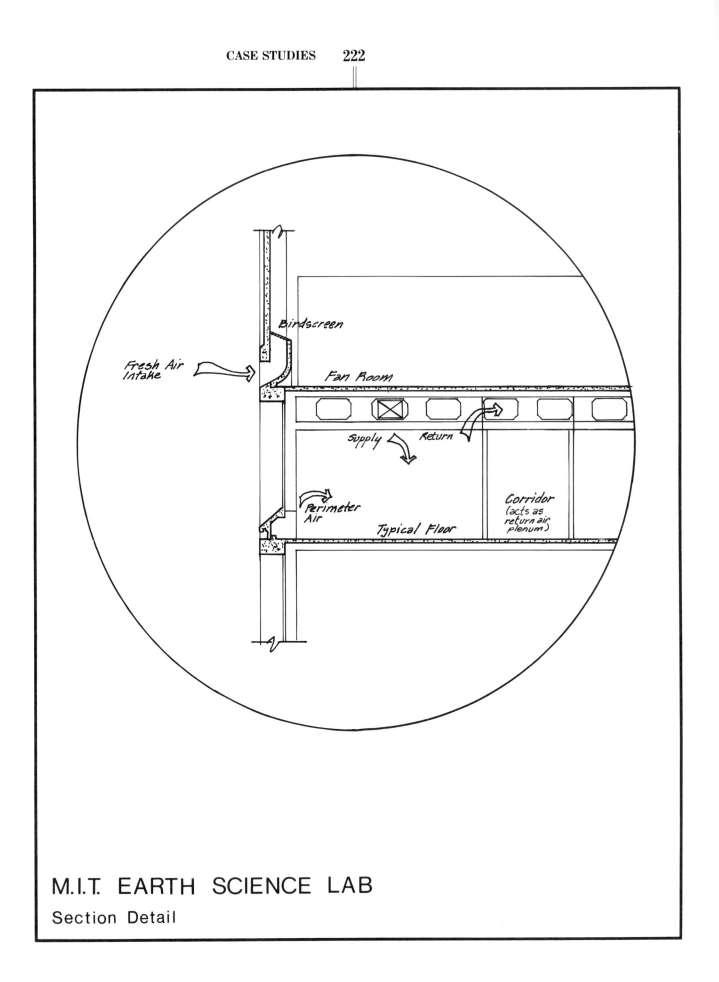

Birdscreen

Fresh Air
Intake

Fan Room

Supply   Return

Perimeter
Air

Typical Floor

Corridor
(acts as
return air
plenum)

M.I.T. EARTH SCIENCE LAB
Section Detail

AMERICAN LIFE INSURANCE

THIS very neatly designed building in Wilmington, Delaware, refines many of the classic detailing tricks that had their roots in the Bauhaus and were developed by the Breuers of the world. This tradition has flowered in this modest building, which is a marvelous example of texture, changes in planes, and shadowing.

In this quietly understated office tower, I.M. Pei has used split end cores in order to obtain maximum contiguous floor space. In the MIT tower, which also had exterior end cores, Pei ran the floor-beam pattern parallel to these cores, across the structure's short dimension, but in the American Life Insurance Company building, the beam pattern runs across the longitudinal dimension of the building, which spans from core to core. This apparently minor change in approach opens up an entirely new array of aesthetic possibilities. By running the beams parallel to the facade, there is no longer a need for columns, either in the facade or anywhere else; the cores themselves serve as the only vertical support. In this configuration, the beams are called upon to span the building's largest dimension. The longer span would normally require the framing to have a proportionally larger depth, and this larger depth might create some problems by increasing the overall floor-to-floor dimension. All of this could have had a major impact on the appearance and overall scale of the facade had not the floor beams been post-tensioned in order to reduce their depth-to-span ratio, thus avoiding the excessive depth that their span would have necessitated. The use of this process has been subtly conveyed to the viewer by sculpturing the beam shape to symbolize the draping pattern of the post-tensioned cable. Additionally, the location of the embedded anchoring of the cables is stated on the exterior with a quiet circle. In fact, the use of a hierarchy of textures on the exposed poured concrete is extremely well handled throughout. This is seen in the change of scale that indicates the marking of wall-form ties versus post-tensioning anchors, as well as in the use of different textures and boarding patterns to distinguish and articulate the foundations, the floor levels, and the sweep of the beams.

The location of the cores, with their mechanical shafts, at the ends of the occupied space, presented Pei with some interesting possibilities in terms of expressing the horizontal aspects of the environmental system. The problem of integrating the duct system with the beam pattern is vastly simplified since the two systems are parallel to each other. What was actually done is a bit disappointing. The 3'-1" deep girders, are supported on piers at the edge of the cores, and the spaces between these piers are used alternately for supply and return risers. At this point one might expect the ducts to run exposed between each pair of girders, which does not happen. First, the architects hung a ceiling between the girders, part way down their depth, which makes the girders look shallower than they actually are. Then they concealed the ducts above the hung ceiling, where they could not contribute to any visual statement. Finally, a series of ribs were located at right angles to the load-carrying girders. These ribs added some cross-bracing stability, but they wound up creating a grid pattern on the ceiling that confuses the image of what is happening structurally. The solution does have two advantages. It provides some accoustical control, as well as a two-directional rib surface against which to terminate subdividing partitions.

Despite some frustration over the unclear expression in the interior of the mechanical/structural mesh, the building's exterior articulation of functions and spaces is clean and elegant. One delightful advantage of having exterior end cores is the possibility of providing a window and a view while waiting for an elevator—a feature that the architects handsomely exploited with changes in planes on the building's exterior concrete surface that relieves the rigid box shape, and creates textures with their shadow patterns. The manner in which the pair of stairs are expressed is also worthy of close attention in order to appreciate how they, too, were articulated without being overdone or cute.

Actually, two separate buildings are enclosed in the structure: the office tower under discussion and a low, horizontal building that houses a bank on the ground floor. The entrance-lobby space does an outstanding job of linking the two masses together while allowing each to maintain its own integrity. This is a most sophisticated building, whose praises somehow remain unsung compared to the majority of Pei's work even though this building is elegantly proportioned and contains some of his best detailing.

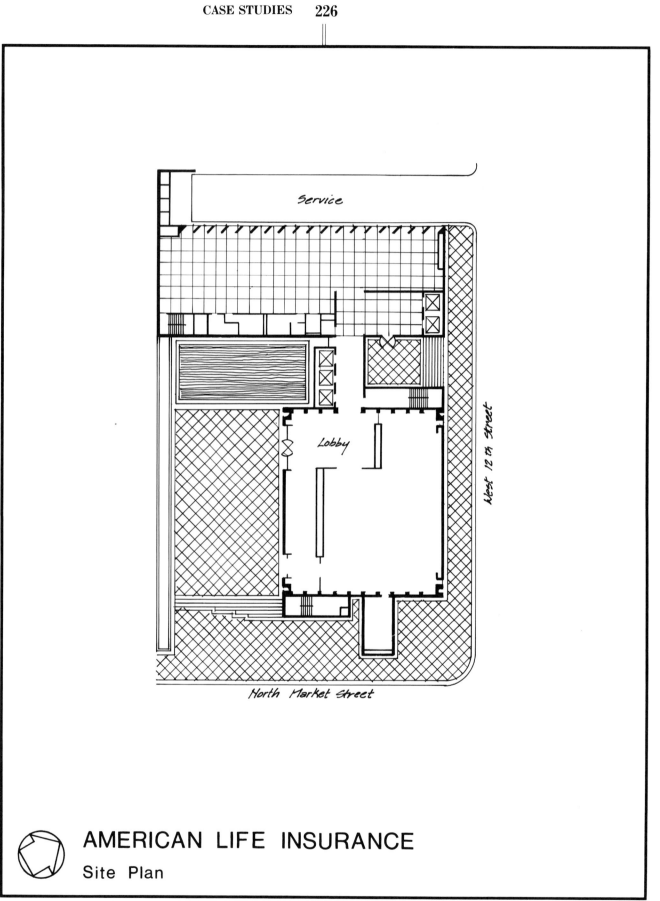

Service

West 12 th Street

Lobby

North Market Street

AMERICAN LIFE INSURANCE
Site Plan

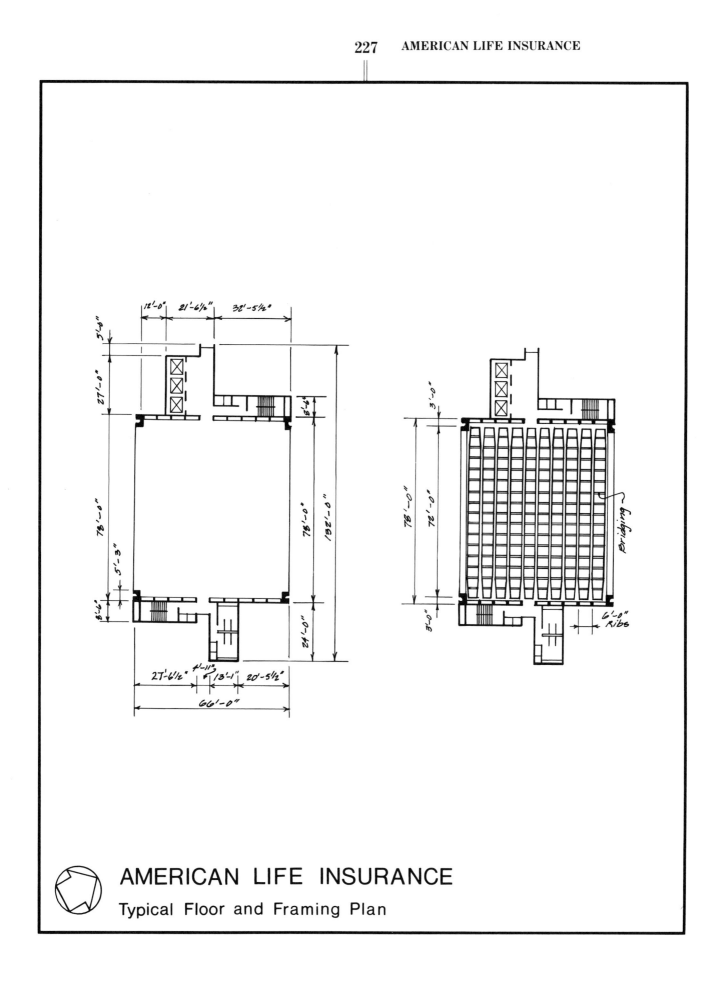

AMERICAN LIFE INSURANCE

Typical Floor and Framing Plan

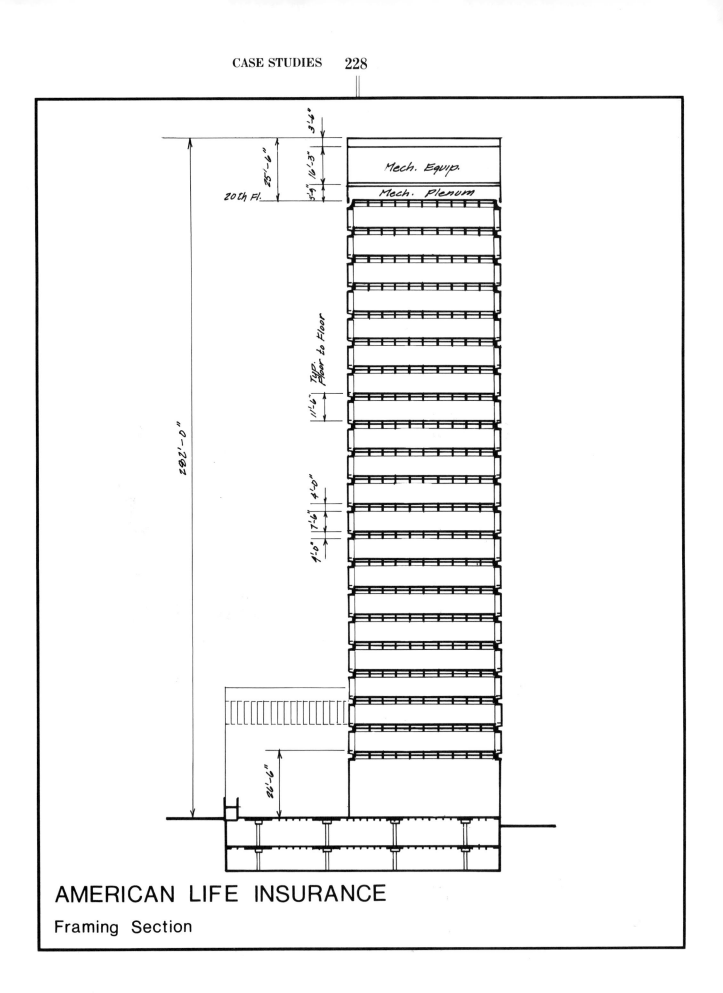

AMERICAN LIFE INSURANCE

Framing Section

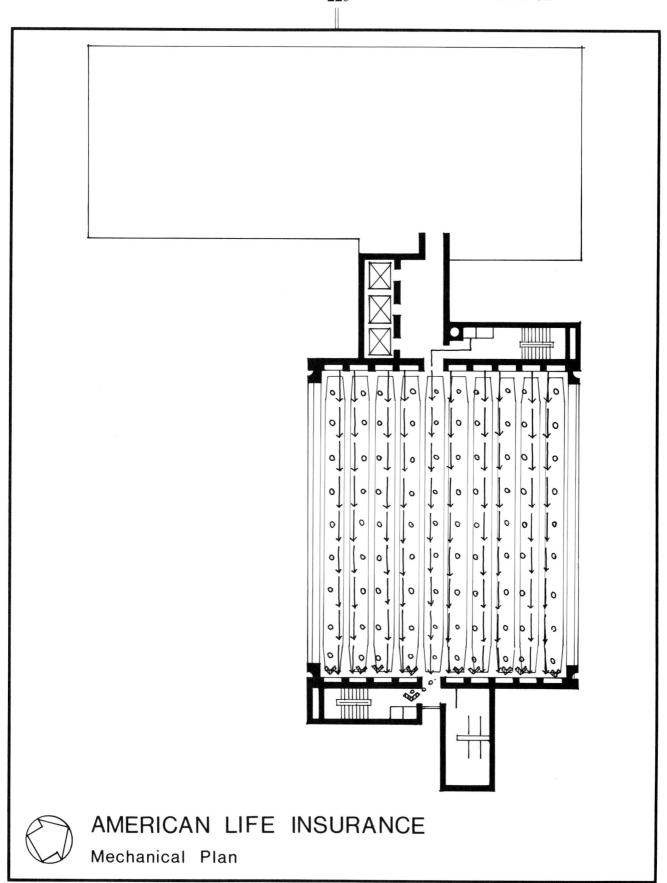

AMERICAN LIFE INSURANCE
Mechanical Plan

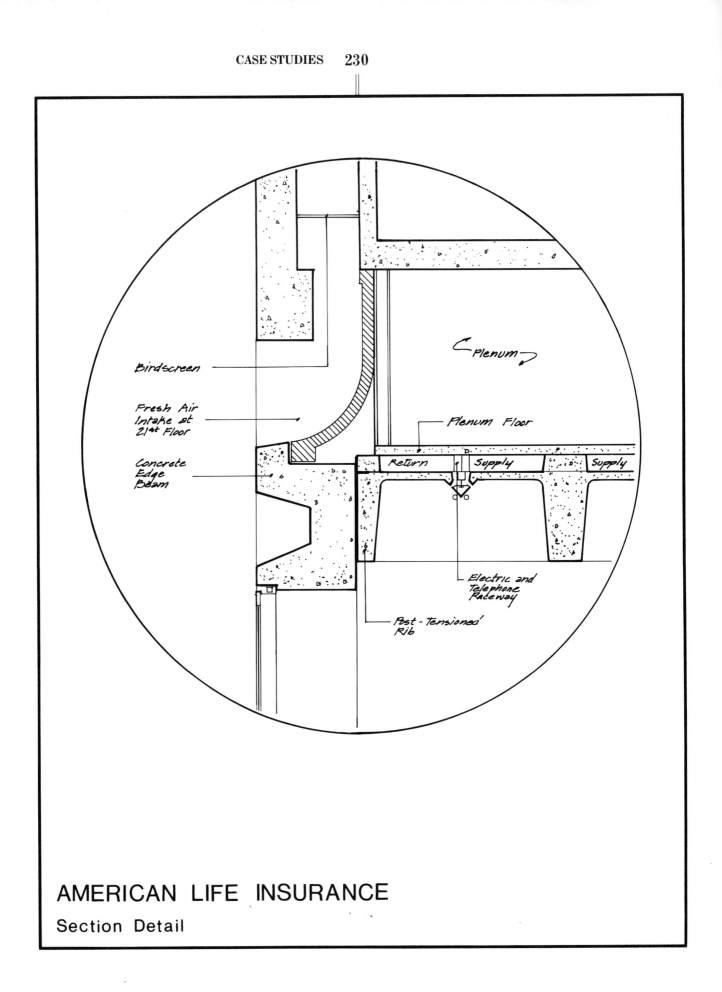

Birdscreen

Fresh Air
Intake at
21st Floor

Concrete
Edge
Beam

Plenum

Plenum Floor

Return   Supply   Supply

Electric and
Telephone
Raceway

Post-Tensioned
Rib

AMERICAN LIFE INSURANCE

Section Detail

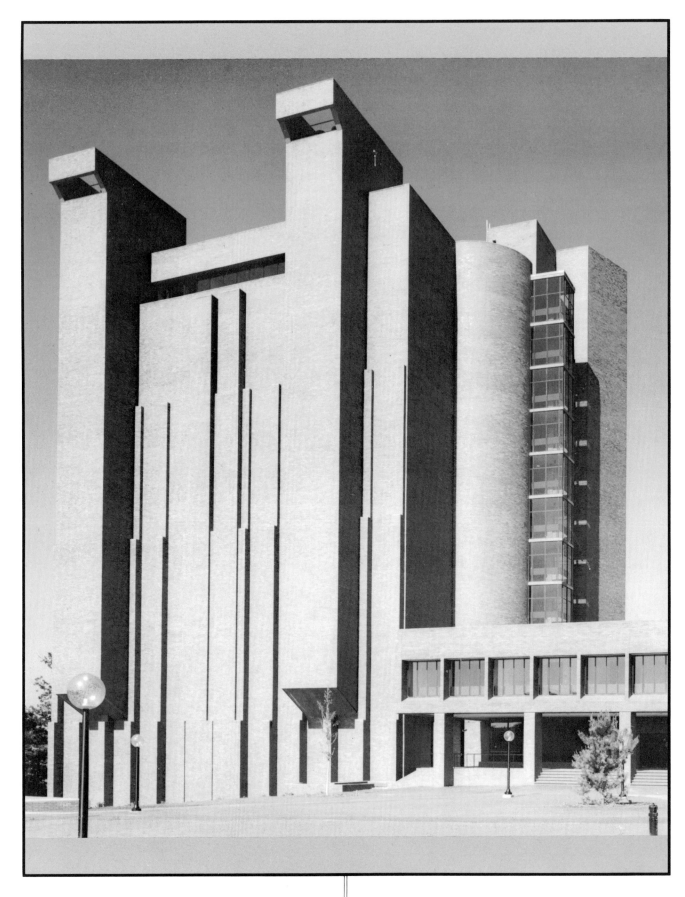

CORNELL
AGRONOMY
LABORATORY

MANY buildings have used their structural bones as their dominating form giver. In the Cornell Agronomy Laboratory, Ulrich Franzen has added shapes that evolved from the dominating amount of shaft area that is required in a research laboratory. Kahn initiated this approach earlier with his exposed assemblage of precast trusses and masonry shafts for the medical laboratory building at the University of Pennsylvania. Franzen's research tower builds on the same concepts as Kahn's tower, solidifying the massing and producing a far more functional building.

In the Cornell Laboratory, the flow of people has been separated from the movement of endless piping, and monstrous laboratory exhaust ducts. The people— and their air supply—circulate vertically at the opposite ends of the building and then horizontally down a central corridor. Laboratory ductwork and piping move vertically along the other pair of exterior walls, and then run horizontally at each floor contained within their own accessible mechanical corridor. The massive exhaust shafts dominate, but do not overwhelm the articulated pipe shafts and subtly diminishing structural piers.

The framing system consists of a poured-in-place concrete skeleton with columns spaced 8'-6" apart and a precast concrete channel floor. The spaces between the exposed ribs of the floor system serve as a recess where the supply piping runs, exposed in the ceiling under the laboratory desks they service, and the ductwork and lights are placed to serve the area beneath them. Since the 4-foot-wide mechanical-services corridors at each side of the building provide for the longitudinal horizontal disbursement of mechanical equipment, there is no need for any of the ducts or pipes to cross the grain of the channel ribs. All the mechanical equipment stays neatly tucked in, forming its own frank statement.

This building proves that in the hands of a strong architect. the mechanical elements of a structure can become as valid a form-giver as the structural elements. The richly articulated texture of brick, traditionally scaled to fit the mason's hand, has been adopted with a powerful and humanizing effect to the requirements of sheathing a modern-day structure. In fact, if this laboratory has any aesthetic weakness, it is that the building appears to be of masonry bearing-wall construction when, in fact, it isn't. The richness of the shadow patterns created by the many, different-sized shafts and stepped, buttress-like columns have created a building with a great deal of dignity.

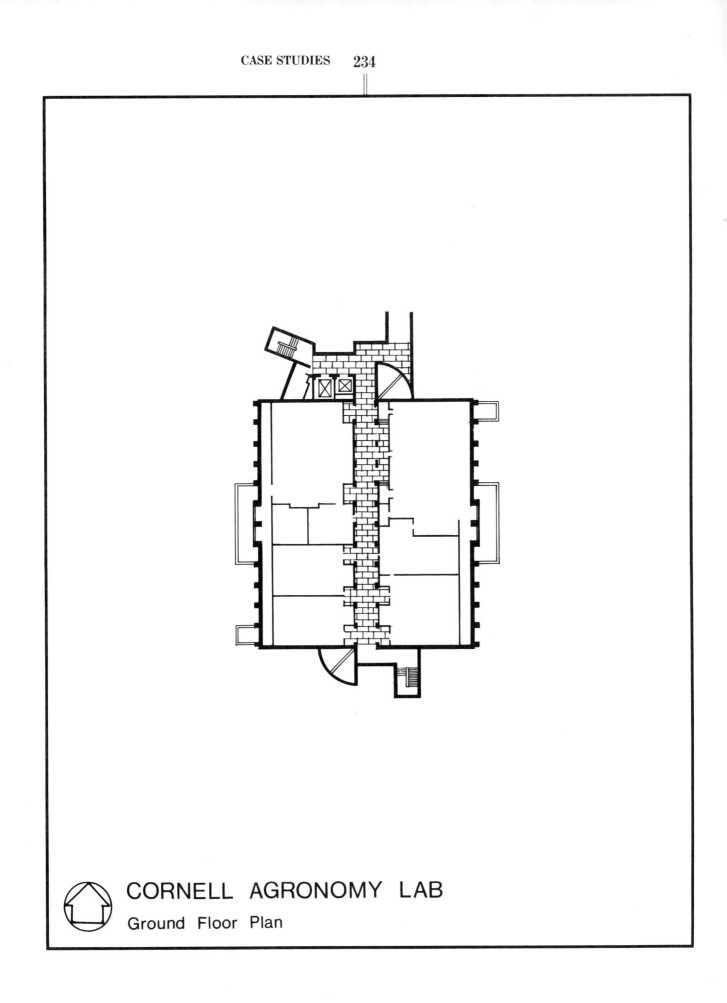

CORNELL AGRONOMY LAB
Ground Floor Plan

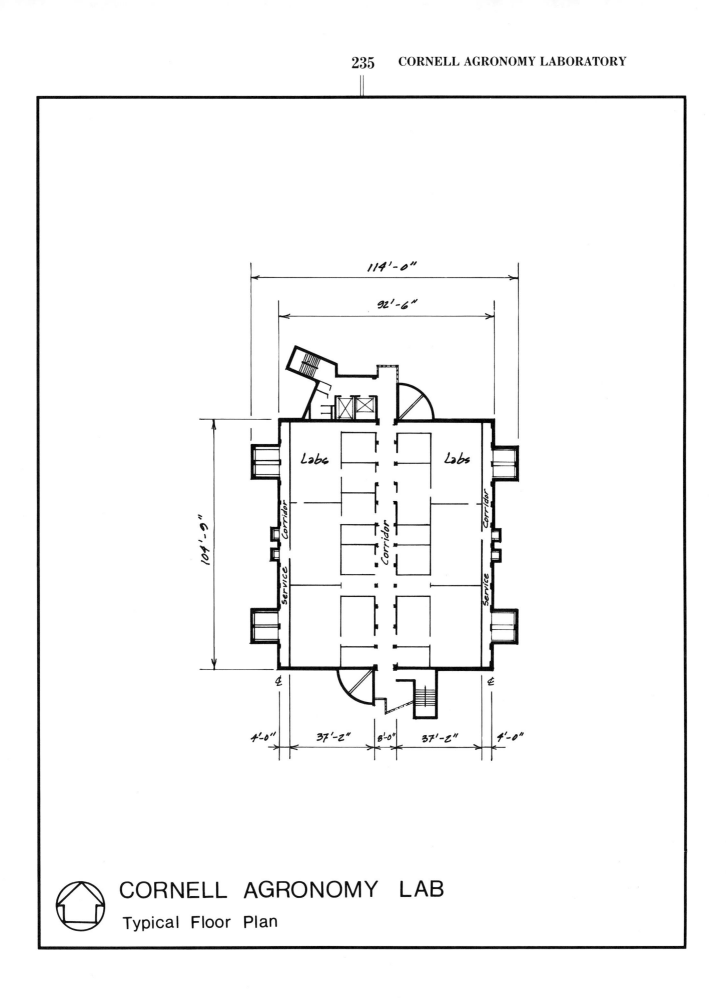

CORNELL AGRONOMY LAB

Typical Floor Plan

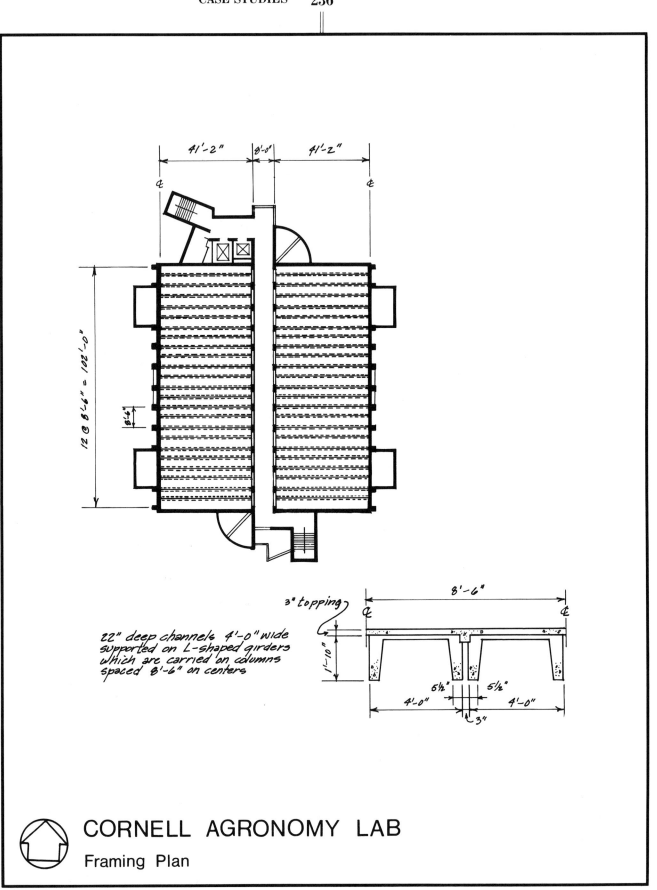

22" deep channels 4'-0" wide
supported on L-shaped girders
which are carried on columns
spaced 8'-6" on centers

CORNELL AGRONOMY LAB

Framing Plan

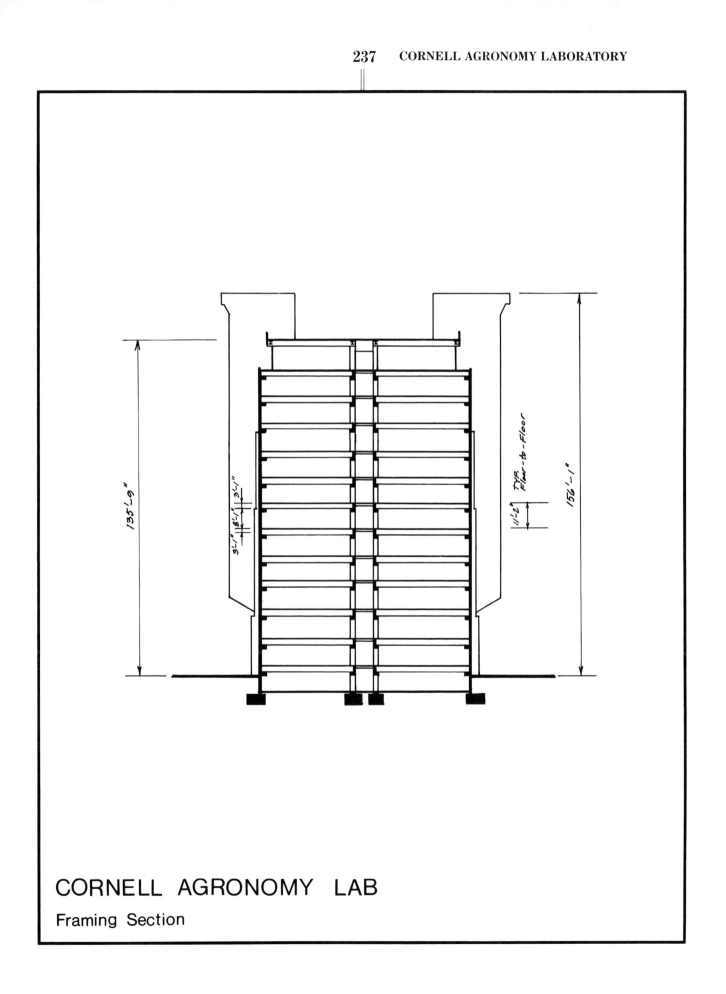

CORNELL AGRONOMY LAB

Framing Section

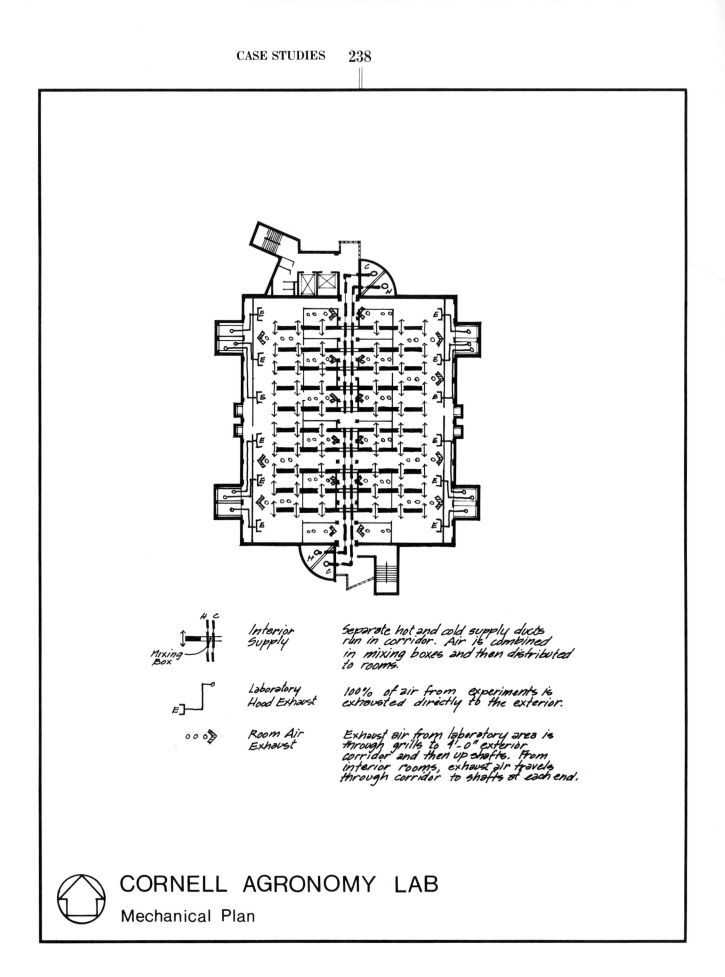

| | | Interior Supply | Separate hot and cold supply ducts run in corridor. Air is combined in mixing boxes and then distributed to rooms. |

Mixing Box

Interior Supply — Separate hot and cold supply ducts run in corridor. Air is combined in mixing boxes and then distributed to rooms.

Laboratory Hood Exhaust — 100% of air from experiments is exhausted directly to the exterior.

Room Air Exhaust — Exhaust air from laboratory area is through grills to 4'-0" exterior corridor and then up shafts. From interior rooms, exhaust air travels through corridor to shafts at each end.

CORNELL AGRONOMY LAB

Mechanical Plan

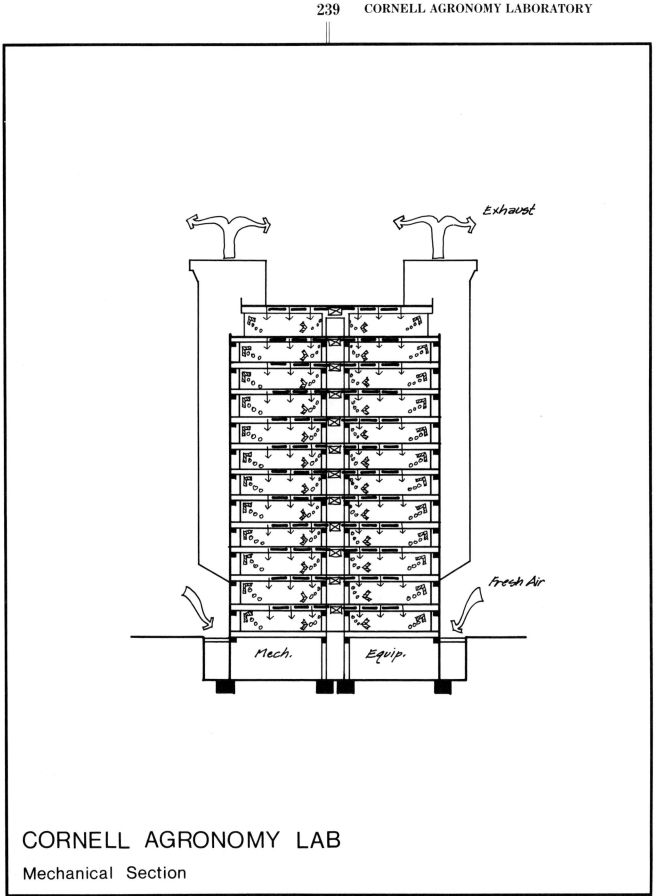

Exhaust

Fresh Air

Mech.   Equip.

CORNELL AGRONOMY LAB
Mechanical Section

780 THIRD AVENUE

THIS granite-covered, 48-story, needle-like tower, somewhat lost among the haystack of New York City skyscrapers, is the world's first high-rise building constructed with an exterior poured-in-place concrete cross-bracing system. The subtle expression of a diagonal bracing pattern on the facade is the building's distinguishing architectural expression.

The exposed exterior bracing system is used to provide both structural stability and architectural expression, drawing upon centuries of experience. Medieval half-timber buildings were delineated with wood bracing filled in with wattle and daub. The exteriors of Gothic cathedrals were surrounded by rows of powerful stone flying buttresses placed perpendicular to the walls they supported. Their filigree, partial arches, and complex shadow patterns became the cathedral's initial and dominant image. Exposed exterior framing was a characteristic of many iron-frame buildings, of which Jules Saulnier's design for a chocolate factory built near Paris in 1871 is a particularly fine early example. Post-World War II high-rise steel structures, exemplified by the Alcoa Building in San Francisco and the John Hancock Tower in Chicago, utilized exterior steel cross-bracing members to provide the primary wind-bracing system, which became the structure's predominant architectural feature. As steel became more expensive and the behavior of concrete better understood, it was inevitable that a poured-in-place concrete high-rise building would be stabilized by an exterior cross-bracing system, thus completing the progression from wood, to stone, to iron, to steel, to reinforced concrete.

The Wang Building, as 780 Third Avenue has been renamed, stands as a modest and staid addition to its mixed neighborhood of office towers, apartment buildings, and low-rise four to eight-story structures. Richly clad in russet granite, it has the courtesy to permit light to reach the sidewalk, the graciousness to provide pedestrians with an oasis of space and seating, and the good sense to pay attention to tidy detailing and choice of materials. From street level, it often takes a deliberate upward glance to notice the criss-crossing paths of missing windows, which appear to have been erased from the facade's checkerboard pattern of alternating soft gray windows and granite panels. The structural pattern creates a design much like a bishop's path on a giant's chessboard. As the pattern wraps around the tower, it only has room to generate half-crosses on the narrow side facades, and produces an offset of the front cross intersections on the rear elevation. These variations enrich the total image and give the building a front and sides that can be sensed and understood from afar. By blocking out windows, Falzur Kahn, the design engineer, was able to create diagonal braces within the planes of the exterior walls. The significance of this accomplishment was a concrete system capable of distributing horizontal wind loads (by means of the diagonal) amongst the columns which march around the tower perimeter between each vertical stack of windows. This system can successfully compete with steel as a framing material for a skyscraper with very slender width-to-height proportions.

Although the Wang Building's total height of 570-feet is modest when compared to some of its "world class" neighbors, its relation to the narrow 70-foot by 126-foot plan dimensions generates a 1:8 width-to-height ratio. This is a startling proportion when compared to the far more modest 1:6 ratio held by 1350-foot-high World Trade Center, and the 38 percent lower 1:5 ratio shared by the Empire State Building and Citicorp Tower.

The Wang building's window pattern provides a sufficient amount of natural light to make the open floors pleasant; however, when the interior office space is subdivided, those areas in the vicinity of a solid infilled window panel face a 14-foot-long stretch of opaque exterior wall—a penalty when compared to an all-glass wall surface, obtainable in a steel frame structure. One compensation is that concrete has a much slower, and thus more energy-efficient, rate of heat transfer than glass. The alternating rhythm of matching 4'-8" panels and windows is the main contributor to the building's comparatively low amount (26%) of exterior glass in relation to its total facade surface.

In order to maintain the purity of the tower form, the architects created a tangential six-story caboose building to house the truck-dock entrance and mechanical equipment space that service the lower part of the tower. This adjunct structure, located off the southwest corner, overlaps part of the tower's west facade. A small amount of office space is also contained within the upper floors of the 22-foot-wide building. The east wall of the low-rise building frames the plaza space on the tower's south side, and the freestanding wall built against the neighboring building similarly frames the north plaza.

Each typical floor has its own individual mini-

HVAC room, located within the building's core. Fresh air is supplied to these rooms from two locations: one at the top of the tower, and the other atop a 23-foot-high set-back at the rear of the six-story annex. The fresh air supply for the upper floors travels down from the roof to the 25th level, with the exhaust and spill air moving up in the opposite direction. The 2nd through 24th levels are supplied with fresh air entering through louvers on top of the offset at the North end of the caboose building. The exhaust and spill air for these floors travel all the way up to the tower roof. Two below grade office levels, the ground floor lobby and mezzanine are serviced by systems which receive their fresh air from the supplementary building, and dump their spill and exhaust air through louvers located on the South elevation above the truck dock. The architectural advantage of this solution is that it eliminates the necessity of placing louvers on the tower's immaculate facade pattern. In fact, the architects deliberately disguised the mechanical equipment spaces on the tower's upper two levels by continuing the office space enclosing facade pattern as a cosmetic screen. This decision, to maintain a relentless unbroken window pattern to the sky, produced windows that face into the rooftop cooling towers.

Individual HVAC units at each floor permit more efficient energy usage and cost control, especially in situations when individual tenants operate beyond the normal building hours, since only the occupied floor's equipment needs to be turned on.

The environmental system for a typical floor consists of two interior zones supplied by ducts located above the hung ceiling. Return air travels back to the mini-HVAC room through the plenum space above the ceiling. The air system is supplemented by a hot water fin-tube perimeter system serviced by supply and return piping at the tower corners.

In order to demonstrate its elegance, the tower needs to be perceived as a freestanding building. While the north, east and south elevations each face directly onto a street, the west elevation backs onto a property line with an eight-story building built against it. Additionally, the lower levels of the tower's west elevation become unavoidably obscured by other existing buildings along 48th and 49th streets. This is a common urban situation, one taken for granted in the intense density of downtown New York. Currently, the majority of the rear elevation continues to soar above the roofs of its lower neighbors, allowing it to demonstrate its relationship with the other three facades.

While the structural pattern of the tower frame remains true, the window voids behind the abutting structures to the West (as well as those located less than 30 feet above their roofs, due to fire codes) literally had to be blocked-up with masonry. Also, the amount of reinforcing steel placed in the vertical spaces (which act as columns between windows), is less in the west facade than in the east. This happens because the load-bearing core is placed eccentrically due to the small size of the office floors, and is much closer to the west facade. The two facades remain visually similar but somewhat different structurally. The architects did the rational thing under the circumstances, as economics dictate that less reinforcing be used where less is needed.

One might wish that such an important precedent-setting building could have had its own slightly larger site, permitting a purer four-sided solution. But, issues and constraints produced a character of its own. What makes architecture challenging and fascinating is that it is an art form that must deal with realities. Realities that include structure, environment, cost, and the particular piece of land the client owns, and all must be dealt with. Given these constraints, Skidmore Owings and Merrill found highly successful solutions. The Wang Building at 780 Third Avenue assumes its place in the evolution of structural form with architectural grace and dignity.

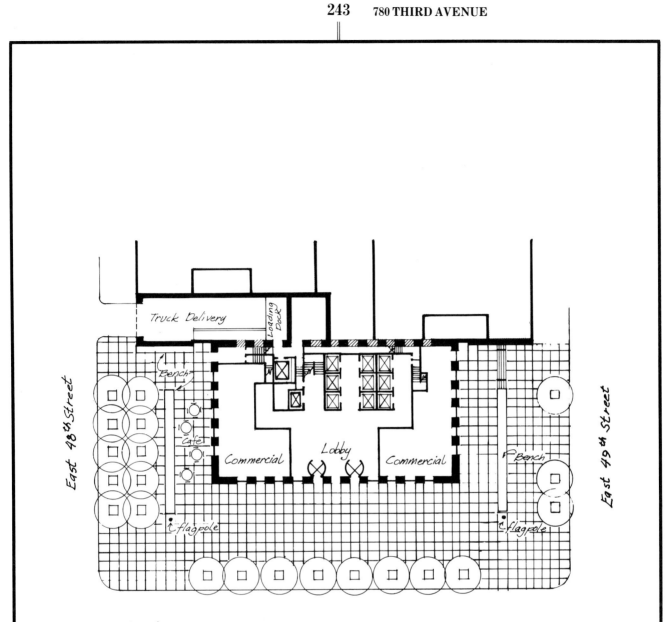

East 48ᵗʰ Street

Truck Delivery

Loading Dock

Bench

Café

Commercial

Lobby

Commercial

Bench

flagpole

flagpole

East 49ᵗʰ Street

Third Avenue

780 THIRD AVENUE
Ground Floor Plan

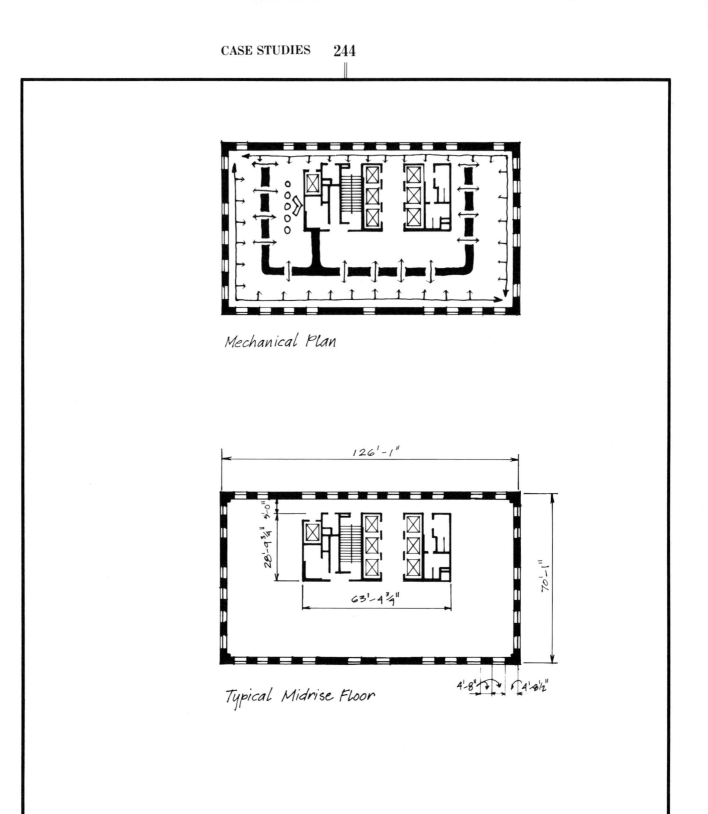

Mechanical Plan

126'-1"

28'-9 3/4"   5'-0"

63'-4 3/4"

70'-1"

Typical Midrise Floor

4'-8"   4'-8 1/2"

780 THIRD AVENUE
Typical Floor and Mechanical Plans

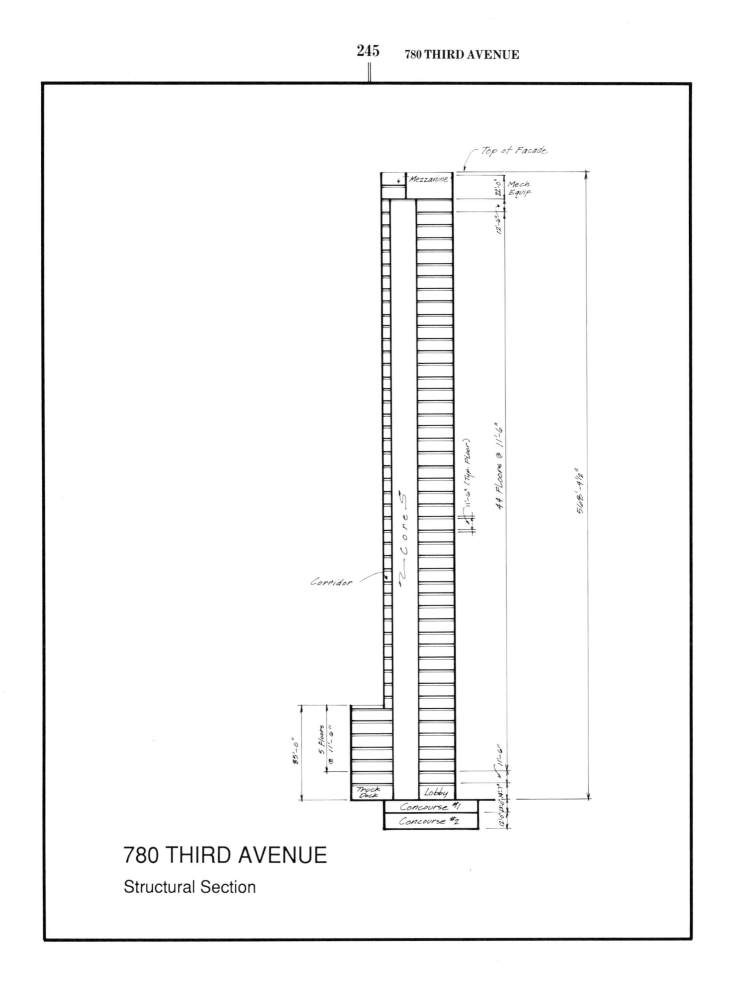

Top of Facade

Mezzanine

Mech. Equip.

22'-0"

12'-6"

44 Floors @ 11'-6"

11'-6" (Typ. Floor)

568'-4½"

Floors

Corridor

85'-0"

5 Floors @ 11'-6"

11'-6"

Truck Dock

Lobby

Concourse #1

Concourse #2

12'-0" 13'-0" 14'-7"

780 THIRD AVENUE

Structural Section

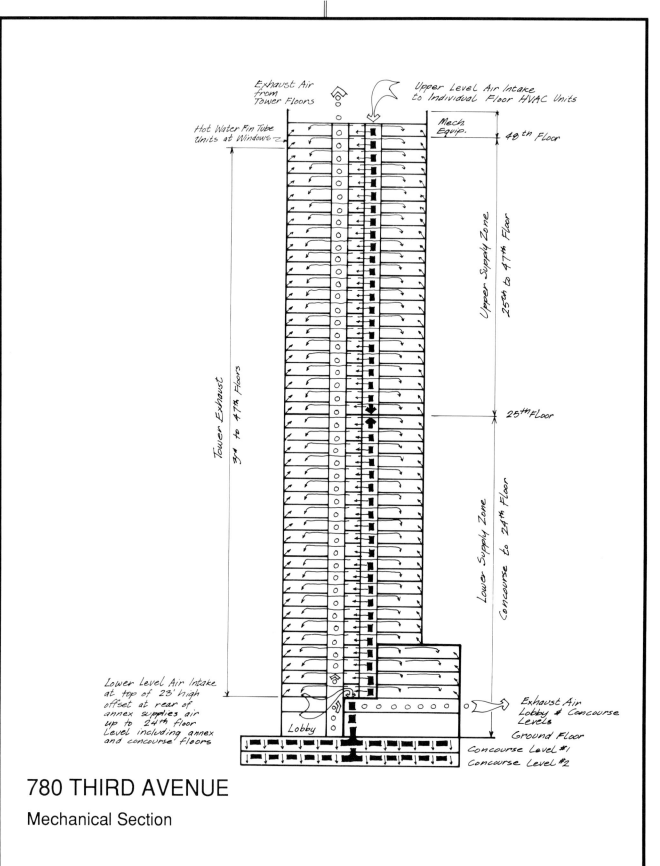

Exhaust Air from Tower Floors

Upper Level Air Intake to Individual Floor HVAC Units

Hot Water Fin Tube Units at Windows

Mech. Equip.

48th Floor

Upper Supply Zone
25th to 47th Floor

Tower Exhaust
3rd to 47th Floors

25th Floor

Lower Supply Zone
Concourse to 24th Floor

Lower Level Air Intake at top of 23' high offset at rear of annex supplies air up to 24th floor Level including annex and concourse floors

Lobby

Exhaust Air Lobby & Concourse Levels

Ground Floor

Concourse Level #1

Concourse Level #2

780 THIRD AVENUE

Mechanical Section

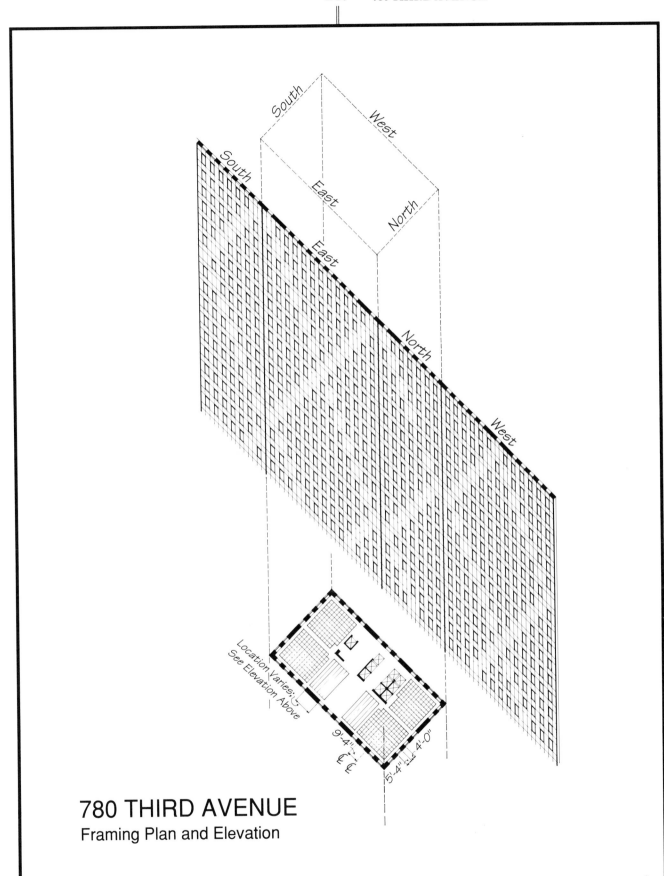

780 THIRD AVENUE
Framing Plan and Elevation

DATA SHEETS FOR CASE STUDIES

A Brief Explanation of Some of the Data Sheet Information Items That Are Not Self-Defining

Section E   Base Building

1. a.   This gives a "Guinness Book of Records" height of whatever knickknack has been stuck into the sky in order to establish a record height.

1. b.   The top of the structural roof beams provides a constant method of comparison.

3. a.   The listed plan dimensions are overall general dimensions that encompass and include all the little bumps and turns. The purpose of these figures is to establish a quick sense of how the building sits on the ground.

3. c.   This is measured to the exterior edge and includes such items as columns that project out past the building's skin.

3. d.   The core area will vary on different floors as the needs and number of elevator and mechanical shafts change. Therefore, a "typical floor" has been defined for purposes of this book, as a floor located where the line of the perimeter of the core area coincides with a structural grid line.

3. g.   Usable area and net area are not necessarily the same. In this text, net area is the gross area less the core area. Usable area could be less than the net area; this is the case, for example, if columns are located beyond the glass line, since the area of the columns would be included in the gross but not subtracted from the core to form the net.

4. c.   This figure provides some indication of the volume of horizontal space that is needed for beams and ducts. When this figure is added to the vertical volume of space consumed by the building core and columns, one begins to realize just how much of the building's volume is devoted to functions other than providing occupiable or habitable space.

5. a.   This gives a sense of a building's appearance and stability.

5. b–c.   These figures are listed only for those buildings for which the designing architect or real estate agent has provided them. They have not been verified from the original working drawings.

Section F   Structure

8. a–c.   The object of this section is to give a sense of the relationship between the depth of a structural system and its span. Many variables also affect this ratio, such as how closely the beams are spaced and the design load they must support. Even with these variables, however, an overall pattern emerges.

9. b–c.   This information can be used to trace the trend to create tall buildings with greater clear spans between vertical supports while using less material. The use of less material reduces the cost, while the greater clear spans increase the flexibility of use. These figures are provided only when the corporation furnishing the structural steel or concrete or some other reliable source has indicated the amount of material that was used and when a total gross building square-foot figure was also available.

Section G   Mechanical

13.   This area includes shafts for ductwork, vents, pipes, conduits, and elevators. Also included are telephone and electric closets and items such as mail conveyors. It does not include washrooms or public corridors and stairs that are part of the total core.

Section H   Exiting and Vertical Transportation

16. a–d.   These numbers show how the codes can affect overall proportions. Section c is not a code item, but perhaps should be, and this is an attempt to show the impact that the shape of a building has on the alternate way out during an emergency.

17. d.   This gives a sense of convenience when used with the occupancy load per floor (3.h.)

A BUILDING: *Seagram Building*

B ARCHITECT: *Mies van der Rohe/with*
   Philip Johnson & Kahn & Jacobs

C LOCATION: *New York, New York*

D DATE OF CONSTRUCTION: *1958*

E BASE BUILDING

1 a Total building height, entrance level to highest point: *515'-8"*
   b First floor level to top of roof beam: *471 ft.*

2 a Total number of occupied floors: *38*
   b Total number of floor levels above grade: *40*
   c Total number of floor levels below grade: *3*
   d Total number of floor levels: *43*

3 Typical Floor
   a Overall dimensions (measured at glass line): *115'-4" × 143'-1"*
   b Overall dimensions of core: *40'-1" × 101'-0"*
   c Gross area: *15,188 sq. ft.*
   d Gross area of core: *4,150 sq. ft.*
   e Net area of usable space: *11,038 sq. ft.*
   f Core area as a percent of total floor area: *27.3%*
   g Usable area as a percent of gross area: *72.7%*
   h Approximate number of occupants on a typical floor: *110*

4 a Floor-to-floor height: *12'-0"*
   b Floor-to-ceiling height: *8'-10½"*
   c Usable height as a percent of total floor height: *74%*

5 a Ratio of building width to height: *1/4.0*
   b Net building area: *530,000 sq. ft.*

F STRUCTURE

6 Type of framing system:
   Steel skeleton with poured-in-place one-way concrete floor slab spanning 6'-11"

7 Dimensions of a typical framing bay: *27'-9" × 27'-9"*

8 Sizes of typical horizontal framing members:
   a Typical girder: *W 27 × 114*
      Depth: *27"* Span: *27'-9"* Spacing: *27'-9"* Depth/Span: *1/12.3*
   b Typical beam: *W 16 × 45*
      Depth: *16"* Span: *27'-9"* Spacing: *6'-11¾"* Depth/Span: *1/20.8*
   c Typical spandrel beam: *W 24 × 76*
      Depth: *24"* Span: *27'-9"* Depth/Span: *1/13.8*

9 How columns structurally and visually accommodate their cumulative change in load-carrying capacity: *Columns are not expressed on facade except at night as a silhouette.*

   Structural columns on upper floors are smaller, but the outside dimensions of the exterior columns are kept visually constant by their fire protection encasement

G MECHANICAL

10 Type of heating and cooling system:
    a Interior: *Dual duct*
    b Exterior: *High-speed induction units*

11 Location of H.V.A.C. equipment rooms:
 a Level   b Floor covered
  Cellar   *Up to 20th*

  39th & 40th   *Down to 21st*

12 Number of H.V.A.C. shafts servicing a typical floor:
 a Interior: *2*   c Return *4*
 b Exterior *5*

13 a Area of the space required for all mechanical equipment and shafts on a typical floor, including H.V.A.C., electric, telephone, plumbing, and elevator shafts and spaces: *2,206 sq. ft.*
 b This area as a percent of the core area: *53.1%*
 c This area as a percent of gross floor area: *14.5%*

14 a Area required for all H.V.A.C. shafts on a typical floor: *328 sq. ft.*
 b Shaft area as a percent of the core area: *7.9%*
 c Shaft area as a percent of the gross floor area: *2.2%*

15 a Glass area as a percent of facade area: *72%*

H   **EXITING AND VERTICAL TRANSPORTATION**

16 a Total number of exit stairways: *2*
 b Maximum travel distance to closest exit on a typical floor: *90 ft.*
 c Maximum travel distance to a second means of exit: *140 ft.*
 d Maximum dead end public corridor length: *Varies with tenant layout*

17 a Total number of passenger elevators: *17*
 b Total number of freight elevators: *1-plus another from garage to lobby*
 c Number of passenger elevators in each height zone:

Zone:	Floors serviced:	Number of elevators:
1	*1–10*	*6*
2	*1 + 10–25*	*6*
3	*1 + 25–38*	*5*

 d Ratio of total number of elevators to number of floors above grade: *1/2.2*

A   BUILDING: *Knights of Columbus*

B   ARCHITECT: *Roche Dinkerloo and Associates*

C   LOCATION: *New Haven, Connecticut*

D   DATE OF CONSTRUCTION: *1969*

E   BASE BUILDING

    1   a   Total building height, entrance level to highest point: *320'-9"*
         b   First floor level to top of roof beam: *319'-0"*

    2   a   Total number of occupied floors: *22*
         b   Total number of floor levels above grade: *23*
         c   Total number of floor levels below grade: *1*
         d   Total number of floor levels: *24*

    3   Typical Floor
         a   Overall dimensions (measured at glass line): *92'-3 × 92'-3"*
                                                131'-1" × 131'-1" overall
         b   Overall dimensions of core: *29'-11½" × 29'-11½"*
         c   Gross area: *10,535 sq. ft.*
         d   Gross area of core: *5 cores = 3,600 sq. ft.*
         e   Net area of usable space: *6,935 sq. ft.*
         f   Core area as a percent of total floor area: *34.2%*
         g   Usable area as a percent of gross area: *65.8%*
         h   Approximate number of occupants on a typical floor: *69*

    4   a   Floor-to-floor height: *13'-0"*
         b   Floor-to-ceiling height: *12'-6½" 10'-10" under beams*
         c   Usable height as a percent of total floor height: *83.3%*

    5   a   Ratio of building width to height: *1/2.44*

F   STRUCTURE

    6   Type of framing system: *Exposed steel spandrel beams supported on concrete corner towers. Exposed steel floor beams span from central concrete core to spandrel beam and support a 5½" concrete floor slab.*

    7   Dimensions of a typical framing bay: *10'-0" × 35'-10"*

    8   Sizes of typical horizontal framing members:
         a   Typical girder: *Diagonal at corner pair of W 21 × 55*
         b   Typical beam: *W 21 × 55*
            Depth: *1'-9"*   Span: *35'-10½"*   Spacing: *10'-0"*   Depth/Span: *1/20.5*
         c   Typical spandrel beam: *W 36 × 194*
            Depth: *3'-0"*   Span: *72'-5"*   Depth/Span: *1/24.1*

    9   How columns structurally and visually accommodate their cumulative change in load-carrying capacity: *Towers serve as vertical supports and are visually constant in diameter. The amount of steel reinforcement decreases with the tower's height.*

G   MECHANICAL

    10   Type of heating and cooling system: *Dual duct, with a mixing box for each zone. Mixing boxes are located in the corner towers at each floor.*

11   Level of H.V.A.C. equipment rooms: *Fan room on roof serves entire structure. City steam supplied to building in cellar. Some equipment for first-floor bank located in corner towers.*

12   Number of H.V.A.C. shafts servicing a typical floor:
   a   Interior: *2*
   b   Exterior: *4*
   c   Return: *Located above doors to corner towers at 2 diagonally opposite towers on each floor.*

13   a   Area of the space required for all mechanical equipment and shafts on a typical floor, including H.V.A.C., electric, telephone, plumbing, and elevator shafts and spaces: *1,540 sq. ft.*
   b   This area as a percent of the core area: *42.7%*
   c   This area as a percent of gross floor area: *14.6%*

14   a   Area required for all H.V.A.C. shafts on a typical floor: *270 sq. ft.*
   b   Shaft area as a percent of the core area: *7.5%*
   c   Shaft area as a percent of the gross floor area: *2.5%*

15   a   Glass area as a percent of total facade area: *90.7%*

H   EXITING AND VERTICAL TRANSPORTATION

16   a   Total number of exit stairways: *2*
   b   Maximum travel distance to closest exit on a typical floor: *70 ft.*
   c   Maximum travel distance to a second means of exit: *90 ft.*
   d   Maximum dead-end public corridor length (when part of basic building layout and not dependent on tenant subdivision): *None*

17   a   Total number of passenger elevators: *6*
   b   Total number of freight elevators: *One—from cellar to first floor only*
   c   Number of passenger elevators in each height zone:

Zone:	Number of elevators:	Floors serviced:
1	*6*	*All*

   d   Ratio of total number of elevators to number of floors above grade: *1/3.8*

A   BUILDING: *One Liberty Plaza*

B   ARCHITECT: *Skidmore Owings and Merrill*

C   LOCATION: *New York, New York*

D   DATE OF CONSTRUCTION: *1973*

E   BASE BUILDING

    1   a Total building height, entrance level to highest point: *743 ft.*
        b First floor level to top of roof beam: *727'-6"*

    2   a Total number of occupied floors: *51*
        b Total number of floor levels above grade: *56*
        c Total number of floor levels below grade: *2*
        d Total number of floor levels: *58*

    3   Typical Floor
        a Overall dimensions (measured at glass line): *163'-4" × 238'-0"*
        b Overall dimensions of core: *65'-6" × 153'-8"*
        c Gross area: *38,865 sq. ft.*
        d Gross area of core: *Including central corridor, 10,065 sq. ft.*
                               Not including corridor, 8,657 sq. ft.
        e Net area of usable space: *28,800 sq. ft.*
        f Core area as a percent of total floor area: *25.9%*
        g Usable area as a percent of gross area: *74.1%*
        h Approximate number of occupants on a typical floor: *288*

    4   a Floor-to-floor height: *12'-6"*
        b Floor-to-ceiling height: *8'-6"*

    5   a Ratio of building width to height: *1/4.56*

F   STRUCTURE

    6   Type of framing system: *Steel skeleton with exterior face of spandrel beams exposed. Corrugated metal floor deck with concrete toping. 2-story-high "K" bracing in split central core.*

    7   Dimensions of a typical framing bay: *46'-8" × 47'-6"*

    8   Sizes of typical horizontal framing members:
        a Typical girder: *W 36 × 194 at corners*
          Depth: *3'-0"*   Span: *47'-6"*   Depth/Span: *1/15.8*
        b Typical beam: *W 27 × 84*
          Depth: *2'-3"*   Span: *47'-6"*   Spacing: *14'-0"*   Depth/Span: *1/21.1*
        c Typical spandrel beam: *Built-up member*
          Depth: *5'-10"*   Span: *46'-8"*   Depth/Span: *1/8.0*

    9   a How columns structurally and visually accommodate their cumulative change in load-carrying capacity: *Actual size of built-up column decreases with building height. Exposed column cover maintains a constant size throughout.*
        b Weight of framing system: *26,000 tons*
        c Weight per square foot of framing system: *23.5 lb./sq. ft.*

G   MECHANICAL

10   Type of heating and cooling system:
  a   Interior: *Constant temperature variable volume*
  b   Exterior: *High-speed induction units*

11   Level of H.V.A.C. equipment rooms:
  a   Level: b   Floors covered:
   15 & 16   *3rd to 29*
   40 & 41   *30 to 53*
   Cellar   *Cellar to 2*

12   Number of H.V.A.C. shafts servicing a typical floor:
  a   Interior: *4*   c   *Return: 4*
  b   Exterior: *4*

13   a   Area of the space required for all mechanical equipment and shafts on a typical floor, including H.V.A.C., electric, telephone, plumbing, and elevator shafts and spaces: *a-1 4,830 sq. ft. a-2 5,883 sq. ft. on lower floors*
  b   This area as a percent of the core area: *47.9% full core with corridor: b-2 Core area less central corridor, 55.8%*
  c   This area as a percent of gross floor area: *c-1 12.4%   c-2 15.1%   Average = 13.8%*

14   a   Area required for all H.V.A.C. shafts on a typical floor: *904 sq. ft.*
  b   Shaft area as a percent of the core area: *10.4%*
  c   Shaft area as a percent of the gross floor area: *2.3%*

15   a   Glass area as a percent of total facade area: *41.1%*

H   EXITING AND VERTICAL TRANSPORTATION

16   a   Total number of exit stairways: *2 double-width stairs*
  b   Maximum travel distance to closest exit on a typical floor: *120 ft.*
  c   Maximum travel distance to a second means of exit: *240 ft.*
  d   Maximum dead-end public corridor length (when part of basic building layout and not dependent on tenant subdivision): *30 ft.*

17   a   Total number of passenger elevators: *36*
  b   Total number of freight elevators: *3*
  c   Number of passenger elevators in each height zone:

Zone:	Number of elevators:	Floors serviced:
1	*6*	*1–11*
2	*6*	*1 + 11–20*
3	*6*	*1 + 20–28*
4	*6*	*1 + 28–36*
5	*6*	*1 + 36–45*
6	*6*	*1 + 45–53*

  d   Ratio of total number of elevators to number of floors above grade: *1/1.4*

A   BUILDING   *Chase Manhattan Bank Central Office Building*

B   ARCHITECT: *Skidmore Owings and Merrill*

C   LOCATION: *New York, New York*

D   DATE OF CONSTRUCTION: *1963*

E   BASE BUILDING

     1   a   Total building height, entrance level to highest point: *812'-5"*
           b   First floor level to top of roof beam: *779'-11"*

     2   a   Total number of occupied floors: *54*
           b   Total number of floor levels above grade: *61*
           c   Total number of floor levels below grade: *6*
           d   Total number of floor levels: *67*

     3   Typical Floor
           a   Overall dimensions (measured at glass line):   *281'-6" × 107'-6"*
           b   Overall dimensions of core: *195'-10" × 36'-0"*
           c   Gross area: *30,561 sq. ft. including columns*
           d   Gross area of core: *7,049 sq. ft.*
           e   Net area of usable space: *23,213 sq. ft.*
           f   Core area as a percent of total floor area: *24.0%*
           g   Usable area as a percent of gross area: *75.9%*
           h   Approximate number of occupants on a typical floor: *232*

     4   a   Floor-to-floor height: *12'-7"*
           b   Floor-to-ceiling height: *8'-10"*
           c   Usable height as a percent of total floor height: *70%*

     5   a   Ratio of building width to height (outside face of column)   *1/6.92*
           b   Gross building area: *2,250,000 sq. ft.*

F   STRUCTURE

     6   Type of framing system: *Steel skeleton with exterior columns. Steel floor deck with concrete topping.*

     7   Dimensions of a typical framing bay: *29'-0" × 33'-3" and 29'-0" × 42'-11"*

     8   Sizes of typical horizontal framing members:
           a   Typical girder: *Paired 3'-0" deep built-up member*
               (1) Depth: *3'-0"*   Span: *40'-6"*   Spacing: *29'-0"*   Depth/Span: *1/13.5*
               (2) Depth: *3'-0"*   Span: *31'-10"*   Spacing: *29'-0"*   Depth/Span: *1/10.6*
           b   Typical beam: *W 18 × 55*
               Depth: *1'-6"*   Span: *27'-9"*   Spacing: *10'-4"*   Depth/Span: *1/18.5*

     9   a   How columns structurally and visually accommodate their cumulative change in load-carrying capacity: *Special built-up columns use a decreasing amount of steel on the upper floor. The visual cover remains constant in size.*
           b   Weight of framing system: *53 tons*
           c   Weight per square foot of framing system: *47.3 lb./sq. ft.*

G   MECHANICAL

     10   Type of heating and cooling system:
           a   Interior: *Variable volume*
           b   Exterior: *Induction units*

11   Level of H.V.A.C. equipment rooms:
       a   Level: b   Floors covered:
           3rd cellar   *Cellars to 2*
           11 & 12 floors   *3 to 22*
           31 & 32 floors   *23 to 31*
           51 & 52   *42 to 61*

12   Number of H.V.A.C shafts servicing a typical floor:
       a   Interior: *2*   c   Return: *4*
       b   Exterior: *6*

13   a   Area of the space required for all mechanical equipment and shafts on a typical floor, including
           H.V.A.C., electric, telephone, plumbing, and elevator shafts and spaces: *4,022 sq. ft.*
       b   This area as a percent of the core area: *57.0%*
       c   This area as a percent of gross floor area: *13.2%*

14   a   Area required for all H.V.A.C. shafts on a typical floor: *904 sq. ft.*
       b   Shaft area as a percent of the core area: *12.8%*
       c   Shaft area as a percent of the gross floor area: *2.9%*

15   a   Glass area as a percent of total facade area: *58%*

H   EXITING AND VERTICAL TRANSPORTATION

16   a   Total number of exit stairways: *4*
       b   Maximum travel distance to closest exit on a typical floor: *135 ft.*
       c   Maximum travel distance to a second means of exit: *175 ft.*
       d   Maximum dead-end public corridor length (when part of basic building layout and not de-
           pendent on tenant subdivision): *50 ft.*

17   a   Total number of passenger elevators: *34*
       b   Total number of freight elevators: *4*
       c   Number of passenger elevators in each height zone:

Zone:	Number of elevators:	Floors serviced:
1	*6*	*1–17*
2	*6*	*1 + 16–27*
3	*8*	*1 + 26–38*
4	*8*	*1 + 37–48*
5	*8*	*1 + 47–60*

       d   Ratio of total number of elevators to number of floors above grade: *1/1.42*

A   BUILDING: *Boston Company Building*

B   ARCHITECT: *Pietro Belluschi with Emory Roth & Sons*

C   LOCATION: *Boston, Massachusetts*

D   DATE OF CONSTRUCTION: *1970*

E   BASE BUILDING

   1   a   Total building height, entrance level to highest point: *602 ft.*
       b   First floor level to top of roof beam: *536 ft.*

   2   a   Total number of occupied floors: *38*
       b   Total number of floor levels above grade: *41*
       c   Total number of floor levels below grade: *1*
       d   Total number of floor levels: *42*

   3   Typical Floor
       a   Overall dimensions (measured at glass line):   *140'-0" × 140'-0"*
       b   Overall dimensions of core: *63'-1" × 57'-0"*
       c   Gross area: *20,449 sq. ft. (143' × 143')*
       d   Gross area of core: *3,596 sq. ft. (lower floors)*
       e   Net area of usable space: *16,004 sq. ft.*
       f   Core area as a percent of total floor area: *17.6%*
       g   Usable area as a percent of gross area: *78.3%*
       h   Approximate number of occupants on a typical floor: *160*

   4   a   Floor-to-floor height: *12'-0"*
       b   Floor-to-ceiling height: *8'-6"*
       c   Usable height as a percent of total floor height: *70.8%*

   5   a   Ratio of building width to height: *1/3.75*

F   STRUCTURE

   6   Type of framing system: *Steel skeleton with braced exterior frame which divides facade into three vertical levels. The vertical loads of each of these zones are transferred by 6'-0" deep tie girders to corner columns. Floor framing spans from center core to facade.*

   7   Dimensions of a typical framing bay: *9'-4" × 42'-0"*

   8   Sizes of typical horizontal framing members:
       a   Typical girder: *Built-up girder at base of vertical zones*
          Depth: *6'-0"*   Span: *140'-0"*   Depth/Span: *1/23.3*
       b   Typical beam:
          Depth: *1'-9"*   Span: *42'-0"*   Spacing: *9'-4"*   Depth/Span: *1/24.0*
       c   Typical spandrel beam: *16 B 26*
          Depth: *1'-4"*   Span: *9'-4"*   Depth/Span: *1/7*

   9   a   How columns structurally and visually accommodate their cumulative change in load-carrying capacity: *Typical facade columns are constant in expressed size and appear almost mullion-like.*
          Corner columns change both in size and shape. They are boxed-out cruciform shaped to the 17th floor, then boxed-out H-columns above.
       c   Weight per square foot of framing system: *21 lb./sq. ft.*

G   MECHANICAL

   10   Type of heating and cooling system:
       a   Interior: *Variable volume*
       b   Exterior: *Induction units*

11   Level of H.V.A.C. equipment rooms:
    a   Level: b   Floors covered:
      41   *cellar to 4*
      17   *5 to 28*
      4   *29 to 40*

12   Number of H.V.A.C. shafts servicing a typical floor:
    a   Interior: *2*   c   Return: *2*
    b   Exterior: *4*

13   a   Area of the space required for all mechanical equipment and shafts on a typical floor, including H.V.A.C., electric, telephone, plumbing, and elevator shafts and spaces: *2,090 sq. ft.*
    b   This area as a percent of the core area: *58.1%*
    c   This area as a percent of gross floor area: *10.2%*

14   a   Area required for all H.V.A.C. shafts on a typical floor: *427 sq. ft.*
    b   Shaft area as a percent of the core area: *11.8%*
    c   Shaft area as a percent of the gross floor area: *2.0%*

15   a   Glass area as a percent of total facade area: *46%*

H   EXITING AND VERTICAL TRANSPORTATION

16   a   Total number of exit stairways: *2*
    b   Maximum travel distance to closest exit on a typical floor: *115 ft.*
    c   Maximum travel distance to a second means of exit: *170 ft.*
    d   Maximum dead-end public corridor length: *Depends on tenant layout*

17   a   Total number of passenger elevators: *18*
    b   Total number of freight elevators: *1*
    c   Number of passenger elevators in each height zone:

Zone:	Number of elevators:	Floors serviced:
1	*6*	*1–15*
2	*6*	*1 + 15–28*
3	*6*	*1 + 29–40*

    d   Ratio of number of elevators to floors served: *1/2.1*

A BUILDING: *Westcoast Transmission Company*

B ARCHITECT: *Rhone & Iredale*

C LOCATION: *Vancouver, British Columbia*

D DATE OF CONSTRUCTION: *1969*

E BASE BUILDING

   1   a Total building height, entrance level to highest point: *232'-7"*
       b First floor level to top of roof beam: *180'-0"*

   2   a Total number of occupied floors: *12*
       b Total number of floor levels above grade: *17*
       c Total number of floor levels below grade: *3*
       d Total number of floor levels: *20*

   3   Typical Floor
       a Overall dimensions (measured at glass line): *110'-1" × 110'-1"*
       b Overall dimensions of core: *37'-2" × 37'-2"*
       c Gross area: *12,118 sq. ft.*
       d Gross area of core: *1,380 sq. ft.*
       e Net area of usable space: *10,738 sq. ft.*
       f Core area as a percent of total floor area: *11.4%*
       g Usable area as a percent of gross area: *88.6%*
       h Approximate number of occupants on a typical floor: *107*

   4   a Floor-to-floor height: *12'-0"*
       b Floor-to-ceiling height: *8'-9"*
       c Usable height as a percent of total floor height: *72%*

   5   a Ratio of building width to height: *core: 1/6.25*
                            overall building mass: 1/1.63
       b Gross building area: *156,035 sq. ft.*
       c Net building area: *138,000 sq. ft.*

F STRUCTURE

   6   Type of framing system: *Steel skeleton system supported on central concrete core and exterior cables draped over core top to outrigger roof beams, from which they hang vertically.*

   7   Dimensions of a typical framing bay: *12'-0" × 36'-3"*

   8   Sizes of typical horizontal framing members:
       a Typical girder: *none*
       b Typical beam: *W 16 × 45*
          Depth: *16"* Span: *35'-8"* Spacing: *12'-0"* Depth/Span: *1/26.7*
       c Typical spandrel beam: *W 24"*
          Depth: *2'-0"* Span: *36'-3"* Depth/Span: *1/18.1*

   9   How columns structurally and visually accommodate their cumulative change in load-carrying capacity: *Constant diameter cables are covered by a uniform encasement.*

G MECHANICAL

   10 Type of heating and cooling system:
       a Interior: *Constant-volume terminal reheaters*
       b Exterior: *High-velocity air*

11   Level of H.V.A.C. equipment rooms:
    a   Level: b   Floors covered:
       Top of core   *All*
       Above main roof

12   Number of H.V.A.C. shafts servicing a typical floor:
    a   Interior: *1*   c   Return: *2*
    b   Exterior: *1*

13   a   Area of the space required for all mechanical equipment and shafts on a typical floor, including
       H.V.A.C., electric, telephone, plumbing, and elevator shafts and spaces: *610 sq. ft.*
    b   This area as a percent of the core area: *44.2%*
    c   This area as a percent of gross floor area: *5.0%*

14   a   Area required for all H.V.A.C. shafts on a typical floor: *164 sq. ft.*
    b   Shaft area as a percent of the core area: *11.9%*
    c   Shaft area as a percent of the gross floor area: *1.4%*

15   a   Glass area as a percent of total facade area: *41%*

H   EXITING AND VERTICAL TRANSPORTATION

16   a   Total number of exit stairways: *2*
    b   Maximum travel distance to closest exit on a typical floor: *60 ft.*
    c   Maximum travel distance to a second means of exit: *120 ft.*
    d   Maximum dead end public corridor length (when part of basic building layout and not dependent on tenant subdivision): *varies with tenant layout*

17   a   Total number of passenger elevators: *4*
    b   Total number of freight elevators: *None*
    c   Number of passenger elevators in each height zone:

Zone:	Number of elevators:	Floors serviced:
1	*4*	*1 + 4–15*

    d   Ratio of total number of elevators to number of floors above grade: *1/3.75*

A   BUILDING: *U.S. Steel Building*

B   ARCHITECT: *Harrison & Abramovitz & Abbe*

C   LOCATION: *Pittsburgh, Pennsylvania*

D   DATE OF CONSTRUCTION: *1970*

E   BASE BUILDING

    1   a   Total building height, entrance level to highest point: *847'*
         b   First floor level to top of roof beam: *841'*

    2   a   Total number of occupied floors: *64*
         b   Total number of floor levels above grade: *64*
         c   Total number of floor levels below grade: *4*
         d   Total number of floor levels: *68*

    3   Typical Floor
         a   Overall dimensions (measured at glass line): *221' × 221' × 221' (three areas @ 221 × 45½)*
         b   Overall dimensions of core: *162' × 162' × 162'*
         c   Gross area: *40,170 sq. ft. (43,754 to exterior frame)*
         d   Gross area of core: *11,314 sq. ft.*
         e   Net area of usable space: *28,856 sq. ft.*
         f   Core area as a percent of total floor area: *28.2%*
         g   Usable area as a percent of gross area: *g-1 71.8% sq. ft. g-2 65.9%*
         h   Approximate number of occupants on a typical floor: *288*

    4   a   Floor-to-floor height: *11'-10"*
         b   Floor-to-ceiling height: *8'-6"*
         c   Usable height as a percent of total floor height: *72%*

    5   a   Ratio of building width to height: *1/3.73*
         b   Gross building area: *2,900,000 sq. ft.*

F   STRUCTURE

    6   Type of framing system: *Steel skeleton. 2 secondary floors supported on each primary floor. Liquid filled exterior box columns.*

    7   Dimensions of a typical framing bay: *13'-0" × 50'-4"*

    8   Sizes of typical horizontal framing members:
         a   Typical girder: *none*
         b   Typical beam: *W 27 × 102*
             Depth: *2'-3"*   Span: *48'-10"*   Spacing: *13'-0"*   Depth/Span: *1/21.7*
         c   Typical spandrel beam: *Box girder every 3 floors*

    9   a   How columns structurally and visually accommodate their cumulative change in load-carrying capacity: *Exposed box columns visually decrease in size with increase in height. 18 columns, total 6 per side, attached to box spandrel beams every 3 floor levels.*
         b   Weight of framing system: *41,659 tons*
         c   Weight per square foot of framing system: *28.7 lb./sq. ft.*

G   MECHANICAL

    10   Type of heating and cooling system:
         a   Interior: *Variable volume with linear diffusers 13'-0" o.c.*
         b   Exterior: *2 pipe induction units*

11   Level of H.V.A.C. equipment rooms:
    a Level: b Floors covered:
       3   *3–18*
       34   *19–48*
       63 & 64   *50–64*

12   Number of H.V.A.C. shafts servicing a typical floor:
    a Interior: *6*   c Return: *5 (some are double shafts—see plan)*
    b Exterior: *4*

13 a Area of the space required for all mechanical equipment and shafts on a typical floor, including H.V.A.C., electric, telephone, plumbing, and elevator shafts and spaces: *5,090 sq. ft.*
    b This area as a percent of the core area: *44.9%*
    c This area as a percent of gross floor area: *12.6%*

14 a Area required for all H.V.A.C. shafts on a typical floor: *1,362 sq. ft.*
    b Shaft area as a percent of the core area: *12.0%*
    c Shaft area as a percent of the gross floor area: *3.3%*

15 a Glass area as a percent of total facade area: *24.8%*

H   EXITING AND VERTICAL TRANSPORTATION

16 a Total number of exit stairways: *3*
    b Maximum travel distance to closest exit on a typical floor: *150 ft.*
    c Maximum travel distance to a second means of exit: *250 ft.*
    d Maximum dead-end public corridor length (when part of basic building layout and not dependent on tenant subdivision): *40 ft. (in core)*

17 a Total number of passenger elevators: *48*
    b Total number of freight elevators: *4*
    c Number of passenger elevators in each height zone:

Zone:	Number of elevators:	Floors serviced:
1	*8*	*2–15*
2	*8*	*2 + 15–25*
3	*8*	*2 + 25–36*
4	*8*	*2 + 36–45*
5	*8*	*2 + 45–54*
6	*8*	*2 + 54–62*

    d Ratio of total number of elevators to number of floors above grade: *1/1.18*

A   BUILDING: *Citicorp Central Tower*

B   ARCHITECT: *Hugh Stubbins with Emory Roth & Sons*

C   LOCATION: *New York, New York*

D   DATE OF CONSTRUCTION: *1978*

E   BASE BUILDING

1   a   Total building height, entrance level to highest point: *914'-9"*
     b   First floor level to top of roof bean: *810'-2"*

2   a   Total number of occupied floors: *46*
     b   Total number of floor levels above grade: *55 plus 4, plus shed area at top*
     c   Total number of floor levels below grade: *3*
     d   Total number of floor levels: *62 plus mechanical shed at top*

3   Typical Floor
     a   Overall dimensions (measured at glass line): *156'-10" × 156'-10"*
     b   Overall dimensions of core: *67'-10" × 70'-4"*
     c   Gross area: *24,596 sq. ft.*
     d   Gross area of core: *4712 sq. ft.*
     e   Net area of usable space: *19,884 sq. ft.*
     f   Core area as a percent of total floor area: *19.1%*
     g   Usable area as a percent of gross area: *79.9%*
     h   Approximate number of occupants on a typical floor: *198*

4   a   Floor-to-floor height: *12'-9"*
     b   Floor-to-ceiling height: *8'-6"*
     c   Usable height as a percent of total floor height: *67%*

5   a   Ratio of building width to height: *1/5.8*
     b   Gross building area: *1,800,000 sq. ft.*
     c   Net building area: *1,100,000 sq. ft.*

F   STRUCTURE

6   Type of framing system: *Steel skeleton with diagonal chevrons framing into mast at center of each facade.*

7   Dimensions of a typical framing bay: *38'-0" × 38'-0"*

8   Sizes of typical horizontal framing members:
     a   Typical girder: *none*
     b   Typical beam: *W 21 × 68*
          Depth: *1'-9"*   Span: *42'-1"*   Depth/Span: *1/24.0*
     c   Typical spandrel beam: *W 21 × 55*
          Depth: *1'-9"*   Span: *38'-0"*   Depth/Span: *1/21.7*

9   How columns structurally and visually accommodate their cumulative change in load-carrying capacity: *Column cross-section varies with load, but this is not visible from the exterior.*

G   MECHANICAL

10   Type of heating and cooling sysem:
     a   Interior: *variable volume*
     b   Exterior: *2 pipe induction with cold water only*

11   Location of H.V.A.C. equipment rooms:
     a   Level: b   Floors covered:
          9th & Mezzanine   *10–30*
          57th & 58th   *31–56*

12 Number of H.V.A.C. shafts serving a typical floor:
    a Interior: *2*   c Return: *2*
    b Exterior: *2 (one serves 3 sides, the other the south elevation only)*

13 a Area of the space required for all mechanical equipment and shafts on a typical floor, including H.V.A.C., electric, telephone, plumbing, and elevator shafts and spaces: *2,471 sq. ft. (10–26 fls.)*
    b This area as a percent of the core area: *52.4%*
    c This area as a percent of gross floor area: *10.0%*

14 Area required for all H.V.A.C. shafts on a typical floor: *450*
    a Shaft area as a percent of the core area: *9.6%*
    b Shaft area as a percent of the gross floor area: *1.8%*

15 a Glass area as a percent of facade area: *46%*

H   EXITING AND VERTICAL TRANSPORTATION

16 a Total number of exit stairways: *2*
    b Maximum travel distance to closest exit on a typical floor: *138 ft.*
    c Maximum travel distance to a second means of exit: *208 ft.*
    d Maximum dead-end public corridor length: *varies with tenant layout*

17 a Total number of passenger elevators: *20 tandem 2-level elevators*
    b Total number of freight elevators: *2*
    c Number of passenger elevators in each height zone:

Zone:	Floors serviced:	Number of elevators:
1	*Lobby + 10–27*	*8*
2	*Lobby + 27–41*	*6*
3	*Lobby + 41–56*	*6*

    d Ratio of total number of elevators to number of floors above grade: *1/2.2*

A   BUILDING: *Burlington Industries*

B   ARCHITECT: *A.J. Odell Jr. & Associates*

C   LOCATION: *Greensboro, North Carolina*

D   DATE OF CONSTRUCTION: *1970*

E   BASE BUILDING (tower only)

     1   a   Total building height, entrance level to highest point: *93'-6"*
          b   First floor level to top of roof beam: *86'-0"*

     2   a   Total number of occupied floors: *7*
          b   Total number of floor levels above grade: *6*
          c   Total number of floor levels below grade: *1*
          d   Total number of floor levels: *7*

     3   Typical Floor
          a   Overall dimensions (measured at glass line):   *153'-0" × 153'-0"*
          b   Overall dimensions of core: *60'-0" × 60'-0"*
          c   Gross area: *23,409 sq. ft.*
          d   Gross area of core: *3,600 sq. ft.*
          e   Net area of usable space: *19,809 sq. ft.*
          f   Core area as a percent of total floor area: *15.4%*
          g   Usable area as a percent of gross area: *84.6%*
          h   Approximate number of occupants on a typical floor: *1 per 100 sq. ft. = 234*

     4   a   Floor-to-floor height: *13'-6"*
          b   Floor-to-ceiling height: *9'-6"*
          c   Usable height as a percent of total floor height: *66.6%*

     5   a   Ratio of building width to height: *1/.56*

F   STRUCTURE

     6   Type of framing system: *Girders span 45 ft. between a rigid steel frame core to perimeter hangers suspended from a diagonal roof grid, which in turn is carried by the core and 4 massive exterior trusses.*

     7   Dimensions of a typical framing bay: *30'-0" × 45'-0"*

     8   Sizes of typical horizontal framing members:
          a   Typical girder: *W 36 × 182*
             Depth: *3'-0"*   Span: *45'-0"*   Spacing: Depth/Span: *1/15*
          b   Typical beam: *W 16 × 45 and W 18 × 55*
             Depth: *1'-4"*   Span: *25'-0"*   Spacing: *9'-0"*   Depth/Span: *1/19*
          c   Typical spandrel beam: *W 27 × 94*
             Depth: *2'-3"*   Span: *25'-0" & 30'-0"*   Depth/Span: *1/1 & 1/13*

     9   How columns structurally and visually accommodate their cumulative change in load-carrying capacity: *Exterior columns are actually hangers, which are supported from the roof grid—the hangers are wide flange sections, concealed behind an opaque curtain wall.*

G   MECHANICAL

     10   Type of heating and cooling system:
          a   Interior: *dual-duct, constant air volume*
          b   Exterior: *variable-volume*

11   Location of H.V.A.C. equipment rooms:
       a   Level: b   Floor covered:
          6 floor   *1 through 6*
          cellar   *cellar*

12   Number of H.V.A.C. shafts servicing a typical floor:
       a   Interior: *1*   c   Return: *2*
       b   Exterior: *2*

13   a   Area of the space required for all mechanical equipment and shafts on a typical floor, including H.V.A.C., electric, telephone, plumbing, and elevator shafts and spaces: *1,181 sq. ft.*
       b   This area as a percent of the core area: *32.8%*
       c   This area as a percent of gross floor area: *5.0%*

14   a   Area required for all H.V.A.C. shafts on a typical floor: *338 sq. ft.*
       b   Shaft area as a percent of the core area: *9.4%*
       c   Shaft area as a percent of the gross floor area: *1.4%*

15   a   Glass area as a percent of facade area: *65.1%*

H   EXITING AND VERTICAL TRANSPORTATION

16   a   Total number of exit stairways: *2*
       b   Maximum travel distance to closest exit on a typical floor: *126 ft.*
       c   Maximum travel distance to a second means of exit: *186 ft.*
       d   Maximum dead-end public corridor length: *none*

17   a   Total number of passenger elevators: *3*
       b   Total number of freight elevators: *1*
       c   Number of passenger elevators in each height zone: *3*

Zone:	Floors serviced:	Number of elevators:
1	*1 through 6*	*3*

       d   Ratio of total number of elevators to number of floors above grade   *1:2*

A   BUILDING: *CBS Headquarters*

B   ARCHITECT: *Eero Saarinen*

C   LOCATION: *New York, New York*

D   DATE OF CONSTRUCTION: *1962*

E   BASE BUILDING

   1   a   Total building height, entrance level to highest point: *494'*
       b   First floor level to top level to top of roof beam: *491'*

   2   a   Total number of occupied floors: *36*
       b   Total number of floor levels above grade: *38*
       c   Total number of floor levels below grade: *1*
       d   Total number of floor levels: *39*

   3   Typical Floor
       a   Overall dimensions (measured at glass line): *155'-0" × 125'-0"*
       b   Overall dimensions of core: *85'-3" × 55'-3"*
       c   Gross area: *19,375 sq. ft. + perimeter = 20,577 sq. ft.*
       d   Gross area of core: *4,710 sq. ft. plus 58 columns @ 1.5 sq. ft. = 4,797 sq. ft.*
       e   Net area of usable space: *14,665 sq. ft.*
       f   Core area as a percent of total floor area: *24.3%*
       g   Usable area as a percent of gross area: *71.3%*
       h   Approximate number of occupants on a typical floor: *146*

   4   a   Floor-to-floor height: *12'-0"*
       b   Floor-to-ceiling height: *8'-9"*
       c   Usable height as a percent of total floor height: *69%*

   5   a   Ratio of building width to height: *1/3.9*
       b   Gross building area: *748,650 sq. ft. (including service structure)*

F   STRUCTURE

   6   Type of framing system: *Combination of poured-in-place one-way rib at side of cores to perimeter and waffle slab at corners.*

   7   Dimensions of a typical framing bay: *5'-0" × 35'-0"*
                                          ribs 2'-6" o.c.
                                          columns 5'-0" wide 10'-0" o.c.

   8   Sizes of typical horizontal framing members:
       a   Typical girder: *none*
       b   Typical beam:
          Depth: *1'-5"* Span: *35'-0"* Spacing: *2'-6"* Depth/Span: *1/24.7*
       c   Typical spandrel beam: *2'-9" wide × 1'-5" deep*
          Depth: *1'-5"* Span: *5'-0"*

   9   How columns structurally and visually accommodate their cumulative change in load-carrying capacity: *Load-carrying changes not expressed. Column area and amount of reinforcement change.*

G   MECHANICAL

   10   Type of heating and cooling system:
       a   Interior: *variable volume*
       b   Exterior: *high-speed induction units, air supplied from alternate columns*

11   Location of H.V.A.C. equipment rooms:
     a   Level: b   Floors covered:
        38 floor   *37–21*
        2 floor   *1–20*

        Note: lower perimeter zone feeds up to 12th floor

12   Number of H.V.A.C. shafts serving a typical floor:
     a   Interior: *2*   c   Return: *2*
     b   Exterior: *27*

13   a   Area of the space required for all mechanical equipment and shafts on a typical floor, including H.V.A.C., electric, telephone, plumbing, and elevator shafts and spaces: *1,840 sq. ft.*
     b   This area as a percent of the core area: *39%*
     c   This area as a percent of gross floor area: *8.9%*

14   a   Area required for all H.V.A.C. shafts on a typical floor: *398 sq. ft.*
     b   Shaft area as a percent of the core area: *8.3%*
     c   Shaft area as a percent of the gross floor area: *1.9%*

15   a   Glass area as a percent of facade area: *37%*

H   EXITING AND VERTICAL TRANSPORTATION

16   a   Total number of exit stairways: *2*
     b   Maximum travel distance to closest exit on a typical floor: *135 ft.*
     c   Maximum travel distance to a second means of exit: *200 ft.*
     d   Maximum dead-end public corridor length: *varies with tenant layout*

17   a   Total number of passenger elevators: *16*
     b   Total number of freight elevators: *1*
     c   Number of passenger elevators in each height zone:

Zone:	Floors serviced:	Number of elevators:
1	*1 + 2–19*	*8*
2	*1 + 19–35*	*8*

     d   Ratio of total number of elevators to number of floors above grade: *1/2.2*

A   BUILDING: *One Shell Plaza*

B   ARCHITECT: *Skidmore Owings and Merrill*

C   LOCATION: *Houston, Texas*

D   DATE OF CONSTRUCTION: *1968*

E   BASE BUILDING

    1   a   Total building height, entrance level to highest point: *711'-3"*
           b   First floor level to top of roof beam: *684'-9"*

    2   a   Total number of occupied floors: *48*
           b   Total number of floor levels above grade: *50*
           c   Total number of floor levels below grade: *4*
           d   Total number of floor levels: *54*

    3   Typical Floor
           a   Overall dimensions (measured at glass line): *132'-0" × 192'-0" (plus column depth, which varies with location and height)*
           b   Overall dimensions of core: *88'-8" × 57'-8"*
           c   Gross area: *25,344 sq. ft. plus perimeter = 26,640 sq. ft.*
           d   Gross area of core: *5,112 sq. ft.*
           e   Net area of usable space: *(540 sq. ft. of core is rentable) 26,640 − 5112 + 540 = 22,068 sq. ft.*
           f   Core area as a percent of total floor area: *19.2%*
           g   Usable area as a percent of gross area: *82.8%*
           h   Approximate number of occupants on a typical floor: *202*

    4   a   Floor-to-floor height: *13'-0"*
           b   Floor-to-ceiling height: *9'-0"*
           c   Usable height as a percent of total floor height: *69.2%*

    5   a   Ratio of building width to height: *1/4.89*
           b   Gross building area: *1,593,448 sq. ft. (including garage)*

F   STRUCTURE

    6   Type of framing system: *One-way concrete ribs span between bearing wall at core on 2 sides, and from girder on 2 sides to outer columns. Corners are framed in waffle slabs. 3½" slab.*

    7   Dimensions of a typical framing bay: *6'-0" 37'-2"*

    8   Sizes of typical horizontal framing members:
           a   Typical girder: *At column line parallel to core—20" × 42"*
               Depth: *3'-6"* Span: *27'-0"*   Spacing: *at core columns*   Depth/Span: *1/7.7*
                      39'-0" to exterior   *only*
           b   Typical beam: *joist 9" × 24"*
               Depth: *2'-0"* Span: *37'-2*   Spacing: *6'-0"*   Depth/Span: *1/18.6*
           c   Typical spandrel beam: *4'-2" deep × 11" wide (23" wide opposite core corner)*
               Depth: *4'-2"* Span: *4'-0"*   Depth/Span: *1/.96*

    9   How columns structurally and visually accommodate their cumulative change in load-carrying capacity: *Column depth decreases with building height. Width remains constant at 1'-10". (Actual column depth varies from 1'-1$\frac{13}{16}$" to 3'-11".)*

G   MECHANICAL

    10   Type of heating and cooling system: *Dual duct. Separate zone for each office.*

11 Location of H.V.A.C. equipment rooms: *Central equipment on top floor and roof. Minor mech space in mezzanine for lobby. Each floor has 2 mechanical equipment rooms.*

12 Number of H.V.A.C. shafts serving a typical floor: *Basically only piping from cooling tower and toilet exhausts.*

13 a Area of the space required for all mechanical equipment and shafts on a typical floor, including H.V.A.C., electric, telephone, plumbing, and elevator shafts and spaces: *1,400 sq. ft.*
   b This area as a percent of the core area: *27.4%*
   c This area as a percent of gross floor area: *5.3%*

14 a Area required for all H.V.A.C. shafts on a typical floor: *311 sq. ft. includes mechanical equipment rooms*
   b Shaft area as a percent of the core area: *6.0%*
   c Shaft area as a percent of the gross floor area: *1.2%*

15 a Glass area as a percent of facade area: *39%*

H EXITING AND VERTICAL TRANSPORTATION

16 a Total number of exit stairways: *2*
   b Maximum travel distance to closest exit on a typical floor: *140 ft.*
   c Maximum travel distance to a second means of exit: *165 ft.*
   d Maximum dead end public corridor length: *Varies with tenant use*

17 a Total number of passenger elevators: *22*
   b Total number of freight elevators: *2*
   c Number of passenger elevators in each height zone:
      (Shuttle elevators to garage from mall and to top 3 floors from 47th floor.)

Zone:	Floors serviced:	Number of elevators:
1	*mall −16*	*6*
2	*mall + 16–31*	*8*
3	*mall + 31–47*	*8*

   d Ratio of total number of elevators to number of floors above grade: *1/21*

A   BUILDING: *Richards Medical Research Laboratories, University of Pennsylvania*

B   ARCHITECT: *Louis I. Kahn*

C   LOCATION: *Philadelphia, Pennsylvania*

D   DATE OF CONSTRUCTION: *1959*

E   BASE BUILDING

    1   a Total building height, entrance level to highest point: *121'-0"*
        b First floor level to top of roof beam: *96'-0"*

    2   a Total number of occupied floors: *8*
        b Total number of floor levels above grade: *7*
        c Total number of floor levels below grade: *1*
        d Total number of floor levels: *8*

    3   Typical Floor
        a Overall dimensions (measured at glass line): *complex 154'-7" × 157'-3"*
                                           individual laboratory building 47'-4" × 47'-4"
        b Overall dimensions of core: *Core in separate building, plus towers, plus links*
        c Gross area: *11,964 sq. ft.*
        d Gross area of core: *2,985 sq. ft. plus corridor in labs = 3,525 sq. ft.*
        e Net area of usable space: *8,439 sq. ft.*
        f Core area as a percent of total floor area: *24.5%*
        g Usable area as a percent of gross area: *70.5%*
        h Approximate number of occupants on a typical floor: *210*

    4   a Floor-to-floor height: *12'-0"*
        b Floor-to-ceiling height: *8'-6"*
        c Usable height as a percent of total floor height: *70.8%*

    5   a Ratio of building width to height: *1/2.03*

F   STRUCTURE

    6   Type of framing system: *Precast, post-tensioned concrete frame with exposed truss system.*

    7   Dimensions of a typical framing bay: *47'-4" × 47'-4"*

    8   Sizes of typical horizontal framing members:
        a Typical girder:
           Depth: *3'-2"* Span: *45'-0"* Spacing: *16'-2"* Depth/Span: *1/14.2*
        b Typical beam:
           Depth: *3'-2"* Span: *15'-0"* Spacing: *7'-6"* Depth/Span: *made to match major truss depth*
        c Typical spandrel beam: *Cantilevered exposed truss, depth varies.*

    9   How columns structurally and visually accommodate their cumulative change in load-carrying capacity: *Columns are visually constant in size @ 2'-10".*

G   MECHANICAL

    10   Type of heating and cooling system:
        a Interior: *Variable volume*
        b Exterior: *Supplemental hot water radiators*

    11   Location of H.V.A.C. equipment rooms:
        a Level: *Penthouse*
        b Floors covered: *All*

12   Number of H.V.A.C. shafts serving a typical floor: *For complex:*
    a *Fresh air intakes: 4—exposed on exterior*
    b *Exhaust shafts: 4—exposed on exterior*
    c *Supply air shafts: 2—interior*
    d *Return air shafts: 2—interior*
    e *Stair shafts are also exposed, but have 2-sided tops to differentiate them from 4-sided air shafts.*

13   a Area of the space required for all mechanical equipment and shafts on a typical floor, including H.V.A.C., electric, telephone, plumbing, and elevator shafts and spaces: *1,340 sq. ft.*
    b This area as a percent of the core area: *44.9%*
    c This area as a percent of gross floor area: *11.2%*

14   a Area required for all H.V.A.C. shafts on a typical floor: *1,007 sq. ft.*
    b Shaft area as a percent of the core area: *33.7%*
    c Shaft area as a percent of the gross floor area: *8.4%*

15   a Glass area as a percent of facade area: *35%*

H   EXITING AND VERTICAL TRANSPORTATION

16   a Total number of exit stairways: *4*
    b Maximum travel distance to closest exit on a typical floor: *70 ft.*
    c Maximum travel distance to a second means of exit: *110 ft.*
    d Maximum dead-end public corridor length: *None*

17   a Total number of passenger elevators: *2*
    b Total number of freight elevators: *1*
    c Number of passenger elevators in each height zone:

Zone:	Floors serviced:	Number of elevators:
1	*1–8*	*2*

    d Ratio of total number of elevators to floors above grade: *1/2.7*

A   BUILDING: *Hoffmann-LaRoche Administration Building*

B   ARCHITECT: *Lundquist & Stonehill*

C   LOCATION: *Nutley, New Jersey*

D   DATE OF CONSTRUCTION: *1967*

E   BASE BUILDING

    1   a   Total building height, entrance level to highest point: *125'-9"*
          b   First floor level to top of roof beam: *112'-9"*

    2   a   Total number of occupied floors: *8*
          b   Total number of floor levels above grade: *8*
          c   Total number of floor levels below grade: *1*
          d   Total number of floor levels: *9*

    3   Typical Floor
          a   Overall dimensions (measured at glass line): *120'-0" × 120'-0"*
                                                at perimeter: 130'-0" × 130'-0"
          b   Overall dimensions of core: *42'-0" × 42'-0"*
          c-1   Gross area: *17,224 sq. ft. including exterior stair and 5-ft. wide perimeter column ring*
          c-2   Gross area to glass lines: *14,624 sq. ft. including exterior stair.*
          d   Gross area of core: *2,088 sq. ft. including exterior stair.*
          e   Net area of usable space: *12,636 sq. ft.*
          f(1)   Core area as a percent of total floor area: *12.1%*
          f(2)   Core area as a percent of floor area to glass line: *14.2%*
          g   Usable area as a percent of gross area: *73.3%*
          h   Approximate number of occupants on a typical floor: *126*

    4   a   Floor-to-floor height: *13'-7"*
          b   Floor-to-ceiling height: *9'-8"*
          c   Usable height as a percent of total floor height: *71%*

    5   a   Ratio of building width to height: *1/0.87*

F   STRUCTURE

    6   Type of framing system: *Waffle slab supported on column strips which divide space into 8 equal bays around central core.*

    7   Dimensions of a typical framing bay: *41'-6" × 41'-6"*
          Ribs 2½ ft. o.c.
          Columns 7½ ft. o.c.

    8   Sizes of typical horizontal framing members:
          a   Typical girder: *43'-3" center line of spandrel to center line of core wall*
          b   Typical beam: *Rib of waffle slab*
              Depth: *2'-0"*   Span: *41'-6"*   Spacing: *2'-6"*   Depth/Span: *1/20.8*
          c   Typical spandrel beam: *2-5⅝" wide × 2'-0" deep to match ribs*
              Depth: *2'-0"*   Span: *6'-8"*   Depth/Span: *1/3.75*

    9   How columns structurally and visually accommodate their cumulative change in load-carrying capacity: *Columns maintain uniform appearance. Amount of reinforcement varies. Each column is 2'-5⅝" × 10"*

G   MECHANICAL

    10   Type of heating and cooling system: *Separate variable volume system for each floor.*

11   Location of H.V.A.C. equipment rooms: *Roof cooling tower serves all floors. Each floor has its own mechanical equipment room.*

12   Number of H.V.A.C. shafts serving a typical floor: *Individual air-handling room each floor. One supply riser and one exhaust shaft. 4 separate zones and supply ducts. 4 return ducts. 8 separate exterior zones and supply ducts. 4 interior zones and supply ducts.*

13   a   Area of the space required for all mechanical equipment and shafts on a typical floor, including H.V.A.C., electric, telephone, plumbing, and elevator shafts and spaces: *914 sq. ft.*
        b   This area as a percent of the core area: *43.8%*
        c   This area as a percent of gross floor area: *c-1 6.2%: c-2 5.3%*

14   a   Area required for all H.V.A.C. shafts on a typical floor: *509 sq. ft. including air-handling area*
        b   Shaft area as a percent of the core area: *24.4% including air-handing area*
        c   Shaft area as a percent of the gross floor area: *c-1 3.45%: c-2 2.95%*

15   a   Glass area as a percent of facade area: *71%*

H   EXITING AND VERTICAL TRANSPORTATION

16   a   Total number of exit stairways: *2*
        b   Maximum travel distance to closest exit on a typical floor: *120 ft.*
        c   Maximum travel distance to a second means of exit: *160 ft.*
        d   Maximum dead-end public corridor length: *Varies according to tenant subdivision layout.*

17   a   Total number of passenger elevators: *3*
        b   Total number of freight elevators: *none*
        c   Number of passenger elevators in each height zone:

Zone:	Floors serviced:	Number of elevators:
1	*all floors*	*3*
	cellar to 8th	

        d   Ratio of total number of elevators to number of floors above grade: *1/2.7*

A   BUILDING: *Yale Art Gallery*

B   ARCHITECT: *Louis I. Kahn with Douglas Orr*

C   LOCATION: *New Haven, Connecticut*

D   DATE OF CONSTRUCTION: *1953*

E   BASE BUILDING

1   a   Total building height, entrance level to highest point: *69'-5"*
     b   First floor level to top of roof beam: *51'-9"*

2   a   Total number of occupied floors: *4 plus cellar*
     b   Total number of floor levels above grade: *varies from 3 to 4½*
     c   Total number of floor levels below grade: *1*
     d   Total number of floor levels: *5*

3   Typical Floor
     a   Overall dimensions: *158'-11" × 81'-6"*
     b   Overall dimensions of core: *24'-6" × 81'-6" plus isolated stair @ 8' × 21'-5"*
     c   Gross area: *12,950 sq. ft.*
     d   Gross area of core: *1,997 + 171 = 2,168 sq. ft.*
     e   Net area of usable space: *10,782 sq. ft.*
     f   Core area as a percent of total floor area: *16.7%*
     g   Usable area as a percent of gross area: *83.3%*
     h   Approximate number of occupants on a typical floor: *269*

4   a   Floor-to-floor height: *13'-3"*
     b   Floor-to-ceiling height: *10'-8"*
     c   Usable height as a percent of total floor height: *80%*

5   a   Ratio of building width to height: *1/.63*

F   STRUCTURE

6   Type of framing system: *One-way rib spanning between girders. Rib sloped as side of 3-way tetrahedron grid. Other ribs of system are nonload-bearing, but provide some distribution and stabilizing help.*

7   Dimensions of a typical framing bay: *19'-9" × 40'-0" column bays*
                                            2'-6" × 37'-0" rib bays

8   Sizes of typical horizontal framing members:
     a   Typical girder:,   *3'-0" wide × 2'-4" deep*
          Depth: *2'-4"*   Span: *18'-2"*   Spacing: *40'-0" o.c.*   Depth/Span: *1/7.78*
     b   Typical beam: *rib 5" × 2'-4"*
          Depth: *2'-4"*   Span: *37'-0"*   Spacing: *2'-5½" o.c.*   Depth/Span: *1/15.8*

9   How columns structurally and visually accommodate their cumulative change in load-carrying capacity: *Not expressed. Amount of reinforcement decreases.*

G   MECHANICAL

10   Type of heating and cooling system:
     a   Interior: *Low speed multiduct variable volume*
     b   Exterior: *Hot water baseboard at glass*

11   Location of H.V.A.C. equipment rooms:
     a   Level: *Penthouse on 5th level*
     b   Floors covered: *All*

12   Number of H.V.A.C. shafts serving a typical floor:
    a   Interior: *One, with two main branches*
    b   Exterior: *Supplemental fin-tube hot water radiators*
    c   Return: *One, exposed ceiling grill in core*

13   a   Area of the space required for all mechanical equipment and shafts of a typical floor, including H.V.A.C., electric, telephone, plumbing, and elevator shafts and spaces: *527 sq. ft.*
    b   This area as a percent of the core area: *24.3%*
    c   This area as a percent of gross floor area: *4.0%*

14   a   Area required for all H.V.A.C. shafts on a typical floor: *114 sq. ft.*
    b   Shaft area as a percent of the core area: *21.2%*
    c   Shaft area as a percent of the gross floor area: *0.9%*

15   a   Glass area as a percent of facade area: *48% on a typical floor*

H   EXITING AND VERTICAL TRANSPORTATION

16   a   Total number of exit stairways: *3*
    b   Maximum travel distance to closest exit on a typical floor: *60 ft.*
    c   Maximum travel distance to a second means of exit: *100 ft.*
    d   Maximum dead-end public corridor length: *No corridors in exhibit areas*

17   a   Total number of passenger elevators: *0*
    b   Total number of freight elevators: *1*
    c   Number of passenger elevators in each height zone:

Zone:	Floors serviced:	Number of elevators:
1	*1–4*	*2*

    d   Ratio of total number of elevators to total numbers of floors above grade: *1/4*

A   BUILDING: *M.I.T. Earth Science Laboratory*

B   ARCHITECT: *I.M. Pei & Associates*

C   LOCATION: *Cambridge, Massachusetts*

D   DATE OF CONSTRUCTION: *1962*

E   BASE BUILDING

    1   a   Total building height, entrance level to highest point: *322'-5" to weather tower*
        b   First floor level to top of roof beam: *274'-6"*

    2   a   Total number of occupied floors: *19*
        b   Total number of floor levels above grade: *21*
        c   Total number of floor levels below grade: *1*
        d   Total number of floor levels: *22*

    3   Typical Floor
        a   Overall dimensions: *111'-6" × 54'-6"*
        b   Overall dimensions of core: *1 @ 12'-3" × 48'-0" (notched)*
                                      1 @ 9'-3 × 48'-0" (notched)
        c   Gross area: *5,922.5 sq. ft.*
        d   Gross area of core: *1,224 sq. ft.*
        e   Net area of usable space: *4,370 sq. ft. (glass line recessed 2'-0")*
        f   Core area as a percent of total floor area: *20.7%*
        g   Usable area as a percent of gross area: *73.8% (usable area plus core is less than gross due to glass line setback.)*
        h   Approximate number of occupants on a typical floor: *43*

    4   a   Floor-to-floor height: *11'-7½"*
        b   Floor-to-ceiling height: *8'-1½"*
        c   Usable height as a percent of total floor height: *69.9%*

    5   a   Ratio of building width to height: *1/5.0*

F   STRUCTURE

    6   Type of framing system: *3'-6" deep concrete I-beams span across the building's width parallel to end cores. Every beam is supported by a column at each end.*

    7   Dimensions of a typical framing bay: *9'-0" × 48'-4"*

    8   Sizes of typical horizontal framing members:
        a   **Typical girder:** *none*
        b   **Typical beam:** *3'-6" I-beam*
            Depth: *3'-6"*   Span: *48'-4"*   Spacing: *9'-0"*   Depth/Span: *1/13.8*

    9   How columns structurally and visually accommodate their cumulative change in load-carrying **capacity:** *No change in visual expression of column. Columns collected at 2nd floor by massive girder.*

G   MECHANICAL

    10   Type of heating and cooling system:
        a   Interior: *Variable volume*
        b   Exterior: *Induction units with air intake at each window*

    11   Location of H.V.A.C. equipment rooms:
        a   Level: b   Floors covered:
           20 & 21   *All*

12   Number of H.V.A.C. shafts serving a typical floor
    a   Interior: *2*   c   Return: *1*
    b   Exterior: *4*   d   Exhaust: *as required for each toxic hood.*
                                        Return air furnished at each exhaust hood area.

13   a   Area of the space required for all mechanical equipment and shafts on a typical floor, including H.V.A.C., electric, telephone, plumbing, and elevator shafts and spaces: *553*
    b   This area as a percent of the core area: *45.2%*
    c   This area as a percent of gross floor area: *9.3%*

14   a   Area rquired for all H.V.A.C. shafts on a typical floor: *182 sq. ft.*
    b   Shaft area as a percent of the core area: *14.8%*
    c   Shaft area as a percent of the gross floor area: *30%*

15   a   Glass area as a percent of facade area: *23.2%*

H   EXITING AND VERTICAL TRANSPORTATION

16   a   Total number of exit stairways: *2*
    b   Maximum travel distance to closest exit on a typical floor: *80*
    c   Maximum travel distance to a second means of exit: *80 ft.*
    d   Maximum dead-end public corridor length: *none*

17   a   Total number of passenger elevators: *3*
    b   Total number of freight elevators: *0*
    c   Number of passenger elevators in each height zone: *3*

Zone:	Floors serviced:	Number of elevators:
1	*1–19*	*3*

    d   Ratio of total number of elevators to number of floors above grade: *1/6.3*

A   BUILDING: *American Life Insurance Company*

B   ARCHITECT: *I.M. Pei & Associates*

C   LOCATION: *Wilmington, Delaware*

D   DATE OF CONSTRUCTION: *1973*

E   BASE BUILDING

   1   a   Total building height, entrance level to highest point: *282'-0"*
      b   First floor level to top of roof beam: *278'-6"*

   2   a   Total number of occupied floors: *21*
      b   Total number of floor levels above grade: *23*
      c   Total number of floor levels below grade: *2*
      d   Total number of floor levels: *25*

   3   Typical Floor
      a   Overall dimensions: *132' × 66'*
             overall office area 78' × 66' = 5,148 sq. ft.
      b   Overall dimensions of core: *Irregular, see plan*
      c   Gross area: *6,473 sq. ft.*
      d   Gross area of core: *1,673 sq. ft. (includes shaft walls)*
      e   Net area of usable space: *4,752 sq. ft.*
      f   Core area as a percent of total floor area: *25.8%*
      g   Usable area as a percent of gross area: *73.9%*
      h   Approximate number of occupants on a typical floor: *47*

   4   a   Floor-to-floor height: *11'-6"*
      b   Floor-to-ceiling height: *8'-2"*
      c   Usable height as a percent of total floor height: *71%*

   5   a   Ratio of building width to height: *1/4.3*

F   STRUCTURE

   6   Type of framing system: *Post-tensioned beams span between cores located at each end of the building.*

   7   Dimensions of a typical framing bay: *6'-0" × 72'-0"*

   8   Sizes of typical horizontal framing members:
      a   **Typical girder:**   *Post-tensioned concrete tapers in width from 1"-4" at top to 11¼" at bottom*
         Depth: *3'-1"*   Span: *72'-0"*   Spacing: *6'-0"*   Depth/Span: *1/23.4*

   9   How columns structurally and visually accommodate to their cumulative change in load-carrying capacity: *Columns are buried in core and are not visible as an element.*

G   MECHANICAL

   10   Type of heating and cooling system:
       a   Interior: *Variable volume*
       b   Exterior: *Induction units*

   11   Location of H.V.A.C. equipment rooms:
       a   Level: b   Floors covered:
         21 & 22   *All*

   12   Number of H.V.A.C. shafts servicing a typical floor:
      Shaft locations in each end core, each shaft approximately 5' × 2'
       a   Interior: *10*   c   Return: *10*
       b   Exterior: *2*

13   a   Area of the space required for all mechanical equipment and shafts on a typical floor, including H.V.A.C., electric, telephone, plumbing, and elevator shafts and spaces: *698 sq. ft.*

       b   This area as a percent of the core area: *41.7%*

       c   This area as a percent of gross floor area: *10.8%*

14   a   Area required for all H.V.A.C. shafts on a typical floor: *180 sq. ft.*

       b   Shaft area as a percent of the core area: *10.7%*

       c   Shaft area as a percent of the gross floor area: *2.8%*

15   a   Glass area as a percent of facade area: *22.3%*

H   EXITING AND VERTICAL TRANSPORTATION

16   a   Total number of exit stairways: *2*

       b   Maximum travel distance to closest exit on a typical floor: *50 ft.*

       c   Maximum travel distance to a second means of exit: *50 ft.*

       d   Maximum dead end public corridor length: *none*

17   a   Total number of passenger elevators: *3*

       b   Total number of freight elevators: *0*

       c   Number of passenger elevators in each height zone:

Zone:	Floors serviced:	Number of elevators:
1	*1–21*	*3*

       d   Ratio of total number of elevators to number of floors served above grade: *1/7.0*

A   BUILDING: *Cornell Agronomy Laboratory*

B   ARCHITECT: *Ulrich Franzen and Associates*

C   LOCATION: *Ithaca, New York*

D   DATE OF CONSTRUCTION: *1968*

E   BASE BUILDING

    1   a Total building height, entrance level to highest point: *156'-1"*
        b First floor level to top of roof beam: *135'-8¼"*

    2   a Total number of occupied floors: *12*
        b Total number of floor levels above grade: *12*
        c Total number of floor levels below grade: *1*
        d Total number of floor levels: *13*

    3   Typical Floor
        a Overall dimensions: *92'-6" × 104'-9"*
        b Overall dimensions of core: *Irregular, surrounds almost entire structure*
        c Gross area: *12,317 sq. ft.*
        d Gross area of core: *4,160 sq. ft.*
        e Net area of usable space: *7,580 sq. ft.*
        f Core area as a percent of total floor area: *33.7%*
        g Usable area as a percent of gross area: *61.5%*
        h Approximate number of occupants on a typical floor: *189*

    4   a Floor-to-floor height: *9'-1"*
        b Floor-to-ceiling height: *11'-2"*
        c Usable height as a percent of total floor height: *81.3%*

    5   a Ratio of building width to height: *1/1.47*

F   STRUCTURE

    6   Type of framing system: *Poured-in-place concrete skeleton with precast concrete channel slabs spanning between beams. 5" poured slab in corridor. Top floor corridor columns and roof are framed in steel.*

    7   Dimensions of a typical framing bay: *8'-6" × 41'-2"*

    8   Sizes of typical horizontal framing members:
        a Typical girder: *L-shaped corridor girder spans between columns spaced 8'-6" o.c.*
        b Typical beam: *4'-0" wide precast channel slabs*
           Depth: *1'-10"*   Span: *41'-2"*   Spacing: *4'-3" o.c.*   Depth/Span: *1/22.5*
        c Typical spandrel beam: *L-shaped girder spans between columns spaced 8'-6" o.c.*
           Depth: *2'-8"*

    9   How columns structurally and visually accommodate their cumulative change in load-carrying capacity: *Columns increase in size. This is expressed on facade as a 1'-0" setback at 3 locations at 3rd, 7th, & 10th levels.*

G   MECHANICAL

    10   Type of heating and cooling system:
        a Interior: *Dual duct system, with mixing boxes located in corridor*
        b Exterior: *Hot water baseboard in lounge only*

11   Location of H.V.A.C. equipment rooms:
     a   Level: *Cellar and roof (campus central steam)*
     b   Floors covered: *All*

12   Number of H.V.A.C shafts serving a typical floor:
     a   Interior: *2 sets of hot & cold risers*   c   Return: *6*
     b   Exterior: *Hot water baseboard*   d   Exhaust: *Separate ducts for each toxic hood*
        at glass areas   *collected into 4 shafts.*

13   a   Area of the space required for all mechanical equipment and shafts on a typical floor, including H.V.A.C. electric, telephone, plumbing, and elevator shafts and spaces: *1,556 sq. ft.*
     b   This area as a percent of the core area: *41.7%*
     c   This area as a percent of gross floor area: *14.0%*

14   a   Area required for all H.V.A.C. shafts on a typical floor: *1,038 sq. ft.*
     b   Shaft area as a percent of the core area: *24.9%*
     c   Shaft area as a percent of the gross floor area: *8.4%*

15   a   Glass area as a percent of facade area: *7.2%*

H   EXITING AND VERTICAL TRANSPORTATION

16   a   Total number of exit stairways: *2*
     b   Maximum travel distance to closest exit on a typical floor: *110 ft.*
     c   Maximum travel distance to a second means of exit: *110 ft.*
     d   Maximum dead-end public corridor length: *none*

17   a   Total number of passenger elevators: *1*
     b   Total number of freight elevators: *1*
     c   Number of passenger elevators in each height zone:

Zone:	Floors serviced:	Number of elevators:
1	*1–12*	*2*

     d   Ratio of total number of elevators to number of floors above grade: *1/6*

A   BUILDING: *780 Third Avenue*

B   ARCHITECT: *Skidmore Owings & Merrill*

C   LOCATION: *New York, New York*

D   DATE OF CONSTRUCTION: *1984*

E   BASE BUILDING

    1   a   Total building height, entrance level to highest point: *575'-10"*
        b   First floor level to top of roof beam: *566'-7" (568'-7" top of parapet)*

    2   a   Total number of occupied floors: *49 (47 above grade)*
        b   Total number of floor levels above grade: *49*
        c   Total number of floor levels below grade: *2*
        d   Total number of floor levels: *51*

    3   Typical Floor
        a   Overall dimensions (measured at glass line):   *126'-1" × 70'-1"*
        b   Overall dimensions of core: *54'-6" × 33'-9¾"*
        c   Gross area: *8,836 sq. ft.*
        d   Gross area of core: *59'-11¼" × 33'-9¾" = 2,026 sq. ft. includes rear corridor*
        e   Net area of usable space: *6,105 (1'-10" perimeter)*
        f   Core area as a percent of total floor area: *22.9%*
        g   Usable area as a percent of gross area: *69.1%*
        h   Approximate number of occupants on a typical floor: *61*

    4   a   Floor-to-floor height: *11'-6"*
        b   Floor-to-ceiling height: *8'-5"*
        c   Usable height as a percent of total floor height: *73%*

    5   a   Ratio of building width to height: *1/8.08*

F   STRUCTURE

    6   Type of framing system: *Poured in place concrete diagonally braced tube. Waffle and one-way floor slabs.*

    7   Dimensions of a typical framing bay: *column centers 9'-4"*

    8   Sizes of typical horizontal framing members:
        a   Typical beam: *waffle and one-way ribs*
             Depth: *1'-3"*   Span: *28'-8"*   Spacing: *3'-0"*   Depth/Span: *1/22.9*
        b   Typical spandrel beam: *2'-11¼" wide*
             Depth: *1'-3"*   Span: *5'-4"*   Depth/Span: *1/4.2*

    9   How columns structurally and visually accommodate their cumulative change in load-carrying capacity: *Diagonal bracing is expressed on facade. Increase in load bearing with height of columns located betweed windows is accommodated by an increase in amount of reinforcing steel and is not expressed.*

G   MECHANICAL

    10   Type of heating and cooling system:
        a   Interior: *individual floor forced air*
        b   Exterior: *hot water fin tube*

11   Location of H.V.A.C. equipment rooms:
    a   Level: *48 main equipment and cooling tower*
    b   Each floor has own mini-H.V.A.C. room

12   Number of H.V.A.C. shafts servicing a typical floor:
    a   Supply: *1*
    b   Exhaust: *1*

13   a   Area of the space required for all mechanical equipment and shafts on a typical floor, including
       H.V.A.C., electric, telephone, plumbing, and elevator shafts and spaces: *940 sq. ft.*
    b   This area as a percent of the core area: *46%*
    c   This area as a percent of gross floor area: *10.6%*

14   a   Area required for all H.V.A.C. shafts on a typical floor: *50 sq. ft.*
    b   Shaft area as a percent of the core area: *2.5%*
    c   Shaft area as a percent of the gross floor area: *0.5%*

15   a   Glass area as a percent of facade area: *26%*

H   EXITING AND VERTICAL TRANSPORTATION

16   a   Total number of exit stairways: *2*
    b   Maximum travel distance to closest exit on a typical floor: *106 ft.*
    c   Maximum travel distance to a second means of exit: *136 ft.*
    d   Maximum dead-end public corridor length: *none*

17   a   Total number of passenger elevators: *10*
    b   Total number of freight elevators: *1*
    c   Number of passenger elevators in each height zone:

Zone:	Floors serviced:	Number of elevators:
1	*1 + 3–19*	*3*
2	*1 + 20–34*	*3*
3	*1 + 35–48*	*3*
4	*1 + concourse 1 & 2*	*1*

    d   Ratio of total number of elevators to number of floors above grade   *1/5.2*

SUMMARY OF SELECTED DATA	1b / 2b — Building Height / Number of Floors	5a — Building Width / Building Height	3g — Useable Area / Gross Area	7a — Dimensions of a Typical Framing Bay	8b — Typical Beam Depth/Span	13c — Mechanical Equipment & Shaft Area / Gross Floor Area	14c — H.V.A.C. Shaft Area / Gross Floor Area	4c — Usable Height / Total Floor Height	15a — Glass Area / Facade Area	17d — Number of Elevators / Number of Floors
Building		Ratio	%	×	Ratio	%	%	%	%	Ratio
Seagram Building	$\frac{516}{40}$	1:4.5	73	27'-9" × 27'-9"	1:20.8	14.5	2.2	74	72	1:2.2
Knights of Columbus	$\frac{319}{24}$	1:2.4	66	10'-0" × 35'-10"	1:20.5	14.6	2.5	66	91	1:3.8
One Liberty Plaza	$\frac{728}{56}$	1:4.5	74	46'-8" × 47'-6"	1:21.1	13.8	2.3	68	41	1:1.4
Chase Manhattan	$\frac{813}{61}$	1:6.9	76	29'-0" × 33'-3" & 42'-11"	1:18.5	13.2	3.0	70	58	1:1.4
Boston Company	$\frac{536}{41}$	1:3.8	78	9'-4" × 42'-0"	1:24	10.2	2.0	71	46	1:2.1
Westcoast Transmission	$\frac{180}{17}$	Core 1:6 Bldg 1:1.6	88	12'-0" × 36'-0"	1:26.7	5.0	1.4	72	41	1:3.8
U.S. Steel	$\frac{841}{64}$	1:3.7	72	13'-0" × 48'-0"	1:22.3	12.6	3.3	72	24	1:1.2
Citicorp	$\frac{915}{56}$	1:5.8	80	38'-0" × 38'-0"	1:24	10.0	1.8	67	46	1:2.2
Burlington Industries	$\frac{86}{6}$	1:.56	85	25'-0" × 45'-0"	1:19	5.0	1.4	66	65	1:2
Averages/Steel Frame Building		1:4.2	77		1:21.8	10.9	2.2	69	53	1:2.3

STEEL FRAME

	$\frac{1b}{2b}$	5a	3g	7a	8b	13c	14c	4c	15a	17d
SUMMARY OF SELECTED DATA	Building Height/ Number of Floors	Building Width/ Building Height	Useable Area/ Gross Area	Dimensions of a Typical Framing Bay	Typical Beam Depth/Span	Mechanical Equipment & Shaft Area/ Gross Floor Area	H.V.A.C. Shaft Area/ Gross Floor Area	Usable Height/ Total Floor Height	Glass Area/ Facade Area	Number of Elevators/ Number of Floors
Building		Ratio	%	×	Ratio	%	%	%	%	Ratio
CBS	$\frac{491}{38}$	1:3.6	71	2'-6" × 35'-0"	1:24.7	8.3	1.9	69	37	1:2.2
One Shell Plaza	$\frac{685}{50}$	1:4.9	83	6'-0" × 37'-2"	1:18.6	5.3	1.2	69	39	1:2.1
Richards Medical Labs	$\frac{96}{8}$	1:2.0	71	47'-4" × 47'-4"	1:14.2	11.2	8.4	71	35	1:2.7
Hoffmann-La Roche	$\frac{113}{8}$	1:0.87	73	41'-6" × 41'-6"	1:20.8	5.3	3.0	71	71	1:2.7
Yale Art Gallery	$\frac{52}{4\frac{1}{2}}$	1:0.63	83	19'-9" × 40'-0"	1:15.8	4.1	0.9	80	47	1:4
M.I.T. Earth Science Lab	$\frac{275}{21}$	1:5.0	74	9'-0" × 48'-4"	1:13.8	9.3	3.0	70	23	1:6.3
American Life	$\frac{283}{23}$	1:4.3	73	6'-0" × 72'-0"	1:23.4	10.8	2.8	71	22	1:7.0
Cornell Agronomy Lab	$\frac{136}{12}$	1:1.5	62	8'-6" × 41'-2"	1:22.5	14.0	8.4	81	7	1:6.0
780 Third Avenue	$\frac{566}{49}$	1:8.0	69	9'-4" × 28'-80"	1:22.9	10.6	0.5	73	26	1:5.2
Averages/Concrete Frame Buildings		1:3.4	73		1:19.6	8.7	3.3	73	35	1:4.2

CONCRETE FRAME

		5a	3g		8b	13c	14c	4c	15a	17d
Averages/All Case Studies		1:3.8	75		1:20.7	9.8	2.8	71	44	1:3.3

PHOTO CREDITS

PART ONE   Page 1: Photo courtesy of Francis G. Mayer Art Color Slides, Inc. Page 2 (top and middle): Photos by David Guise; (bottom) photo courtesy of The Kamen Collection. Page 3 (top): Photo courtesy of Warren Ogden/Art Resource, Inc.; (bottom) photo courtesy of The Kramer Collection. Page 4 (top): Photo courtesy of Granger Collection; (bottom) by David Guise. Page 5 (left column, top right photo): Photos by Robert Galbraith; (bottom right) photo courtesy of Bethlehem Steel. Page 6 (top): Photo by Elizabeth Church; (Bottom) photo by Ezra Stroller. Page 8 (top): Photo courtesy of Geiger-‹Berger Associates; (bottom) photo by AP/Wide World. Page 11: Photo by Robert Galbraith. Page 14: Photo Courtesy of Western Wood Products Association. Page 19 (top): Photo courtesy of Ezra Stroller; (bottom) photo by David Guise. Page 21: Photo courtesy of CCNY Architectural Collection. Page 23: Photo courtesy of CCNY Architectural Collection. Page 25: Photos courtesy of Prestressing Industries. Page 27: Photo by Lynchnere, courtesy of Rhone & Iredale. Page 51: Photo courtesy of CCNY Architectural Collection. Page 55: Photo courtesy of CCNY Architectural Collection, Page 58 (top): Photo courtesy of CCNY Architectural Collection; (bottom) photo by Ezra Stroller. Page 67: Photo courtesy of CCNY Architectural Collection. Page 68 (top): Photo by Jack Horner; (bottom) photo courtesy of CCNY Architectural Collection. Page 69: Photo courtesy of CCNY Architectural Collection. Page 70: Photo courtesy of CCNY Architectural Collection. Page 71: Photo by David Guise. Page 74: Photo by David Guise. Page 76: Photo by David Guise. Page 77 (top): Photo courtesy of Larsen's Manufacturing Co.; (center) Photo courtesy of Elkhart Bros. Manufacturing Co. Inc.; (bottom) photo courtesy of CCNY Architectural Collection. Page 78: Photo courtesy of Bobrick Washroom Equipment, Inc. Page 79: Photo by David Guise. Page 83: Photo courtesy of Otis Elevator Co.

PART TWO   Page 89: Photo by David Guise. Page 92: Photo by Ezra Stroller, courtesy of Joseph E. Seagram & Sons, Inc. Page 100: Photo by David Guise. Page 102: Photo courtesy of CCNY Architectural Collection. Page 106: Photo courtesy of Roche, Dinkerloo, and Associates. Page 112: Courtesy of Galbreath-Ruffin Corp. Page 122: Photo by Sam Fair, courtesy of Chase Manhattan Archives. Page 130: Photo by Gorchev and Gorchev, courtesy of CC and F Property and Management Company, Inc. Page 138: Photo by Jack Lindsay, courtesy of Westcoast Transmission Co., Ltd. Page 140: Photo by Schwang Studio, courtesy of Gunner Bickerts Architects. Page 144: Photo by Lynchnere, courtesy of Rhone & Iredale. Page 146: Photo courtesy of Galbreath-Ruffin Corp. Page 148: Photo courtesy of CCNY Architectural Collection. Page 156: Courtesy of Citibank, N.A. Page 157: Photo courtesy of CCNY Architectural Collection. Page 163: Photo by David Guise. Page 164: Photo courtesy of Burlington Industries. Page 174: Photo by David Guise. Page 175: Photo courtesy of Myron Goldsmith. Page 177: Photo by David Guise. Page 180: Photo by Robert Galbraith. Page 186: Photo by Richard Payne. Page 187: Photo courtesy of CCNY Architectural Collection. Page 194: Photo by John Ebstel, courtesy of Louis Kahn Collection. University of Pennsylvania. Page 196: Photos courtesy of CCNY Architectural Collection. Page 202: Photo by Robert Galbraith. Page 204: Photo by Robert

ART CREDITS

TABLE CREDITS

INDEX